THE BECKONING SILENCE

Summit

Mittellegi Ridge

Summit Ice Field

Corti Bivouac   Exit Cracks

Spider
Traverse of the Gods

Ramp Ice Field   Brittle Crack
Brittle Ledges

Waterfall Chimney

Ramp

Third Ice Field   Death Bivouac

Flat Iron

Second Ice Field

Ice Hose
First Ice Field   Röte Fluh
Swallow's Nest   Hinterstoisser Traverse

Difficult Crack

Gallery Window

Shattered Pillar

First Pillar

Start

THE
BECKONING
SILENCE

JOE SIMPSON

THE MOUNTAINEERS BOOKS

Published by
The Mountaineers Books
1001 SW Klickitat Way, Suite 201
Seattle, WA 98134

First North American edition: first printing 2003, second printing 2004

First published in the United Kingdom in 2002 by Jonathan Cape
The Random House Group Limited
20 Vauxhall Bridge Road, London SW1V 2SA

Published simultaneously in Great Britain by Cordee, 3a DeMontfort
Street, Leicester, England, LE1 7HD

Manufactured in the United States of America

Text design and layout: Jennifer LaRock Shontz

Cover photograph by Andrea Forlini
Frontispiece map: *Features and routes on the north face of the Eiger*
    (Jost van Allman; reproduced in *Eiger: The Vertical Arena,*
    ed. Daniel Anker)

Acknowledgement is due for permission to quote from *The Wildest
Dream* by Peter and Leni Gillman (Hodder Headline Ltd), *The White
Spider* by Heinrich Harrer (Flamingo/HarperCollins Publishers), *Into
Thin Air* by Jon Krakauer (Pan Macmillan), and "No Woman, No Cry"
(Words & Music by Vincent Ford) Copyright © 1974 Fifty-Six Hope
Road Music Ltd./Odnil Music Ltd./Blue Mountain Music Ltd. (PRS). All
rights for North and South America controlled and administered by
Rykomusic, Inc. (ASCAP) and for the rest of the world by Rykomusic
Ltd. (PRS). Lyrics Used By Permission.

A catalog record for this book is on file at the Library of Congress

♻ Printed on recycled paper

To Ian "Tat" Tattersall

"We miss you, kid."

Climb if you will, but remember that courage and strength
are naught without prudence, and that a momentary
negligence may destroy the happiness of a lifetime.
Do nothing in haste; look well to each step; and
from the beginning think what may be the end.

Edward Whymper,
Scrambles Amongst the Alps

*In memory of Matthew Hayes and Phillip O'Sullivan
whose dream stretched to the very end.*

CONTENTS

1   GAMES ON A DANGEROUS STAGE   11

2   INTIMATIONS OF MORTALITY   31

3   HIGH ANXIETY   57

4   GIVEN WINGS TO FLY   73

5   THE COLDEST DANCE   91

6   RITE OF PASSAGE   119

7   BECAUSE IT'S THERE   131

8   THE STRETCHED DREAM   141

9   THE EIGERWAND   157

10   AGAINST THE DYING OF THE LIGHT   167

11   HEROES AND FOOLS   181

12   TOUCHING HISTORY   199

13   DO NOTHING IN HASTE   223

14   LOOK WELL TO EACH STEP   241

15   THE FATAL STORM   261

16   THE HAPPINESS OF A LIFETIME   271

17   HALF SILENCES   291

Acknowledgments   309

Selected Readings   313

GAMES ON A DANGEROUS STAGE

THE ICE WAS THIN AND LOOSELY ATTACHED TO THE ROCK. I could see water streaming beneath the opaque layer undermining its strength. I glanced down to the left and saw Ian "Tat" Tattersall hunched over, stamping his feet at the foot of the ice wall. He was cold and I was taking far too long. I could sense his impatience. This first pitch of Alea Jacta Est, a 500-foot grade-V ice climb looming above the valley of La Grave in the Hautes Alpes, France, should have been relatively straightforward. It had felt desperately difficult and precarious.

I looked down at where I had placed my last ice screw in a boss of water ice protruding from a fractured and melting ice wall 35 feet below me. If I fell now I would drop 80 feet and I knew the ice screw would not hold me. The ice boss would shatter and it would be instantly ripped out. It had quickly become apparent that the route was in poor condition. Lower down I had found myself moving from solid ice onto a strange skim of water ice overlaying soft, sugary snow. It was just strong enough to hold my axe picks and crampon points but it would never hold an ice screw. Hoping for an improvement I had climbed higher and moved diagonally towards the right side of the wall. Then the ice began to resemble something more commonly found furring up the icebox in my fridge. I moved tentatively over rotten honeycombed water ice and onto frightening near-vertical slabs of rime ice—a feathery concoction of hoarfrost and loosely bonded powder snow. It was now impossible to downclimb safely and I tried to quell a rising tide of panic as I headed gingerly towards the ice boss that was gleaming with a wet blue sheen near where a rock buttress bordered a rising curtain of ice.

As I twisted the ice screw into the boss, I watched in dismay as a filigree pattern of cracks spread through water ice. I saw water seeping out from beneath the fractures and stopped winding the screw. Clipping the rope to the screw I tried to ignore the fact that it was my first point of protection and that it wouldn't hold my weight let alone a fall. If I fell, I knew that I would hit the ground from over 100 feet. I glanced back at Tat but he wasn't looking at me. It was surprising how very lonely you can suddenly feel.

I moved up slowly, gently hooking my axe picks in melt holes in the ice, careful to pull down and not out. My right foot slipped away as wet ice sheared from the rock and I shuddered down, then stopped. I breathed deeply and stepped up again, forcing the single front-point of my crampons into a shallow crack in the rock and balancing on it as I reached higher and planted my axe into a marginally thicker layer of ice. There was a cracking noise as the ice flexed free of the underlying rock, then silence as it held my weight. I held my breath and pulled steadily on the axe shaft.

The route description mentioned a near-vertical wall of ice trending rightwards. I remembered the old adage about ice climbing, which stated that 75-degree ice feels vertical and vertical ice seems overhanging. I felt physically strong but mentally my resolve had begun to crumble. It had been a slow, insidious leeching away of my confidence directly proportional to the height I gained. Above me a rock wall reared up and the ice curved into a short corner. I spotted a small piece of red tape poking out from beneath a fringe of wet snow. *The belay*, I thought with relief, *protection, safety at last*.

My spirits rose at the welcome sight and I made delicate moves up the ice wall until I was perched cautiously on the tips of my crampon points digging into a moustache of frozen moss and turf. I was alarmed to notice that the turf was not part of a rocky ledge but simply a tuft of vegetation glued to the rock wall. I reached up with my axe and carefully pushed the pick through the small loop of red tape. An experimental tug indicated that it was a solid anchor and I relaxed as the tension ebbed away.

"I've found the belay," I shouted over my shoulder. There was no answer from below. I swept the dusting of snow from around the tape, hoping to reveal a couple of strong bolts. My heart sank as I saw two knife-blade pitons that had been driven half their length into a hairline crack in the rock. The tape had been tied off around the blades to reduce the outward leverage that would have been exerted if the eyes of the pitons had been clipped. I looked quickly around for some other protection to back up this worryingly feeble belay. There was nothing. No cracks for wires or pitons and the nearest ice was too thin and weak to take an ice screw.

I looked down past my boots. A rocky buttress plunged away beneath my crampon points. There was now a fall of over 150 feet if the two blade pegs ripped out. I began to feel nervous. A shout from below was muffled by the sound of a passing truck on the nearby road.

"What?" I yelled.

"Are you safe?" Tat yelled.

I glanced at the two pegs and my stomach tightened. *This isn't good,* I told myself sternly. *We're on holiday. This is supposed to be fun!*

"I'm not sure," I muttered to myself, then leaned out and shouted. "Okay, Tat. Be careful. The ice is crap and the belay isn't much better."

"What?"

Great. He can't hear me.

"Climb!" I yelled, trusting that Tat was too good a climber to fall off the pitch. When he reached the last ice screw and was in earshot I told him about the belay.

"Is it in the right place?" he asked.

"Well, I think so, but having said that I was expecting bolts, so maybe not."

"Why didn't you carry on?" Tat asked. His tone was critical.

"I was a long way above a bad runner, the ice was bad, and I saw what I thought was the belay," I said, sharply angered that my efforts on the first pitch hadn't been appreciated. I knew that to follow it with the security of a rope from above would have presented few problems to a climber of Tat's skill but surely he must have noticed the poor ice and lack of protection?

"I thought it was pretty hairy down there," I added with a note of petulance in my voice. It had unnerved me and I felt embarrassed to have displayed such weakness. Tat remained unconvinced. "And I didn't like the look of that," I added, nodding at the vertical 20-foot rock corner draped on its left side with mushy, crumbling ice. In truth, I was scared. The pitch below had seemed insecure and although I had climbed it competently I had constantly been aware that it was much harder than it should have been. The conditions were deteriorating and the short corner looked horribly risky.

"I don't think this is in good nick," I said as Tat climbed up to stand level with my feet.

"No," Tat said as he examined the corner.

"You'll have to get a runner in before you try that," I cautioned. "Otherwise you will be falling directly onto the belay." I leaned to the side so Tat could see the knife blades.

"Two pegs. What's wrong with that?"

"They're tied off. I don't even like putting my weight on them." I glanced at the drop to the foot of the climb. "They won't hold a fall."

Tat shrugged. He didn't seem as concerned as I was. *Maybe I'm being a wimp? Perhaps it's not so bad?* I reasoned to myself but the bluff didn't work. I knew it was bad. I was climbing well, feeling strong, but doubts were crowding in on me. *Trust your judgment. It's your life.*

I passed a bandolier with ice screws down to Tat. He swung it around his neck and moved to the left, making a long stride out with his boot to get his crampons onto the ice. A large plate of ice cracked off and tumbled down and over the buttress. I watched it, mesmerized, as it wheeled out into the sucking, empty space beneath my feet.

I tensed and grabbed Tat's shoulder to steady him. He tried the stride again and I watched intently as he made precise, soft placements with his axes, weighted them, and shifted to the left until he could stand directly over his left foot. He made a perfunctory examination of the ice then reached up with his axe. Clearly there was no chance of placing an ice screw.

I shifted uneasily. Tat was tall and probably weighed 175 pounds. There was no way I could hold him without putting heavy force on the belay.

"Gear, Tat," I said tensely.

"I'll look under that roof," he said and nodded towards where a small overhang of rock jutted from the rock corner. "There may be a crack underneath it."

He lifted himself smoothly up on his right axe and braced the front-points of his right boot against the back of the rock corner. There was a cracking sound and Tat dropped down as the ice disintegrated and his left foot detached again. I gasped with shock and instantly braced for the fall. He stopped moving and calmly replaced the boot slightly higher.

"Jesus, Tat, get some gear in."

He said nothing.

I felt sick with anxiety. Tat was absorbed in the technical difficulty of climbing while I could only watch and worry and try not to think about the pitons. Any fall would kill us. An edgy hysteria was beginning to flood through me. *This is bad. This is really bad.* Yet I did nothing. I stared, transfixed by Tat's movements, scarcely daring to breathe, trying to will his axes and crampon points to hold firm.

After what seemed an age I found myself looking directly upwards at the red plastic soles of Tat's Footfang crampons. If he fell he might hit me. The impact would knock me off my frail stance. If he slid past me he would fall 20 feet straight onto my harness and then the belay. It would rip out. The frozen turf would not take the strain and the moment it collapsed I would lunge down onto the tied-off knife blades. Then we would be airborne.

I had immense respect for Tat's ability as an ice climber. Indeed I deferred to him, happy to acknowledge his superior experience, although I would never admit this to him. I felt that I was more powerful and probably fitter than Tat but he had the cunning of vast experience and that was worth a great deal. We were climbing at the same standard and I was confident that I could accurately assess what we could and could not do. This now put me in an awkward position. I urgently wanted to tell him that he should back off, that the climb was in a very dangerous state, that it was too hard for him. But he was the leader. This was his pitch, his choice, and I would have to hope he would come to the same conclusion. I didn't want to force the issue.

Another part of me wanted to scream at him to stop. *What is this crap? This isn't just about losing face. This is a bad call he's making and you care more about your precious ego than you do about your life. We're friends, for God's sake. This isn't some hero trip. Tell him. He won't hold it against you.* I kept silent. I was unsure whether the suggestion might antagonize him into continuing; the last thing I wanted.

"Can you get anything in?" I suggested anxiously. Tat was now level with the roof. His left arm was stretched above it, gripping his hammer. I could see that the pick was gripping a few millimeters of filmy ice glued to the left wall. He craned his head to the right and tried to peer under the roof. He let his ice axe dangle from his wrist leash and unclipping a bunch of wires from his harness he tried to fiddle a small metal chock into a crack that he had spotted beneath the roof. The strain on his left arm was making him breathe hard. I stared fixedly at crampon points, trying to anticipate them shooting into space. I doubted his pick placement was doing anything other than keeping him balanced. It would not hold his weight if his feet sheared off. The wired chock jammed and Tat tugged down hard to seat it into the thin crack. On his second pull it flew out and the sudden jerk nearly toppled him from his perch. I swore and jerked my left arm out as if somehow I thought I might be able to catch him.

"It's no good," Tat gasped. "The crack's shallow."

"Will it take a peg?"

"Doubt it," Tat muttered and I heard a hint of irritation in his voice. I knew that he wanted to go for the corner and make the four or five moves needed to reach where the ice was thicker. One good axe placement in that thick ice would be enough for him to haul himself to safety. I knew what he was thinking but I thought it too risky. I watched as he turned to face the wall rising left of the corner. He flipped his axe shaft into his right hand and lodged the pick on a tiny rock edge on the wall. He hauled gently at first and tried weighting the tool. The pick shot off and Tat jerked backwards. I flinched.

Anger began to flush away my fear. I wasn't being given a choice. *This is stupid. We could die on this. Just one slip and we're gone.*

"Tat." He paid no attention. "Tat," I repeated sharply. "That's it. I'm not giving you any more rope until you get a good piece in."

He said nothing but I could sense from his head movement that he didn't like the ultimatum. He turned again to the roof and again attempted to place the wire. It ripped free when he jerked on it. As I watched him struggle to stay in balance a shower of ice crystals pattered onto his shoulder. I looked up to see the air above us filled with a fine rain of ice particles. I knew that it meant that the sun had reached the top of the climb and that there would now be a steady fall of this granular ice. It posed no threat but it meant that conditions would only get worse as the sun heated the already melting ice.

"I can do it," Tat said. "It's only two moves . . ."

"The ice is terrible, Tat. It's pouring with water for God's sake!" He glanced over his shoulder at me. "Fuck it," I snapped, angry now. "If you fall we're dead. Simple as that."

"I won't fall, kid."

"I don't want to die."

"I won't fall."

"Maybe . . . maybe not," I shrugged. "I'm sorry. I'm not taking that risk. Okay? I don't want to do this. I don't need this."

Tat turned and looked speculatively up the corner and I felt even angrier that he might still be risking my life. *What can you do if he insists? I mean, you can't pull him off. That would kill us. If he insists, then you'll have to unrope. Jesus! Tell him that.*

"Tat?" I said quietly, hearing the fear in my voice.

"Okay, okay . . ." He carefully made a move down, lowering himself gently from his left axe. I breathed a sigh of release as he edged towards me. Within a few minutes he was back at the stance beneath where I stood.

"Look, I'm sorry Tat," I said.

"I thought it would go."

"Yeah, and I thought we would go." I glanced at the wash of ice particles showering my arms. "It's way too late for this route anyway. It's too hot. The top gully line would be falling apart."

"Can we rappel off those pegs?" Tat ignored my explanation. I could see that he was disappointed but I could also detect an underlying anger. I was surprised, even though I knew how competitive Tat could be as a climber. I looked at the pegs and bent my legs until most of my body weight came onto them. They flexed.

"Pretty flaky," I said. "But if we move slowly and smoothly they might hold."

"Can you back them up?"

"No." I looked directly at him. "And unless you want to stand there untied you'll come with me if they pull out."

"Right," Tat glanced at the small edge of crusty ice that he was standing on. "Well, I don't trust this stuff. Here," he passed me a carabiner on a sling, "clip me in."

"Anyway," I said as I clipped the sling into the two knife-blade pegs, "I've never had a rappel fail yet." I grinned encouragingly at Tat who stared bleakly back at me.

"I have," he said. "Twice."

We sorted the ropes out in silence, knotting them together after threading them through the loop of red tape, untying from our harnesses, checking which color rope to pull down, double-checking the pitons. It was a routine we had gone through count-less times. We were methodical, efficiently calm. I was nervous about the pitons but said nothing. We had climbed ourselves into this position, now we had to get out of it.

"Pull on green," I said as I lowered myself slowly onto the rappel rope, keeping it locked off on my belay plate. I stared intently at the pitons as they flexed and then stilled. I exhaled slowly. Tat grinned at my expression.

"Okay, pull on green," Tat echoed. "Careful, kid," he added in a gentle voice and I looked at him anxiously.

"You too," I said as I slid down past him, concentrating on releasing the ropes smoothly. No jerks, no sudden stops to stress the weak anchors. I watched as the distance to the ground gradu-ally lessened. When I was 80 feet above the snow slopes at the foot of the rocks I began to relax. It was survivable. A few minutes later my feet touched down and I unclipped from the ropes. A short tug on the green rope proved that it would pull down smoothly.

"Okay," I yelled and watched Tat reach out for the ropes and clip his belay plate in place. I hurriedly moved away from the base of the rocks, feeling guilty as if I were betraying Tat by getting out of the way of his fall line. *He'd kill you from that height,* I reminded myself.

We trudged down the avalanche slopes, following our tracks to the road. As we packed the hardware, ropes, and harnesses into the boot of the car and flung in our axes and crampons I was painfully aware of the silence between us.

I had let Tat down. I had ruined the climb for him by insisting that we retreat. Now that we were safely on the ground I began to question my decision. *Maybe those pegs were okay? I mean they held the rappel. No. They would never have held a fall.* I glanced at Tat as he drove up towards the village of La Grave.

"Do you think the pegs would have held a fall?" I asked.

"No," Tat said bluntly.

Yet you were still prepared to carry on, to push it to the limit? I thought. *Why not me?* The simple answer was because I was too scared. I didn't have such blind faith in Tat's ability.

"I wouldn't have fallen," Tat added as if reading my thoughts. I said nothing.

A game of chess and several large beers on the sunny terrace of a café relaxed us sufficiently to begin talking about what had happened. Tat still seemed strangely reluctant to admit that it had been such a perilous enterprise—so much so that I began to have my own doubts. I wondered whether the frightening ice conditions on the first pitch had so unnerved me that by the time I found myself hanging on the knife blades I was psychologically defeated. Ice climbing is very much a head game and there is a fine balance between confident boldness and being in a blue funk.

Yet when I thought of my reasoning at the time it seemed irrefutable. I felt that I had made a sound mountaineering decision. I knew that one of the hardest things to learn is when to back off, when to retreat ready to fight another day. It was not a matter of injured pride, or cowardice.

I tried to explain this to Tat but he dismissed me with a smile.

"I know all that," he said. "I was just disappointed . . . oh, and checkmate!"

He happily knocked my king over with the base of his queen. "Three—one in the La Grave Open," he added with a triumphantly raised forefinger.

"Bugger," I muttered disconsolately.

"And by the way, I've been thinking."

"Oh?" I replied, apprehensive of whatever climbing adventure he was about to suggest. I knew our failure on the climb that morning would only have spurred him on to try better things. Tat couldn't be put off that easily. "Let me guess." I said. "The Valley of the Devils?"

"Oh, no," Tat looked genuinely surprised. "I was thinking about this morning, about Alea Jacta Est."

"Really?" I said warily.

"Well, you were right about the conditions. We started too late and it was obviously deteriorating. Once the sun hit the top we were in trouble. Now if we get up really early, say five o'clock . . . five-thirty . . . "

"Five-thirty?" I was aghast. "This is a holiday, Tat . . . "

"Well, okay, six then. We'll grab a quick coffee for breakfast and we should be on the first pitch by seven . . . "

"You want to try it again?" I asked, taken aback.

"It'll be freezing hard at that time."

"That's as may be but the ice conditions on the first pitch won't change. It will still be cruddy sugar ice and the screws will be nonexistent."

"One," Tat said. "You had one on the first pitch."

"That wouldn't have held a falling fruit fly and you damn well know it."

He grinned and nodded agreement. "Well, yes, that's true, but you could lead that pitch again. You climbed it well, I thought. A bit slow, mind . . . "

"A bit slow?" I protested. "Of course I was bloody slow. It was falling apart."

"Yeah, but you never looked like falling did you? You were solid."

"Maybe not," I conceded, flattered by his praise.

"You could do it again, no problem."

"But it's a virtual solo without those screws," I complained. "And there's no way it's grade V. We've done stacks of climbs that hard, even harder, and that thing today was desperate. Grade VI more like and bloody serious, crap gear, crap ice . . . "

"Yeah, but what a line," Tat enthused and pointed at the open guidebook. "Look at that couloir cutting through the top rock wall. It looks brilliant, doesn't it?"

"Yeah, it does actually," I agreed. "Rather like a Scottish line, isn't it? And I'll bet we can get good protection in those rock walls."

"Exactly, so it's only that short bit that's stopping us. We can do it." His enthusiasm was infectious and I could feel myself becoming intrigued and excited. Tat was an excellent persuader and he was right. It had been a disappointment to have retreated. We had a score to settle.

"You've been on it now," Tat continued, sensing that I was weakening. "You know the score. You'll be ready for it."

"Yeah, and I've been on those bloody tied-off knife blades."

"That's what I've been thinking about," Tat leaned forward conspiratorially. "You see, I was above the roof and trying to put gear in underneath it. I was off balance and I couldn't really see what I was doing. Tomorrow I'll put the gear in before I commit myself to the corner, then it's just a few moves and we'll be up."

"Or off," I murmured. "I'm not sure, Tat. I really didn't like it today."

"At seven o'clock it will be freezing hard. Totally different ball game. Come on, what do you think?"

"Okay, but on one condition," I said reluctantly. "If you can't get good protection, and I mean good fall-proof gear, then we back off. No questions asked?"

"All right, if you insist."

I smiled and nodded assent.

Tat looked delighted and leaned over to give me one of his trademark hugs. He stood up looking excited and energized. There was no trace of the depressed, silent figure that had trudged gloomily down to the car. "Six o'clock start, then?" he asked, just to check I wasn't going to back out.

"Yeah," I said glumly.

"Don't worry, I'll wake you up."

"I thought you might."

It was cold and the route was silent. There was no meltwater running under the ice. Tat had been right about the first pitch and although I climbed cautiously I dispatched the rope length in about half the time. I quickly climbed over the snow-ice sections, not wanting to waste time looking for protection. I began to feel confident that maybe Tat's plan for an early start was all that we had needed to succeed.

As I neared the belay on the two knife-blade pitons, however, my newfound enthusiasm waned. I clipped into the pitons, arranged my feet on the cramped, frozen turf, and stared gloomily at the corner. It looked desperate. Even in the freezing conditions the shattered sections of thin water ice looked fragile. I glanced at the pitons again, hoping they might not look as bad as they had the day before. If anything, they were worse.

As I took in the ropes and Tat climbed rapidly towards me I tried to work out how on earth I had managed to convince myself that this would be any different from the day before, less than fifteen hours earlier. I had walked away from the climb glad to be alive and now I was back here in exactly the same position. *You must be bloody mad! Nothing has changed. You're belayed to the same two wobbly pitons again, the ice is still crap, and now Tat is working himself into a veritable lather of excitement. What on earth were you thinking?*

"Not bad, is it?" Tat said cheerfully as he reached the belay. "Told you it would be right." I gaped at him in amazement. "Right, let's get on while it's still cold," he added quickly.

"Listen, Tat." I was going to tell him that I wanted to go down.

"Here, hand me those screws."

I passed the bandolier to him. "I was thinking . . . "

"Have you got the pegs?"

I searched on my harness, unclipped the pegs, and passed them to him.

"This belay still won't hold anything," I said. "You know that?"

"Yes, yes, I'll get something in, don't worry."

"I am bloody worried!"

"Right, watch me, kid," Tat said and he bridged across the corner before I could protest further. My heart sank. My stomach felt empty and ached. *That's because it is bloody empty. We didn't have any breakfast because this idiot wants to kill us again,* I thought as I watched Tat fiddling with wires and pitons under the roof. *Don't let him move if he can't find good gear, not an inch.*

It took forty-five long minutes of experimentation before Tat managed to lodge a tiny wired metal wedge, little more than a match-head thick, into the crack below the roof.

"Okay, watch me."

"Is that any good?" I asked hurriedly.

"Sort of," Tat said as he carefully placed his left axe pick against a tiny edge of rock. There was a slick patina of ice shining on the surface of the smooth compact limestone.

"Will it hold?" I said anxiously, as he lifted himself up level with the roof.

"Maybe," he grunted, and that was it. I could do nothing. It was clear that he was committed to the corner. His crampons scratched against the rock as he sought to place them on tiny irregularities. His right arm reached up high and he tapped the axe gently against the ice. I heard the distinct sound of metal on stone. He tried again, swinging blind.

"Further right," I said. "There's a weep of thicker ice a foot to the right." He grunted acknowledgment and swung again. The pick held. His right crampons clawed up the corner seeking purchase. One front-point lodged in a nick cutting into the rock. He weighted the point and I stared at it intently, willing it to hold.

There was a clicking metallic sound and I watched in frozen dread as the tiny, wired metal wedge detached from the crack and slid down the rope on its carabiner to fetch up against my hand. Horrified, I stared at it and then at Tat spread-eagled across the corner. I knew he couldn't reverse the moves and I knew he didn't know that his only piece of protection had just fallen out. I kept silent and braced myself nervously against the pressure of the ropes holding me to the insecure grip of two tied-off knife blades.

Tat raised himself with steady care until both his arms were locked at the elbows, hands gripping the axe handles as they pressed against his chest. I watched as he bridged his left boot out to the side, searching for thicker ice. He kicked gently and the points bit into half an inch of brittle water ice glued to the wall. For a long contemplative moment he hung there, sensing his points of contact, trying to assess whether they would hold and then he unweighted the left axe from its tenuous purchase with the rocky edge. I held my breath as he slowly raised the axe to his full arm length. I could see that it was almost in reach of a smear of thicker, stronger-looking water ice. *Come on, Tat, get it, get it,* I urged, as he strained to reach a little higher.

As he swung the pick against the ice and I saw it bite solidly, there was a harsh scraping sound and the clattering rush of falling ice as his left foot shot into space. I winced, tensing as he swung away from the wall like an opening door. He teetered off balance, hanging grimly onto the left axe that he had just placed. Then, very carefully, he began to haul up on his left arm. His left boot swung back, scratched against the rock, found purchase with another sheet of loosely bonded ice, and held.

I was scarcely breathing, weak with the shock of seeing Tat almost fall. I felt sick as the realization that I was about to be ripped off the stance flashed through my mind. I wondered whether I could survive such a fall. Would the snow cone at the foot of the wall cushion the impact? I almost laughed at my desperation.

Tasting the bile in my throat I wondered whether I would vomit and felt relieved to have missed out on breakfast.

Tat was breathing hard with the effort of trying to remain balanced and maintain a constant, even pressure on his ice picks. There was nothing I could do to help and I felt too paralyzed with anxiety even to think of saying something encouraging. All I could think to say was *Don't fall off*, an inanity that I guessed Tat could do without.

I watched as he detached the right axe and lifted it up to a point just above the placement of his left pick. As he was about to swing I spoke as calmly as I could.

"It's too close to your left axe, Tat," I said. "It'll shatter the ice. You'll be off instantly."

He hesitated then replaced the pick carefully into its original position. I watched as he glanced at the front-points on his right boot. One inside point remained on a tiny edge of ice. He lifted his foot and with careful precision placed the same point in a thin crack 1 foot higher up the corner. He twisted his boot heel out to the left, increasing the torque so that the point bit securely into the crack. I heard the rock crunching under the pressure of the steel point. Straightening his right leg gave him enough height to stretch his right axe well above his left axe placement and he chopped it with firm confidence. The pick buried itself in solid water ice.

"Yes!" he said triumphantly. His feet scrabbled for purchase as he pulled up and planted the left axe high and to the left in even thicker ice. The danger was over. The route was in the bag. I was going to live a little longer.

I exhaled and shook my head. Unclipping the wire chock from the ropes with unsteady hands I felt a tremor of anger. I had just made the most stupid judgment call of my life. Nothing had been different from the day before but I had still let it happen. No runners, no belay, and bad ice. Why? The answer was obvious. I hadn't wanted to back down a second time in front of Tat. Not wanting to appear weak or frightened, I had risked everything to save face. That was not how decisions should be made and I knew I was a fool.

I was torn between anger and joy. I felt happy for Tat. He had got what he wanted and I admired all the skill and nerve and poise he had just displayed under immense pressure. Now that he had succeeded, he could reasonably argue that it was a good decision.

It wasn't and I was angry with myself for saying nothing. It had put me in an invidious position and I had had to stand there and watch while the rest of my life was determined by the shaky adhesion of a few millimeters of frail, melting ice and the dubious friction of a tiny point of metal scratching against a flake of rock. In the past I might have felt that this was what it was all about. This was where you defined yourself, balanced tenuously between life and death. As I stood shakily on a fragile ledge of frozen vegetation all my justifications for climbing seemed suddenly meaningless.

It had been nothing more than a gamble. And for what? The right to say we had climbed a grade V ice route in a dangerously unstable condition. We could justifiably claim that it was grade VI, even grade VII. Technically we had both climbed harder routes but never at such risk. Accidents happen because we are all fallible. We make mistakes, we misjudge conditions, we overreach ourselves, but after all the years of accidents and deaths and mountains climbed, we should at least have learned when to back off. It wasn't as if the situation suddenly engulfed us and we had no choice but to deal with it. We knew everything was wrong and yet we came back, ignored our intuition, and did it anyway.

It wasn't worth our lives. The whole notion of "deep play"— the gambling theory of extreme risk-taking when the gambler stands to lose far more than he could ever possibly win—may well be an apt description of some levels of climbing, but playing the game in reality now seemed a conceited and ridiculous enterprise.

However, when I reached Tat's stance it was difficult not to be infected by his bubbling enthusiasm and pleasure.

"Hiya, kid," Tat smiled and gave me a vigorous one-armed hug that nearly knocked me off the stance. I grabbed at the belay slings to steady myself.

"Good lead, bloody good lead," I said.

"It was thin."

"The wire fell out," I said bluntly.

"Thought it might," Tat nodded cheerfully.

"I thought you were off, you know?"

"It was close," he agreed. "But the placements felt good. You climbed it pretty fast."

"Two pints of adrenalin helps," I retorted. "As does having a rope above you. I don't think we should have done that. We nearly died." I looked hard at Tat and he was suddenly serious.

"Maybe." He seemed defensive, as if recognizing that we had gone too far.

"I thought you were tired of risks. You said dying wasn't worth it."

"Never has been." Then he shrugged and couldn't suppress the grin. "But we're not dead and we have done it, so what's the problem, eh? Come on, let's do the rest of it." He handed me the wires, pitons, and ice screws, impatient to get on. "Up and to the left and then it curves round into that narrow rocky gully." He pointed across a short ice flow leading into an obvious rocky gash.

Forty-five minutes later I was rappelling from a tied-off ice screw back down to where Tat was belayed. A shower of ice particles was sweeping the gully. The sun had hit the top of the face.

"Sorry, Tat," I said, feeling ashamed of my second retreat in two days. "The ice ran out. It was good at first then became wet and thin. After that there was nothing—just a 15-foot-high, smooth rock gully. No cracks, no wires. I couldn't climb it."

"Right," Tat smiled at me, still buzzing from his success. "Better get out of here."

"Eh?" I was taken aback. "But don't you want to try it?"

"No." He began sorting the tangle of ropes into two separate coils. "If you couldn't do it, I probably couldn't. Come on, let's go."

We rappelled swiftly back down to the safety of the snow cone. As we trudged down to the car I marvelled at Tat's equanimity. I had expected a repeat performance of yesterday's moody disappointment. At very least I had expected some criticism about letting him down again. As we bundled the gear into the boot, Tat stopped to look up at the route.

"We'll do it next year," he announced.

"If it's in condition," I qualified warily.

"Of course."

I knew there was no "of course" about it. Knowing Tat as I did, we would be back the next year and we would do it.

"Do you know what Alea Jacta Est means?" Tat asked as he drank deeply from a cold pint of beer.

"No," I said, thinking about the name of the climb. "It's Latin, isn't it?"

"Yeah, that's why I asked," Tat said. "You were taught Latin, weren't you?"

"I was so bad at Latin I spent most of the classes standing in the corner for failing to know the past pluperfect conjugation of some obscure verb. Never even understood what past pluperfect meant, let alone gerundives. And those damn stupid sentences you had to translate, 'Labienus, having sacked Gaul, returned to Rome.' Who the hell was Labienus? That's what I wanted to know but nobody knew. He was just this guy with a vaguely embarrassing name who kept sacking things and then going home. It used to drive me mad . . . "

"But you're not bad at languages," Tat interrupted my rant. "You speak French and Spanish."

"I understand more Spanish than I can speak and I used to be able to speak French, but not Latin," I replied. I finished my beer. "So what do you think it means?"

"I'm not sure. My Latin is a bit rusty, just what I learned as a medical student, but I think it means, 'Only yourself to blame.' Good, eh?"

"It's about right," I laughed. "Except I would have been blaming you," I added.

"Only for as long as it took for us to hit the ground."

The following winter Tat and I returned to find Alea Jacta Est in much better condition. We climbed the route without problems and Tat was proved right. It was a superb climb. It was also the last ice climb we were to do together.

I later learned from Margaret Colwell that the name "Alea Jacta Est" actually meant "The die is cast." Margaret said it was a loose translation but she was sure the word *jacta* was the Latin verb "to throw" and *Alea* meant "dice," hence a gamble, a wager. A literal translation would be, "the die is thrown, or cast." In good conditions the route name did not seem especially apt but in the dangerous state that we had first attempted the climb it was all too true. In effect, it was something that I felt it had always been—an unacceptable gamble, a last throw of the dice, a wintry version of Russian roulette.

Alea jacta est had seemed a naggingly familiar phrase, reminding me vaguely of my miserable Latin lessons. Later I was to learn that the reason it was familiar was that it was what Julius Caesar famously uttered as he crossed the Rubicon, a river that no Roman general was ever allowed to cross as it was tantamount to a revolt against the Republic. Once he'd thrown the dice by crossing the river he had no choice but to press on, overthrow the Republic, and set up his Imperium. He was then assassinated in Rome for precisely this act.

It was a huge gamble that Caesar took, knowing the implications of his decision and knowing also that there was no turning back. I wish I could have claimed to have been so decisive.

INTIMATIONS OF MORTALITY

I HADN'T LIKED THE LOOK OF THE SERACS AT ALL. Through the binoculars they had appeared even more threatening than when seen with the naked eye. I had turned away from the view of Chaupi Orco's south face and glanced towards where Yossi Brain was crouched by the gas stoves. A huddle of tents had been pitched on the gritty ice of the glacier. A few parallel crevasses bordered the farthest tent and beyond that the glacier swept in a sinuous crescent down towards the green pampas of the Lago Soral valley.

"Yossi," I called and he looked up from the steaming pans. "Have you got a moment?" I nodded my head to one side to indicate that I wanted to speak with him in private, out of earshot of the clients. Yossi stood up and ambled over to me. He was a tall man, thin-faced with a shock of long straw-blond hair tied back in a ponytail.

"What's the problem?" he asked as we walked a short distance across the glacier.

"Well, I may be paranoid but I don't like those seracs." I passed him my binoculars and he scanned the serac band. At the foot of the southeast face of the mountain the glacier spilled down in a crevassed, snow-covered hump, flowing between two great rock buttresses. On the right side the rock walls towered up in a series of pinnacles and blocky towers. Directly above the rocks a beautiful conical snow summit flanked the right side of a distinct snow saddle, separating this smaller peak from the round-shouldered mass of Chaupi Orco's 6044-meter (19,829-foot) summit on the left. Where the glacier rose up to this saddle it was squeezed into a series of short ice falls interspersed with loose screes and boulders. From what Yossi had told me, we would be climbing in the dark early the following morning up through the screes and then traversing beneath the largest of the ice falls towards a spit of scree running down the right or eastern flank of the mountain. It was certainly not technically difficult and I knew that if we moved fast we could minimize the risk of a sudden avalanche. And there lay the problem. I was not confident that the group was fit enough to move that fast.

We had spent the last two and a half weeks trekking in the remote Cordillera Apolobamba region of the Bolivian Andes. I was leading a group of trekkers and climbers on a three-week exploration of this rarely visited Bolivian mountain range for High Places, a Sheffield-based adventure trekking company. Yossi Brain, a former journalist and now a resident of La Paz, had drawn up the itinerary for the treks and climbs. We had climbed one mountain, Cuchillo (5660 meters, or 18,570 feet), a striking pyramid peak that had presented no great problems. The view across the Altiplano of the Cordillera Real had been superb and at the time I had thought our hopes for three more summits in this wonderfully remote area were not overambitious. Yet by the time we had made the long, heavily laden trek up to our high camp on the glacier below Chaupi Orco we had not managed any more summits.

The trekking had been superb. There were only four villages of any size in the area and consequently we had run into a number of logistical problems on our trek, mainly concerned with resupply of food and fuel and the difficulty of hiring sufficient donkeys, mules, and llamas. The sense of remoteness had been heightened by the harsh arid conditions of the area and the grinding poverty that the local Indians endured with resigned stoicism.

Midway through the trek I found myself crossing some high pampas, having passed by the small mining settlement of Viscachani. After crossing a pass of nearly 5000 meters (16,404 feet) with the group I went ahead towards a deserted gold mine high on a rocky bluff, overlooking the decrepit and ugly settlement at Sunchuli. I was listening to Van Morrison on my personal stereo, occasionally glancing back to mark the progress of the group. I had gone a little too fast, something I have always been guilty of, but I was happy that both Yossi and Pira were bringing up the rear, and I planned to wait for everyone at the old gold mine. Far in the distance I noticed the small figure of an Indian walking diagonally away from me with what appeared to be a strange gait. A little while later I noticed he had changed direction and was walking directly towards me at some pace. When he was about a quarter of a mile from me he began waving his arms and gesticulating towards his head in a worryingly animated manner. I glanced back, suddenly anxious at being on my own with what appeared to be the only lunatic in an otherwise unpopulated area. I slowed to a halt and warily observed the man approaching. I noted that along with the arm gestures he was sporting a disturbingly manic grin. I gripped my ski poles a little tighter. They were useful for warding off attacking dogs and I was just wondering how I could fend off the man with them when he arrived quite breathless in front of me and shook a little transistor radio at me, which had previously been fixed to his left ear. He swept his poncho clear of his shoulder and raising his radio to the sky, he declared, "France two, Brazil nil."

I stared at him in bemusement. "Football, World Cup, si!" he announced with great satisfaction. "Brazil nil! Heh, heh!" He chortled, then, without another word, he strode purposefully off into the emptiness of the pampas. I listened to his laughter and the occasional yips of excitement as he raised a hand to punch enthusiastically at the sky. A complete stranger had just deviated a mile out of his way to inform me that France was winning the 1998 football World Cup.

I remembered a similar incident that Tom Richardson had told me about when he had been resting on the plains below Mount Kenya after having developed high-altitude sickness. A lone figure approached from an empty horizon. A speck at first, dust rising from his feet, the figure grew taller and more dominant as he strode directly towards Tom. Tom looked around, hoping the stranger might be meeting someone else, but to his alarm he too noticed that he was quite alone. As the figure came close Tom realized it was a very tall and imposing Masai warrior dressed in his traditional red robes, a stately and somewhat intimidating figure, armed as he was with a long-shafted spear. When he drew up beside Tom he inclined his head and announced in a gravely somber voice, "Elvis Presley is dead." He then strode off into the distance without another word, leaving Tom speechless.

The Cordillera Apolobamba, an extension of the main Cordillera Real range, lies to the north of Lake Titicaca and crosses the border into Peru. It had not been visited by any mountaineering expeditions until 1957 and there were still many unclimbed peaks over 5000 meters (16,404 feet). It was relatively unmapped at any useful scale, underpopulated, and difficult to access, and many climbers—or anyone else for that matter—had been dissuaded from exploring the area. Yet there were literally thousands of new routes to be climbed, as Yossi enthusiastically told me in La Paz when he had been showing me the proofs of his forthcoming climbing guidebook of Bolivia.

By the time we were to make our attempt on Chaupi Orco, the highest peak in the Apolobamba range and only climbed successfully once before, we did not have the high-altitude fitness I had hoped for. To add to our woes, half the group—who were awaiting our return at the campsite on the large pampa below Paso Yanacocha—were struggling with an unforeseen lack of fuel and minimal food. Some of Yossi's logistical planning had gone awry. It was a two-day trek to the nearest village of Pelucho, so clearly we were about to go on a diet.

We were fit from days of trekking over high passes. In fact we had crossed twelve passes over 4500 meters (14,764 feet) in our circuitous approach to the mountain but I had hoped that we would have had at least two, maybe three, summits between 5500

and 6000 meters (18,045 and 19,685 feet) to our credit by the time
we attempted Chaupi Orco. We were fit to cross high passes but
not necessarily to scale a 6000-meter (19,685-foot) mountain.
Now, when we needed to move quickly, I was worried that some
of the group would not be fast enough. Of the main party of ten
clients only a handful had reached the high camp, and of these one
had already decided to withdraw from the ascent. Yossi was coming down with flu. Pira, our incredibly fit Spanish guide, and I were
left to guide the remaining three clients.

Yossi lowered the binoculars and squinted at the bright glare
of the afternoon sun on the south face.

"The seracs don't look too bad to me," he said. "It's the way it
was climbed before."

"Yeah, well, that doesn't necessarily mean it's the right way."

"They look a bit nasty on the right side but once you have
moved over to those screes you should be okay." He handed me
the binoculars. "There would only be small stuff coming off them
anyway."

"Small is a relative term, Yossi, when you are talking ice cliffs.
It doesn't take much 'small stuff' to kill you."

"It'll be fine." He turned and strode back towards the stoves.
"I've got the tea to make. Sort it out with Pira." He seemed
remarkably blasé about my worries. Then again, he had just
announced that his impending fever had ruled him out of guiding
on the summit attempt.

I turned and studied the seracs again. *Maybe he's right? Maybe
it's just me?* I thought. *I'm getting too cautious for this game.* Most
often you simply have to accept a degree of objective danger in the
mountains. You can try and minimize it by being fast, or climbing
at night when it is freezing and the loose rocks are bonded safely
together by ice and the seracs are not subject to the expanding heat
of the midday sun. But the danger can never be eliminated and if
you are unlucky there is nothing you can do about it.

Only three years before, two friends, Paul Nunn and Geoff

Tier, had been killed on Haramosh in the Karakoram when a seemingly stable serac had collapsed. Their two companions, who had reached their high camp on the glacier before them, heard their voices chatting in the distance. As they prepared a brew of tea the heavy rumble of the ice avalanche broke the afternoon calm and the voices fell silent. Paul and Geoff had disappeared.

Paul Nunn was a big man in so many ways, not simply in stature and legendary physical strength, but in the breadth of his climbing experiences. He had climbed in an era when the accident and fatality rates were frighteningly high. Paul had come through it all unscathed with a wealth of experience, close shaves, and dramatic tales to tell. At the time of his death he was the president of the British Mountaineering Council and the former vice president of the Alpine Club. Widely respected and admired throughout the sport, he was just as happy in the company of young and ambitious climbers as he was with grizzled old-timers. I counted him as a friend but he was also a man I admired and respected immensely. The combination of experience and sheer physical presence made him seem indestructible. A dangerous notion, I know, but it felt true of Paul. I remember thinking that of another friend and wondering whether it might be tempting fate to think in such terms. Then he was killed in a plane crash in the hills surrounding Kathmandu.

The news of Paul's death was starkly sudden and incomprehensible. It left a lasting impression on me and I wondered at the time that if someone like Paul, who deserved to live into a long and disgracefully happy old age, could be killed so easily, then what of the rest of us? I remember Geoff Birtles, the editor of *High Mountain Sports* magazine, saying, "White stuff kills, end of story," and he was right. It comes down to probability in the end. If you keep putting your head in the lion's mouth one day he's going to shut it and it won't matter how good or strong or lucky you think you are. It was the way that Paul could be wiped from the face of the earth without leaving a trace after climbing a relatively safe mountain that shook me to the core. Once that thought had wormed its way into my mind I began to find it increasingly difficult to psych myself up for this climbing game. The news of Alison Hargreaves's death in a sudden violent storm high on K2 a week later was another blow.

I was no stranger to the random dangers of rockfall and ava-lanches but I had always felt that good judgment and experience could hugely minimize the risk. Even after Roger Baxter Jones was killed with his client on the north face of the Triolet when the serac bands avalanched, I still reasoned it was a risk that could be accepted. When I triggered an avalanche in 1981 near the summit of Les Courtes in the French Alps the experience had been terri-fying but had left me convinced that it was my fault. I had been tired, dehydrated, and consequently not paying sufficient attention to the potential danger of the snow conditions. After falling nearly 2000 feet to the glacier below, probably the fastest descent of the Courtes to date, I knew that the uncomfortable truth was that I had been a damn fool and very, very lucky to survive. The positive side of the experience is that I had developed a healthy, almost paranoid, suspicion of anything with avalanche potential.

Nevertheless, it did seem unfair that years of experience and learning to climb at extreme standards on rock and ice could be wiped out in the sudden collapse of an ice tower or the random impact of a single falling stone as had happened to Alex McIntyre on the vast south face of Annapurna in 1982. Then again, moun-tains are not especially well versed in the notions of fairness. It wasn't as if I hadn't always known and willingly accepted this simple fact, but increasingly I felt unhappy about choosing such risks. The attrition of friends over the years had begun to eat away at my confidence, at my nerve, if blind disregard for unavoidable risk can be described as such. Maybe I was growing out of climbing as my father had confidently predicted over twenty years before, telling me it was time I found a proper job.

We packed our gear and settled in for a few short hours of sleep before our dawn start. I lay unsleeping, listening to the sharp reports of ice cracking as the glacier shifted uneasily beneath my tent and worrying about the seracs. *You're scaring yourself into a corner,* I told myself sternly. *Stop fixating on one problem—find the solution to avoid it and then tackle the next one. Stop looking at the big picture.* It didn't do me much good. I kept thinking of Paul and the avalanche on Haramosh. *Do I really want to be doing this?* I was no longer sure.

I watched my crampons as they bit into the hard névé of the upper glacier in the weaving beam of my head torch. The coils of rope in my right hand tightened momentarily as Alison Claxton paused in her ascent. Somewhere above me Pira was leading another client, Malcolm Minchin, across the scree band. I watched the bobbing yellow dot of his light and tried to make out which line he was taking, without success. Far above him I could just make out the faint shape of the saddle and the right-hand summit as dawn began to lighten the early morning sky. Below the summit ridge we moved cautiously in darkness. To the right of Pira's light a black shadow revealed the looming presence of the pinnacles on the right-hand rock buttress. Up and to the left, directly in line with where I stood, lay the ice cliffs. Although I couldn't see them, I sensed them hanging above us, biding their time.

I waited as Alison approached me. She stopped and leaned over the head of her axe to catch her breath.

"How are you doing?" I asked and reached around her to grab the rope connecting her to her partner Brian Mucci.

"Oh, fine," she replied. "A bit tired, you know?"

"Aye, well, if we just keep to this steady pace we should be okay."

I had guided Alison and Brian on a trip to the Cordillera Blanca in Peru and they had been easily the strongest and most able of the group. They were both doctors—Brian a radiologist and Alison a microbiologist—living in the Lake District. They were keen hill walkers, skiers, and low-grade rock climbers, and had completed many guided ascents in the Alps including the Matterhorn, Mont Blanc, and the Eiger. Having climbed twelve 4000-meter (13,123-foot) peaks and the same number of 5000-meter (16,404-foot) peaks in Nepal and South America, as well as three of 6000 meters (19,685-feet) including Chimborazo, the highest mountain in Ecuador, their steadiness and ability gave me no concern. In Peru I had felt that they could just as easily have achieved their climbing ambitions without the aid of a guide. I suspected that their busy lives meant it was easier for them to join an organized trip than to waste time with all the normal irritating planning and logistics that they would otherwise have to deal with. Brian came up briskly, looking strong.

"No sign of Pira and Malcolm?" he asked.

"Up there, on the scree band. Not too far away." I gathered some coils of rope and turned back into the slope. "If we crack on now and get above the seracs before first light we should be able to take a breather at the ice slope just below the saddle." I didn't wait for a reply and climbed off towards the scree slope running down into the glacier.

I don't know why I chose to traverse left across the screes at half height. Intuition maybe, or luck. The scree was loose and awkward to move over and the ground had been better on the right. I knew that higher up we would just have to traverse all the way back again, so it didn't make sense. I was increasingly conscious of what was hanging above us. I could feel my shoulders tensing.

When I reached the far side of the scree slopes where the ice of the glacier formed a small boundary wall against the loose rocks I stopped by a boulder. It was just big enough to stand behind and if I ducked my head forward its outward lean offered more protection. I heard the stones rattle as Alison came across towards me. Her head torch flickered erratically as she negotiated the rocks, slipping occasionally as they slid away. It was tiring ground.

As she approached, I moved out to let her get in by the shelter of the ice and the boulder. Brian quickly came across and we chatted as we chewed chocolate and energy bars.

It was as I was about to set off directly up the edge of the glacier that the avalanche struck. I glanced up, saw nothing, then swiftly hid behind the boulder again.

The sound of ice cliffs collapsing is unmistakable. You can do nothing. The explosive force of a large avalanche can kill you with its air blast before the snow and ice have even touched you. It is loud, violent, and disorientating and you know that you are seconds from being pulverized out of existence. You are momentarily completely out of control—numb and helpless. Your fate will be determined by luck and nothing else. It is a deeply unpleasant experience.

This one came out of the darkness without warning, falling from far above us in a gathering roar. I heard a suppressed squeal of fright and realized it came from me. As the first cracking sound snapped down from the night air I was consumed with fear. The rumble stilled my senses and for a long helpless moment my mind seemed frozen into silent resignation. I had been expecting it. I had convinced myself it wouldn't happen and I now wished I had listened to my instincts. I cursed my complacency and felt sorry for myself.

As the sound of crashing ice blocks rose to a furiously discordant crescendo I ducked in against the boulder and braced myself for the impact. A small weak voice quailed inside asking plaintively, *Will it hurt?* I knew that it would.

Tiny charges seemed to pulse through my limbs and my mind was as empty and as shockingly aware as if I had been plunged into icy water. I was unbearably tense, filled with dread. Yet it was not unpleasant. As the avalanche swept down I felt frozen—a chilled numbness—yet I was recoiling at sounds, mouth tightening, staring wide-eyed through huge pupils, searching for death in the darkness. I was suspended in an insensate limbo, oblivious of my body as if detached from my senses. I had the unnerving sensation of looking down watching my body about to die.

Time seemed to extend as the avalanche rushed past, expanding as the ice blocks exploded into crystals and bloomed down the rocky couloir. It took only seconds from explosive start to the random knocking thumps as the last chunks tumbled slowly to a halt. I never took a breath. I simply stood in the dark waiting to die. It was a very long wait.

Then I rose up unsteadily as if from a sleep, from a panicky dark clenching fear that held me in thrall. Only then did time begin to move again. I peered around dazed, reprieved, uncomprehending. I was alive. That was all I knew: alive.

There was for a moment an immense simple self-satisfied pleasure at being there. The stars moved. I could hear again. I listened to my heart beating. It was a wonderful comfort, a balm soothing the ebbing terror. Breathing was good. I heard my companions breathe and I felt the living warmth of their backs as I released the protective pressure of my arms. The aliveness made me quiver. I realized with a start that I was never more alive than when I was almost dead. I let out a long unsteady breath and heard nervous giggles in the darkness. I felt that I was on the verge of tears and was glad of the dark.

We had pressed together listening as the ice scoured its way down through the darkness. I had stopped breathing and leaned against Brian and Alison, partly to offer them some protection but mainly to get myself under cover.

I had listened intently to the sound of the avalanche, trying to detect some hint about its size and direction. As I had crouched closer to the boulder I heard someone giggle. I didn't know whether it was Alison or Brian but I remembered thinking *What are you laughing at? This is real, for God's sake!* Maybe it was simply a nervous reaction but I remember being inordinately angry. I was deeply scared, and somehow it was annoying that someone might think it was a joke. When it was over I felt ashamed at my fear. *We're safe. It was nothing. What were you bothered about?* Although I tried to convince myself that I had overreacted it didn't work. Adrenaline was surging through my body. I had an image in my mind of Paul and Geoff chatting as they crossed a snowfield and then the obliterating violence of the ice avalanche that swept them away, never to be seen again. I knew I had every reason to be horrified. This was a lottery.

It was that endless moment, in Bolivia during the summer of 1998, as the avalanche thundered down from the darkness above me, that marked the point at which I began to realize that I no longer loved the mountains.

I glanced hurriedly to the right and searched in the darkness with my head torch, looking for signs of fresh ice. I saw nothing. The loose screes we had just crossed were untouched. The avalanche had swept down the line we had been climbing only fifteen minutes before and I knew from the proximity of the noise that it would certainly have hit us. I couldn't judge how heavy it would have been. It may only have been the rush of ice crystals but something told me that it would have been altogether more lethal than powder snow. I had heard the hard impacts of heavy blocks coming from my right and from below.

"Right, let's get out of here," I said, trying to hide my shock. "That was much too close."

I wanted to get moving, to put distance between myself and the others. Already a reaction was setting in and I heard the tension in my voice. I felt jittery and it annoyed me intensely. It seemed pathetic to react so childishly. I set off up the screes above the boulder, hugging the edge of the glacier on the left and trying to climb fast. I wanted to get off the screes and up level with a terrace that seemed to offer an intricate way through the ice cliffs. From there we would be safe from any further avalanches. I felt the rope tighten in my hand and then relax as first Alison and then Brian began to follow me.

As dawn spread a soft light across the glacier far below, I reached the terrace to find Pira and Malcolm sitting amidst a jumble of rocks.

"Was that near you?" Pira asked, nodding in the direction of the seracs.

"Near enough," I muttered. "It went down the right side . . . just after we had crossed over." Pira nodded.

Above the terrace a 300-foot ice slope of spiky *penitentes* barred the way up to the saddle. The *penitentes,* peculiar it seemed to Andean mountains, were caused by intense thawing and freezing and formed a jagged series of shark-fin spikes of ice jutting in serried ranks across the slope. When frozen hard, as these were, they made for relatively easy, if occasionally stilted, upward progress. Pira and Malcolm were soon up near the saddle but Alison seemed to have slowed down enormously. I wondered whether I had pushed the pace too hard after the avalanche and tired her out. As she struggled to the halfway point on the slope of *penitentes* I could see that she was breathing hard and her face was drawn from the effort. I was surprised, given that she had climbed so strongly in Peru the previous year, but when she slumped down beside me on an ice shelf she shook her head and said in a flat resigned voice that she wanted to go down. She had not had the chance to acclimatize as fully as she had in Peru.

Brian came up quickly and looked fresh and strong. He gave Alison a comforting hug as I tried to work out what to do.

"Do you want to continue?" I asked and Brian looked from me to Alison and back. I could see that he was torn by his loyalty and concern for his partner and his desire to carry on.

"Don't worry about Alison," I reassured him. "I'll go down with her. It'll be all right."

"Why don't I wait here and you go on with Brian?" Alison asked. "I would be safe waiting here." She was obviously anxious that we should all still have a go at the summit. For a moment I was tempted by the idea and then dismissed it. There was no way I would consider leaving a client waiting alone and unroped while I continued the climb. Although I had no doubt that we could give the summit a go and come back safely there were no guarantees that something might not go wrong. I glanced up the ice slope and wondered how far the top was from the saddle. My altimeter watch showed that we were close to 5900 meters (19,357 feet), which put the summit only 150 meters (492 feet) higher, but judging from what I had seen on the glacier I guessed it might well be a long way horizontally from the saddle.

"No, it would be best if we stick together." Brian looked a little deflated. "But you could go on, Brian. Pira can drop a rope down and you go with Malcolm."

I turned to see Pira and Malcolm close to the top of the wall and yelled to attract their attention. After a brief discussion with Pira a rope came snaking down the slope and Brian tied himself into it. I coiled the spare rope and Alison slung it around her shoulders.

"Come on, then, we'll take it easy on the way down." I watched as Brian set off confidently up the slope and felt surprised at how unconcerned I was not to be continuing. A second ascent of the biggest peak in the range would normally have been a powerful incentive.

Alison rose tiredly to her feet, slipping her hand into the wrist loop of her ice axe. I think she felt a little guilty that I was having to descend with her and I should really have told her that I was not bothered at all. We made fast progress down and across the terrace, heeling down the loose screes on the edge of the glacier until we had to traverse back over to the right-hand side. I paused and looked up towards the seracs that were now bathed in morning sunlight. They were splintered and unstable, yet they appeared remarkably innocuous. I could only imagine small chunks peeling off the ice walls and began to doubt my alarmed reaction to the avalanche. *Maybe it just sounded louder because of the dark? Or did I let myself get too worked up about the threat before we set off?*

I increased the pace as we hurried across the traverse, slipping on the loose rocks and encouraging Alison to move, which she did efficiently and calmly. We were both aware of what was hanging above us and just as I had convinced myself that we had never been in any danger I saw the heavy, blue ice blocks, some as big as anvils and probably as weighty, strewn down the rocks we had climbed up in the night. It might not have been a huge avalanche but it was a sobering realization to see how lethal it could have been. Blocks of ice of such mass and weight did not have to be traveling very fast to kill you.

We were in the right place at the right time, I told myself, but I knew instinctively that there was a lot of luck involved. I could argue that I had noticed the threat the day before when I had questioned Yossi about the safety of the route. I chose to cross over to the left so maybe, conscious of the potential threat, I had made a good decision. Yet if I was truly honest with myself, I knew that deep down we were just plain bloody lucky. That was all it came down to in the end.

We were drinking tea outside the tents when we saw the tiny figures of Pira, Malcolm, and Brian appear on the ice slope below the saddle. They made quick progress down onto the glacier, by which time we had struck camp and loaded heavy rucksacks for the long carry down to the tents in the pampas.

Pira approached looking relaxed. He was extremely fit and doubtless could have summitted alone in a quarter of the time they had taken. He was a delightful man, talented, modest, cheerfully affable, and strikingly good-looking.

"Hey, guys, good to see you," Yossi called out and went over to shake Pira's hand. "Did you top out then?"

"No, no," Pira shook his head, smiling wistfully. "It was too far back. We would not have been fast enough to get back down before dark. So . . . " He shrugged expressively.

We had only planned for one night camped on the glacier and Pira knew that we had to get back down to the lower camp that day. For those of us who had made the summit attempt it was going to be a long day. Brian and Malcolm looked tired but were content with the decision.

"Here, there's a brew on," Yossi said. "We're mostly packed so we can get moving as soon as you have had a drink."

I waited until Yossi had moved away from the group before approaching him.

"Did you hear the avalanche?" I asked.

"Yes," he replied. "But I couldn't be sure whether it was near you."

"Went right past us."

"Was it big?"

"Big enough to kill."

"They usually are," he said dismissively and emptied the dregs of his tea onto the ice. "It comes with the territory." He shrugged eloquently.

"I think I had already worked that one out."

I turned away and went to fetch my rucksack. Either I was too cautious or Yossi was too brave. I didn't know, of course, that by the following summer Yossi would be dead, killed in an avalanche that swept over him and his Canadian climbing partner, Darner Witzel, as they set off up an unclimbed face on El Presidente (5700 meters, or 18,700 feet). They didn't do anything wrong, didn't take any excessive risks. They were unlucky. Wrong place, wrong time. It came with the territory.

I stepped out of the shower and walked into the hotel bedroom drying my hair. The group had flown home that morning and Tat and Kate Phillips were due to arrive that afternoon. We hoped to attempt some new routes in the Cordillera Real and Yossi had already pointed me in the direction of a long unclimbed ridge on Illimani, which at 6440 meters (21,129 feet) is Bolivia's highest mountain. Although Yossi had failed on the route the previous year he was keen to have another attempt. I was pleased for him to join us on the climb as his extensive knowledge of the mountain would be invaluable.

As I moved to the side to step past a plastic barrel full of climbing equipment, I stubbed my toe against one of the bed legs. For a moment the pain was excruciating and I howled obscenities at the wall as I hopped around the room. I sat on the bed and examined the toes on my right foot, quickly identifying a tender spot on the bone of one toe. I had broken a toe before in just as stupid an accident. The last time had been kicking a parking cone that I hadn't realized was covering the stump of a concrete lamppost. The time before had been as a kid slipping at the side of a swimming pool and accidentally stubbing my toes on a metal pole. Atop the pole had been a sign helpfully informing me that it was slippery. I put my sandals on and hobbled out of the hotel, trying to convince myself it was simply a painful bruise.

By the time Tat and Kate had arrived that evening there was a livid black swelling on the side of the toe, an indication of hemorrhaging at the site of a fracture. Tat, drawing on years of medical experience as a general practitioner, gave it a painful prod and announced gleefully that it was in fact broken.

"Trust me, I'm a doctor," he added and burst out laughing.

"Bugger," I replied morosely and contemplated my throbbing toe. "Why now, for God's sake?" I moaned. "I've had three weeks looking after ten clients, striding manfully over high passes, playing hopscotch with passing avalanches and now I break my bloody toe walking out of the shower?"

"Because you're an idiot," Tat said succinctly. "Come on, let's go and get something to eat. I'm starving."

The next day we boarded a rickety bus and headed out for a sightseeing tour of Lake Titicaca. It wasn't something we would normally do but given that La Paz, the capital of Bolivia, is at the astonishing height of 3632 meters (11,916 feet), making it the highest capital in the world, it seemed advisable to take things easy for a couple of days to allow everyone to acclimatize.

The drive out to Lake Titicaca took us up onto the dry and dusty Altiplano, a bleak and inhospitable region where Indians struggle to survive, rearing flocks of ragged-looking sheep and llamas and tilling the dry soil for root vegetables. The bus wound its way down through lakeside villages, eventually arriving at Tiquina where it was driven onto an unstable and overloaded ferry that took us across the Straits of Tiquina to the small town of Copacabana. Here we searched out a cheap hotel and Tat and Kate checked out the tour boats at the small quay and chose to take a tour of the Island of the Sun.

Early the following morning they boarded a tour boat that ferried them out to a landing on the lakeshore at Pilkokaina. Walking along the ancient Inca terraces past the Tiwanaku Temple of the Virgins of the Sun they passed some ancient Inca springs, now a tourist attraction bedevilled with the usual horde of handicraft sellers and hawkers. In the distance the snow-covered peak of Nevado Illampu rose above the great sapphire-blue body of Titicaca's waters and the dried yellow grasslands and reed beds bordering the lake. Illampu is a *nevado* sacred to the Incas and was a mountain on which we had hoped to climb a new route. The white peaks of the Cordillera Real were a dramatic backdrop to the views across the lake. The five-hour walk to the beach at Challa, a small village on the northern tip of the island where they caught another boat back to Copacabana, provided ideal acclimatizing exercise.

I, on the other hand, was nursing my blackened toe and quite sick of walking after three weeks trekking. My throbbing toe meant an early return to the village and an opportunity to drink beer in the sun, practice my appalling Spanish, and read up on the local culture.

I discovered through a useful trekking guide that the inhabitants of Copacabana seemed to be utterly obsessed with trucks. The town has long been a sacred place, in earliest times the spiritual site of the Tiwanaku culture and then of the Inca. However, I doubt the thrust of their religions was quite so slavishly materialistic as that of the modern Copacabanians. In the Capilla de Velas attached to the left side of the main church local people burn candles to the Virgin Mary to support their prayers, emphasizing the importance of their requests by writing and drawing on the walls in candle wax. The most sought-after gift was a truck. "Volvo" had been carefully spelled out in wax to make quite sure that the Virgin Mary got the point—the unspoken message was a clear suspicion that, as a woman, she may know nothing of such things. It would appear that Copacabana's inhabitants spent their entire waking and praying hours thinking about trucks.

Two days later, we stepped from a four-wheel-drive jeep at the tiny settlement of Tuni and set off on the three-hour walk—or hobble in my case—to a campsite beneath the towering icy summit of Condoriri. We pitched our tents by the shores of Laguna Condoriri where the surrounding mountains were beautifully reflected in the mirror-smooth surface. The following morning we set off up a long spine-backed scree ridge, steadily gaining height until a glacier crossing led us towards the rocky summit of El Diente. An hour later we were solo climbing up the icy *penitentes* of Pequeno Alpamayo's conical summit. Kate and Tat were coping excellently with this early visit to altitude. It boded well for our plans on Illimani.

As we descended to our tents I discovered that climbing down with a broken toe was considerably more painful than ascending and I gradually fell quite a way behind my companions. I noticed how bare and dry many of the surrounding peaks were compared with the photographs I had seen of them. Yossi had said the mountains were in the driest condition for thirty-five years. I was mulling over the likely effect these conditions would have on our proposed line on Illimani when the lake and tents came into view.

"Hiya, kid," Tat called out as I dumped my sack by the tent. "There's a brew on here."

"Thanks." I gratefully accepted the mug of sweet tea and sat down in the shelter of the rock wall we had built around the tent. A brisk wind was blowing off the lake. Unlacing my right boot I pulled it from my foot, wincing as it caught my bruised toe.

"How is it?" Tat asked solicitously. "I'll bet that front-pointing on the summit slopes was fun."

"It was bloody murder."

"It'll fade in a week or so," Tat said. "It might help if you strapped it to another toe."

"Yeah, one on my left foot maybe," I muttered.

"Ooh. Lovely," he murmured as I pulled the sock off and examined the blue-black digit morosely. He reached out and gave it a poke with his finger and I yelped. "Yup, definitely broken." I shuffled out of range of his medical expertise.

The following morning dawned clear and bright and I thought of suggesting to Tat and Kate that an attempt on Condoriri might be good training for Illimani. Tat had been uncharacteristically quiet and reflective. I tried to think what I might have said to upset him. *It's usually me,* I thought. I can be quite abrasive sometimes, particularly with close friends, without realizing that I might be causing offense. Unable to think of anything I walked over to where he was sitting on a boulder overlooking the lake. I sat down beside him.

"Are you okay?" I asked. "You seem a bit down, youth. Something I said?"

"Eh?" Tat seemed surprised to have his reverie broken. "Oh no, not at all. It's not you."

"What then? You're not a happy bunny."

"I don't know how to put this," Tat looked distracted. "Look, this is going to sound really stupid given that I've only just arrived, but . . . well, I don't want to be here."

"What?" I looked around. "It's not a bad place. I mean, I know it wasn't much of a climb but it was just to get you guys acclimatized."

"I don't mean the mountain. That was fun. I mean here. Bolivia. This expedition thing."

"Right, understood," I nodded, not understanding anything. "So you're saying you've flown all the way out to Bolivia to tell me you don't want to be in Bolivia?"

"Sounds stupid, eh?" Tat said. "It's been bugging me for a

while now and it was only when I arrived out here that I knew it was over and I didn't want to do this anymore."

"Do what?"

"Climb," Tat said quietly and I sat there, stunned into silence.

"My heart's not in it anymore, not like it used to be. It's all changed now, nothing like when we started."

"Yeah, well things do change, Tat . . . "

"Oh, I know that, but I don't think I'm doing anything different anymore. It always seemed to be uniquely ours. There weren't so many people doing it. Now everyone and his mother does it. It's not special, not like it was . . . "

"Hey, hang on," I said abruptly. "So other people do it too. What's the problem with that? We can just go where they're not, do things they haven't done. That was the point, wasn't it?"

"Oh, hell, I'm not saying this right." Tat grimaced. "I mean I've done everything I ever wanted to do in the mountains. More, in fact, than I would ever have dreamed possible. So have you. We've been everywhere. We're not going to do any better. At least I'm not. I've done new routes. I've had all the epics and the fun. I'm not going to beat that. I don't want to."

"This is a bit sudden," I murmured. "Your timing does seem a bit off."

"Hey, I'm sorry, Joe. I don't want to screw up your plans. I mean, I know you want to do this route. I just don't love it any more. I don't want the risks; don't want the effort. I'm tired of these trips. I'd rather go on a whole load of one-week holidays than do this. You know, a week paragliding, a week skiing with the boys, maybe some ice climbing in La Grave, that sort of thing. It's more fun."

"Ice climbing?" I interrupted. "So you do still want to climb?"

"Well, yeah, that doesn't count really. I mean a bit of sport climbing in Corsica or some ice cascades in Italy . . . well, that's fun. But not this, not this mountaineering anymore. I'm sorry to drop this on you, kid, but I just want to go home."

"Right, okay." I wasn't sure what to say. "Have you mentioned this to Kate?"

"Yeah, she was okay with it. She understood."

Give up climbing! Is this how it happens? I thought as Tat stood up and wandered back to the tents. *I suppose you have to stop someday. I mean you always told yourself you would. When the legs hurt too much, you said. Do they hurt enough now? Yeah, they do, if I'm honest. Maybe he has a point.*

I thought of the ice avalanche on Chaupi Orco only a week before and how it had unsettled me. I was tired of all the deaths. They seemed inexorable, as if they were moving in, moving closer. How many times recently had I looked around and thought, *Who next? Will it be Richard, or John, Tat, or Ray? Will it be me?*

The previous year on April 23 Mal Duff had died suddenly of a heart attack at Everest base camp. Whether it was the hard work at altitude that had brought it on we'll never know, but it shocked me. Mal had always been so fit and strong, hard in the old way, a man who had successfully undergone the SAS training course while serving in the Territorial Army, a friend who had carefully taken control after the terrible fall on Pachermo in 1991 that had left me with a shattered left ankle and a face surgically rearranged with my ice axe. His strength, sense of humor, and calm, unruffled mountaineering skill had undoubtedly saved my life that night.

I thought of his funeral in the little church in Culross—one of the rare few I had ever attended for friends who had been killed in the mountains. Most bodies were never recovered. Andrew Grieg, Rob Fairley, Andy Perkins, and I had carried his coffin out of the church. I remembered with a wry smile the muffled curse that Andy had muttered as we had taken the full weight of the coffin off the bier. He weighed a ton. We walked gravely and with slow dignity out of the church, mainly because we could barely cope with the weight. As we stepped onto the loose gravel I felt my knees buckle momentarily and thought that Mal was about to go flying onto the driveway. I knew he would have laughed his head off. At last we gratefully slipped the coffin into the back of the hearse.

"Good God," Andy said. "Has he got half the Khumbu glacier in there or what?"

And that was Mal gone, into a hole in the earth, a poem read out by a bareheaded Tat, and Liz Duff by my side as she lowered the man she loved into his grave.

Less than six weeks later, on June 3 came the news that Brendan Murphy had been killed in an avalanche while descending Changabang in the Garwhal Himalaya after the successful first ascent of the north face. As Andy Cave, Steve Sustad, and Mick Fowler had been standing to one side Brendan had moved unroped to the right to fix an ice screw in a more direct descent line. In stormy weather powder snow avalanches had been sweeping down the mountain with incessant regularity but had not normally been heavy enough to carry them off. Then when Brendan was in an exposed position a much heavier rush of powder came down. Brendan's only hope was to cling to the ice screw with his hands but the force was too much and he was swept down a steep gully and over a series of ice cliffs. There was nothing that his friends could do for him. Mounting a search was impossible and they had to fight for their lives to get off the mountain safely. I always wondered what had happened to Brendan. I could never get the thought out of my head that he might have survived the avalanche and ended up hurt on the glacier below. I hoped he was killed instantly.

Ray Delaney, Kate Phillips, Brendan Murphy, and I had climbed Ama Dablam in 1990 on an expedition with wonderful happy memories. Four years later, Tat, John Stevenson, and Richard Haszko joined us on a trip to the north face of Gangchempo in the Langtang region of Nepal. Brendan was an extraordinary climber—committed, bold, immensely talented, he climbed to the very limits of his skill. Yet it was on easy ground, demanding no great skill, that he was killed. Bad luck, wrong place, wrong time. It was becoming a recurrent theme.

I walked over to the tents to find Tat packing his rucksack.

"Come on, then," I said cheerfully. "Let's go home. I've had enough of this."

Tat looked up in surprise. "You as well?"

"It's been bugging me for a while now. You just vocalized it."

"So that's it, then? End of mountains?" He seemed confused.

"Well, it was your bloody idea," I retorted.

"Yes, I know, but it was my choice, for me. I didn't expect you to join me."

"It was a surprise for me too." I told him about the avalanche and the accidents and the deaths and the painful legs and began to feel that I was trying a little too hard to justify my decision. I felt as if I was betraying something special. It made me feel guilty.

"I just don't want to do it any more. Simple as that," Tat said firmly. "I've had a few close shaves but nothing like you, no injuries, and the deaths, well . . . " He shrugged helplessly. "They've always been dying. We know that."

"Yeah," I agreed. "I'm just finding it harder to accept. And there's so many of them, and they're getting closer."

"Don't let it bug you. It's simply because we know so many people climbing at such high standards, pushing the limits. It's not representative of climbing per se. I'll bet there are loads of people who have never lost friends, let alone had a serious accident."

"I know all that," I snapped. "It's an explanation, not a reason to accept it."

"Are you sure you want to quit?" Tat looked suspiciously at me. "You're not just doing this for me, making it easy?"

"Yes, I'm sure. At least I think I am." I looked up at the summit of Condoriri bathed in sunlight. *It would be good to be up there,* I conceded, but then shook my head. "I'm happy to go home now. I'll think about it when I get back. Maybe I'll change my mind. There are still a few things I want to do, you know, loose ends to tie up, a few things on the tick list. After all, you've been doing it almost ten years more than me, you ancient old goat. I bet you change your mind as well."

"No." Tat shook his head decisively and I knew he meant it. "That's it with mountaineering. I'm going to do something fun, something safe. I want to paraglide more. You should try it again. It's different now."

"No, I don't want any more broken legs, thanks."

"Less likely now," Tat said. "Why not give it a go when we get home? You'll get your pilot license back in no time."

"Maybe," I said uncertainly. "Sounds a bit like jumping out of the frying pan and into the fire if you ask me."

Within twenty-four hours we were on a flight home. Tat looked relaxed and content on the way back. He was at peace with his decision.

I, on the other hand, couldn't make up my mind. I couldn't shake off the uneasy sense of being a traitor for even considering giving up on the mountains.

I knew Tat loved the newly embraced thrills of paragliding. His enthusiasm was infectious. John Stevenson had already given up climbing in favor of flying. Richard Haszko, now a paragliding instructor, had done virtually the same. Highly talented climbers such as John Sylvester and Bobby Drury were now world-class paragliding pilots who had taken their taste for extreme mountain adventure into the booming thermals in the skies above the Himalayas. Perhaps there was more to life than mountains, which was something I could never have admitted only a few years ago.

I wondered whether writing *Dark Shadows Falling* had made me cynical, a bit more jaded with some aspects of modern mountaineering. Certainly the ethics and morality of mountaineering on Everest in particular had nothing to do with the motivations that had spurred my friends and me on to our various climbing adventures. No, the Everest circus had no bearing whatsoever on us. We had no desire to be anywhere near that mountain. Most of our friends were making extraordinary ascents on spectacularly difficult mountains and climbing new routes all over the world—from big walls in Patagonia and Baffin Island to alpine-style ascents in the Himalayas and beyond. Standards in mountaineering had never been higher. It should have been a time of great anticipation and ambitious plans. What had made me lose the passion? The loss of friends, too many accidents, a cumulative building up of fears that I now found hard to deal with? As Mal and Brendan had been picked off I experienced a growing certainty that it was simply a matter of probability before I, too, would end up crushed beneath a mound of icy debris.

I looked out of the oval window at the blinding white beauty of the Cordillera Real wheeling past as we carved an arc through the sky above La Paz and wondered where it had all gone wrong.

HIGH ANXIETY

"PARAGLIDING IS TOTALLY DIFFERENT NOW," John Stevenson insisted as he passed me a pint of Black Sheep Special. "The wings today are amazing."

"Wings?" I was puzzled. "I thought they were canopies?"

"Same thing. It's just that a wing is a better description. It is what it does. It flies like a wing, unlike a parachute canopy, which simply lowers you to the ground . . ."

"Not always so gently."

"But these wings go up. They want to fly. It's not like those tanks we were flying ten years ago."

"Good God! Was it that long ago?"

"Yeah, we're getting old, lad."

"Tell me about it," I replied, thinking of my fortieth birthday. "So how long have I been away from flying then?"

"After you smashed your leg on Pachermo. 1990?"

"1991," I said. "I decided that flying was a bit risky with two knackered legs and no undercarriage."

"There was more to it than that," John interrupted. "I mean, I gave up flying for a couple of years as well. The wings were useless back then and to get anywhere we had to sacrifice safety for performance. Some would collapse for no good reason."

"Yeah, a lot of people were hurt," I agreed. "I always thought it was like using a climbing rope that had a fifty-fifty chance of snapping."

"I know, but it was the only way for the sport to progress. Hang gliders were lethal when they were first developed and it took a lot of risks to get them to today's standards. When we were flying in the late 1980s we didn't really have a hope of getting anywhere. We could only soar in gale-force winds and none of us ever left the hill. Now we can fly cross-country, moving from one thermal to another. We can stay up on the lightest breezes when before we would have dropped like a house brick."

"That was true," I said, remembering the high winds we used to try flying in. "I don't know how we survived it all. We didn't have a clue."

"Yeah, but it was fun, wasn't it?" John smiled. "I thought it was the most exciting thing I'd ever done. Remember our first lesson? Jumping off a chair to simulate a parachute landing roll and then Geoff just threw us off the hill and bang, we were flying."

"Not for long, mind," I added. "We used to hit the ground—fast."

"True, but put it into perspective. When we first started flying the British cross-country distance record was 18 kilometers (11 miles), now it's over 175 (109 miles)."

"Bloody hell! I didn't know it was that far."

"The world record," Richard Haszko added, "is 330 kilometers (205 miles). And despite the limits being pushed so far, it's still relatively safe."

"Oh, yeah," I snorted derisively. "I've heard that one before. Anyway it's not saying much, is it? Within eighteen months of John and I starting we knew seven people who had crush fractures to their backs and Geoff Birtles had broken his neck. It nearly bloody killed him."

"I know, but it is safe now." John was passionate about his paragliding. It was about all he did, having given up climbing and mountaineering trips. "Well, as safe as any of these sports can be. I mean you choose the level of risk. You choose how much you want to push it."

"So it's similar to mountaineering, then?" I said. "Climbing is as dangerous as you make it."

"Exactly," John agreed, "the only difference being that the fatality rate of the top fliers doesn't compare with that of top mountaineers."

"So how many pilots get killed?"

"Hardly any, really," Richard replied. "Most commonly it's through midair collisions or low-altitude collapses, that sort of thing. It's about two or three a year, I suppose."

"Yeah, but there's not as many people doing it as mountaineering."

"Quite, but you also have to remember that our experience of climbing isn't really the norm," Richard pointed out. "I mean we came from a community of climbers, many of whom were climbing at the very highest standards. In the end we experienced a far greater loss of friends than someone who came from a less competitive climbing culture. That made it seem more dangerous than it is."

"Well, yes, I see your point," I said. "But the climbing didn't *seem* more dangerous. It *was* more bloody dangerous."

"Yes, but by choice," John said. "This doesn't happen in flying accidents. Pilots don't suddenly get banged on the head by rocks, or struck by lightning, or inexplicably buried under tons of snow . . . "

"No, you just fall out of the sky and hit the ground at a stupendously painful speed." I finished my pint. It was my round and I wandered towards the bar.

I thought of what Gaston Rebuffat had written in *Starlight and Storms:* "I like difficulty. I hate danger." To his mind testing the very limits of his climbing skills, pushing the "outside of the envelope" as test pilots say, was the essence of climbing. Dying had nothing to do with it. Rebuffat understood that danger was a component risk and did his best to avoid it, but he never embraced it for its own sake and never chose to do something simply because it was very risky. He had put up countless bold and difficult ascents all over the world and had survived to a ripe old age, outwitting the mountains, until cancer eventually stole him away.

John and Richard, often in tandem with Tat and Les Wright, a fellow Sheffield-based pilot, had been extolling the wonders of paragliding for the last few years and encouraging me to give it another go. Often, as they sat drinking beer after a good flying day, they would chatter away excitedly, demonstrating with flailing hands and arms whatever heart-stopping maneuvers they had experienced, laughing at moments that had, in truth, been terrifying. They had that same manic edge about them with "heads full of magic" that great days on the hill gave to climbers. I could see in their intense and passionate enthusiasm exactly the same reactions that I had seen in the company of climbers and it fascinated me.

Clearly there was something enlivening about this sport they loved, something vital that touched them deeply. As a sport it was difficult to learn, obviously dangerous, had no practical purpose, and was potentially very expensive. It wasn't developed as an off-shoot of some military or commercial function. It had no point other than being a source of fun. To be a good pilot one needs to be a fanatic, a completely obsessed control freak, and be prepared to put in a great deal of physical, mental, and financial effort. The rewards are intangible and transient. Many hours could be spent sitting on a hillside waiting for the right wind conditions. Excitement levels were intense and draining. Situations could change with alarming speed. A gentle wafting flight on smooth air could rapidly become a frightening battle with vicious turbulent thermals hurling you around the sky. The adrenalin rush of a two-hour cross-country flight requiring intense concentration and intelligent, high-speed decision-making could leave the pilot drenched in sweat and physically exhausted even though the muscular input was relatively low. It was a scary, exciting, beautiful, and downright idiotic thing to do. It made them live. I was very tempted.

There is something primeval in man's urge to fly. Anyone who has stood on a hillside and watched a hawk rise silently aloft, borne up effortlessly without a beat of its wings, cannot fail to admire the graceful freedom of flight. Who wouldn't want to join the hawk and swing in lazy circles rising above the world, riding the wind? There was something magical about the ability to harness the power of the sun, to step off this earth into a fluid and powerful medium, play games in the sky, to walk on the wind, and read the clouds like a road map. If you watch the movements of smoke from a chimney, spot insects and grass rising on invisible currents of thermic air, and see birds wheeling in circles above them, it is like coloring the air. If you are a good pilot you can read these invisible signs and then gently step off the world.

The forces involved are immense. Understanding them and applying your skills as a pilot to the dynamics of this slippery, restless force is far from easy. Flying had changed enormously since I had quit nine years earlier and I felt anxious that it had left me far behind. I half suspected that I knew how to fly myself into trouble but I didn't know enough to fly out of it.

There seemed to be so many things to learn that we had never bothered with before. Indeed it was worrying how ignorant we had been in the early days, flying blindly in dangerously strong winds, blithely unaware of quite what could happen at any moment.

I remembered standing on a col at the top of the north face of the Aiguille du Midi high above the Chamonix valley one winter's day with my canopy laid out in the snow, wondering whether I had the nerve to run off the edge. There was a cold wind blowing into my face from the depths of the 3000-foot drop, but that was not why I was shivering. When I ran forward, arms outstretched above me with the front risers against my palms, the wing came up smoothly as the steep snow slope dropped away beneath my feet and suddenly I was off into space and swooping out into frosty winter air, marveling at the precipitous sight of the mountains as I had never seen them before. It had been so simple.

Years later I sat and listened to my friends talking excitedly about what they had done and inevitably the subject of close shaves and dangerous moments came up. Exactly as with climbing, the stories, many of them seriously alarming, served as lessons to everyone else. Pilots were forever making mistakes, some minor and some major, and their errors created a wealth of hilarious tales, yet there was usually a reason and therefore an understanding gained of what had gone wrong. The more frightening the story the better the lesson was learned. Like climbers, pilots had a black sense of humor not as a wayward disregard for danger but a way of coping with it.

It is easy to get lyrical about the aesthetic beauties of flying, but the elemental power of the air can also smash you down with frightening force, punching your floppy fragile wing into little more than a bag of dirty washing. It has the power to pull you up into the sky at 2000 feet per minute and it can drop you in sinking air with equally violent rapidity.

I heard stories of pilots being sucked into thunderstorms that have the power to wrench the hapless soul up to 30,000 feet and more. Wind shear and downdrafts create extreme winds within the cloud. If these don't get you then there is a very good chance of freezing to death, being struck by lightning, or rendered unconscious by the pounding of huge hailstones. These clouds are best avoided.

A friend of ours had been caught in the "cloud suck" beneath a thunderhead when flying in central Spain. She had done everything she could think of to lose height, but in desperation she was eventually forced to put her wing into a full stall. If this maneuver had been executed in still air she would have found herself freefalling instantly. If she kept her brake lines fully extended and maintained the stall she would plummet earthwards.

As she instigated the stall she was alarmed to realize that far from free-falling she was still slowly being pulled upwards. After ten frantic minutes she dropped slowly out from beneath the cloud base and once free of the sucking power of the cumulonimbus she was able to fly away to safety, chastened by the notion that there was enough power in these aerial monsters to lift her bodily upwards, despite having no wing flying above her.

I was fascinated and repelled by the sport. Strangely enough that was exactly how I had felt when I had read Heinrich Harrer's *The White Spider* at the age of fourteen. I was appalled by the grisly stories and the black-and-white photos of doomed climbers while at the same time fascinated by what they were trying to do. I was certain that the last thing I would ever do was try to climb the north face of the Eiger, yet at the same time I was inexorably drawn to the experiences of these remarkable men. It seemed that they must live in an extraordinary world. They must see things and sense emotions that few others would ever wish to experience. There was something mesmerizing about climbing extreme mountain faces.

It was the same with paragliding. I could sense the lure of it dragging me forward like the hypnotic attraction that great drops induce when you stand close to the edge of a chasm. I wanted to go with it and see where it would take me and I was scared of where it might lead. It had an irrational attraction. The heady mixture of anticipation and anxious dread was common to mountaineering. I kept reminding myself that I had experienced enough frights in the mountains to last me a lifetime and it didn't make a great deal of sense to swap the known dangers of climbing for the unknown alarms of flying. I had continued to resist the urge to start flying again but my resolve was crumbling. I found myself thinking about the advantages of taking up the sport and studiously ignoring the disadvantages.

Paragliding opened up a whole new set of adventures at exotic sites all over the world. One of the things I knew I would miss if I stopped mountaineering was the sheer fun of travelling off with a group of close friends and having an adventure together. It seemed to me that the essence of these trips was not necessarily the climbing or the summits reached but the laughter and friendship and storytelling that they generated. Paragliding might be the sport that could fill the emptiness that giving up mountaineering would leave. Having said that, I wasn't even sure that I wanted to give up mountaineering. *Why not cut back on how much you do?* I reasoned. *Just climb a few selected routes you always admired. Make a sort of tick list of the last few objectives you feel you should experience.* Paragliding had the advantage that if the day came when injuries or doubts meant that I did stop climbing I would have the flying to take its place. I'd always wondered about being unable to climb. *What on earth would I do with myself?* Well, now I knew. I'd take to the air. I would fly over the mountains instead of climb them.

It was hard to accept that I was seriously contemplating giving up the mountains after all I had experienced in them, but it seemed that with the deterioration in my legs it was a decision I would inevitably have to make some day. I had osteoarthritis and in the winter my knee hurt. In fact my left ankle, shattered on Pachermo, was now causing more pain than the knee. I knew that some day soon I would have to get the ankle fused.

I had had fourteen years of climbing all over the world, which the doctors had said I would never have, so I could afford to be philosophical about giving up something that had been at the center of my adult life. It had enhanced it immeasurably, defined who I now was, something for which I would always be grateful. It would be very hard to leave.

In my heart I knew that I was less enthusiastic about climbing than I had ever been and Tat's decision had made me think about why I was doing it. Simply to be asking myself such a question was an admission that much had changed. On a practical level there were fewer and fewer friends of mine still in the climbing game. Those who hadn't died had taken up paragliding. Apart from Ray Delaney, and more recently Bruce French, there were no other climbers I especially wanted to go away with.

When I wrote *This Game of Ghosts* in 1994 it had been an attempt not simply to explain why climbers climbed but also to explore the strange paradox that climbing presents. It was, after all, a passion for me, something I loved fiercely, and yet it had hurt and unnerved me so much and had killed so many friends. I tried without much success to understand this conflict between pleasure and attrition. I recalled a conversation with John Stevenson about the attrition rate and he had guessed that it was about a death a year.

When I had finished the book I had thought that perhaps this was an exaggeration and that the passing of the years would prove me wrong. Sadly, it was, if anything, a conservative estimate. In the six intervening years seven more friends had died.

In the same period three people, whom I had met briefly, also died. Although not close friends they were inspirational role models for whom I had immense respect. I was in awe of their climbing achievements yet all three were killed by the sudden, random rush of avalanching snow slopes. In 1996, when I was trekking into the Annapurna base camp with Tom Richardson to attempt the south ridge of Singu Chulu, I met the famous French mountaineer Chantal Maudit. There had been a time when Chantal and I were to be filmed climbing together in the French Alps for one program in the six-part television series called *The Face,* which was aired on BBC2 in 1997. Her work commitments meant that this never happened and I climbed instead with Ed February in the Cederberg range in South Africa. Richard Else, the producer for Triple Echo Productions, hoped that Chantal and I might be able to climb together on camera at a later date and I looked forward to it.

We chatted briefly and she mentioned that she had enjoyed reading *La mort suspendue,* the French edition of *Touching the Void.* She was charming and friendly company and we exchanged news of mutual friends in Chamonix as we drank tea and rested at a lodge. She told me of her plan to make an alpine-style ascent of the south face of Annapurna and I was astounded at its boldness. She made a joke about me being accident-prone. We parted company with a cheery wave and I watched as she walked briskly up a forested track. I hoped we might meet again in Kathmandu but it was not to be.

I never heard how she fared on Annapurna but eighteen months later, in mid-May 1998, I received a phone call from Richard Else telling me that Chantal had died on Dhaulagiri. She and Ang Tsering were found buried in their tent at Camp 2 on the Normal Route. It was never clear whether they had been hit by a small avalanche, or simply buried by fresh snow, which they neglected to clear, and had been asphyxiated as a consequence. However, Chantal was later found to have a broken neck, which suggested the crushing impact of an avalanche was the likeliest explanation.

I had met Anatoli Boukreev briefly at the Banff Film Festival in Canada in November 1997. To my mind Anatoli was one of the world's greatest climbers. His list of ascents was impressive. He had climbed eleven of the world's fourteen 8000-meter (26,247-foot) peaks without oxygen and had summitted Everest three times. Indeed he had summitted solo on many of the world's highest peaks, in less than a day, in winter, and always without oxygen.

His part in saving three stranded climbers in a storm on Everest in 1996 that was to claim eight lives was one of the most astounding rescues in mountaineering history. Not only did he perform the rescue single-handed in the dark of a storm-swept night on the South Col, but he had only recently climbed Everest without oxygen. Yet of all the guides and clients sheltering in tents on the South Col at the time, he was the only man strong enough, or willing enough, to attempt the rescue.

Although Jon Krakauer's exceptional book about the Everest tragedy, *Into Thin Air,* referred to Boukreev's strength and past achievements, he seemed to play down Boukreev's efforts. Indeed he was roundly critical of some of Boukreev's actions during that day and the consequent storm-blasted night. Somehow he overlooked his own relative inexperience at high altitude as compared to Boukreev's phenomenal record of ascents. I never did comprehend how someone, quite understandably exhausted by his own oxygen-assisted ascent of the mountain, could sleep through the events of that night and then later write critically of Boukreev. Boukreev made repeated solo forays into the teeth of a blizzard to rescue three climbers who otherwise would certainly have died in the stormy darkness at 26,000 feet. I admire Jon Krakauer hugely, both as a climber and a highly talented writer, but I felt his treatment of Boukreev did him no credit whatsoever.

It was a great honor for me when Anatoli signed my copy of *The Climb*—"Joe, enjoy the life and mountains." He asked about Simon Yates, my climbing partner on Siula Grande in 1985. Simon had worked as a guide with Anatoli and they were firm friends. It seemed a small world. Less than eight weeks later, on Christmas Day, Anatoli died in an avalanche on the south face of Annapurna I.

Ray Delaney and I were drinking beers in P.K.'s lodge in Namche Bazaar when a familiar-looking American offered some friendly advice about potential areas for exploration. We had chatted briefly and inconsequentially and it was only later as Ray and I had set off down the valley towards Phakding that I realized that we had been speaking to Alex Lowe. Ray wasn't convinced and we bickered about this as we headed down the switchbacks below Namche. I regretted not having spoken to Alex for longer. Without doubt he was one of the driving forces of American climbing, a spirit that inspired my generation. He was one of the world's most exceptional climbers. His list of ascents and the standards of technical skill he displayed on both rock and ice was extraordinary.

On October 5, 1999, Alex Lowe, David Bridges, and Conrad Anker were on a quick training hike up towards the foot of their intended route on the south face of Shishapangma, an 8000-meter (26,247-foot) peak in the Tibetan Himalaya. It was supposed to be a rest day and they had set out for some exercise to get the blood circulating and the muscles working hard.

I had met Conrad at the same Banff festival in 1997 where I had encountered Anatoli Boukreev. He struck me as a friendly and

approachable man and I was impressed with his relaxed attitude
to life and climbing, which belied the incredible drive and talent
that enabled him to climb some of the world's hardest and most
formidable routes.

An hour after the party had left their advance base camp a
huge area of wind-slab snow broke loose from the col between
Shishapangma and the peak of Punga Ri 6000 feet above them.
Within thirty seconds it had billowed into one of those lethally
massive avalanches often seen in the Himalayas. Instinct took over
and the three men ran for their lives. Alex Lowe and David Bridges
ran down the slope of the low-angle glacier beneath the south face
and Conrad, without consciously deciding to do so, ran across it.
All three men were caught in the avalanche and Conrad was lucky
to be bundled 70 feet down the slope before being ejected. But
Alex and David disappeared. As he desperately searched for his
friends, knowing the hope of finding them was waning with each
passing minute, Conrad slowly realized that they were gone forever.
He later wrote:

> I knew they were buried yet it felt to me as if they had
> vanished into the sky, lifted by a force far greater than
> humans and carried to a place we can only imagine.

Alex Lowe had been a close friend and a mentor to Conrad for
almost a decade and it must have been a shattering blow to lose
him so violently and so instantly. In a moving tribute published in
Climbing magazine Conrad celebrated Alex Lowe's life and tried
to find some meaning in this stark and brutal loss.

> The old questions we ask ourselves about climbing took on
> new meaning. We knew the risk. Should we have done
> something different? Are the risks we take worth the
> rewards they bring? What drives us to climb? The explo-
> ration of the unknown has led humanity to where we are

today. The quest for knowledge, the willingness to accept
risk for an unknown outcome, has allowed people to
progress spiritually and intellectually. The thrill of discov-
ering new reaches remains with many of us, in all walks
of life. Those of us who found this calling and pursue it
in the mountains are fortunate. For Alex this is what
climbing was about, the exploration of the soul, the trust
and learning gained from attempting something difficult
and improbable.

For me this had always been the essence of climbing but
something had now changed within me, making it harder to accept
the inevitability of such random risks. Some people may regard me
as a highly experienced climber since I have climbed all over the
world and completed difficult technical first ascents, but set
against the climbing standards that Anatoli and Alex had achieved
I was a complete beginner. That they could vanish so easily was hard
to grasp. Alex Lowe had written a dispatch to the *MountainZone*
website prior to the avalanche:

Thinking back . . . I appreciate why I come to the moun-
tains; not to conquer them but to immerse myself in their
incomprehensible immensity—so much bigger than we
are; to better comprehend humility and patience balanced
in harmony, with the desire to push hard; to share what
the hills offer and to share it in the long term with good
friends and ultimately with my own sons.

There is something about mountains that moves the soul. They
arouse a powerful sense of spiritual awareness and a notion of our
own transient and fragile mortality and our insignificant place in
the universe. They have about them an ethereal, evocative addic-
tion that I find impossible to resist. They are an infuriating and
fascinating contradiction. Climbing rarely makes sense but nearly

always feels right. As Syd Marty, the Canadian mountain poet, wrote in his poem *Abbot:*

> Men fall off mountains because
> they have no business being there
> That's why they go, that's why they die

It made a strangely beautiful sort of sense to me. I almost understand it but it fades quickly. Like the thread that makes the cloth I can never tease it all out without it unraveling and losing the deeper meaning. It can only be lived.

I had scarcely known Chantal, Anatoli, and Alex but it was distressing to see how these superb mountaineers could be wiped out so casually. Their talent could not save them. If they could die so easily what were the chances for me? If it came down to probability then the odds were exactly the same and that perhaps was even more disturbing.

I struggled back from the bar clutching four pints of bitter, easing my way tentatively through the throng of customers. Richard, John, and Les were still enthusing about paragliding.

"Are you still banging on about it?" I asked as I passed the pints around.

"Yeah, well you should get back into it," John said.

"Actually, I was coming round to thinking that myself."

"You wouldn't believe how it's changed," Richard Haszko added. "Totally different sport now."

"But at what risk?"

"Just think of what we flew with in the old days," John added. "We had no harnesses, just glorified webbing bra straps. Our idea of a harness was to clip a wooden plank to our risers and sit on it." He laughed at the memory.

"And now we have air bags, kevlar plates, preformed foam padding, the lot. We even have reserve parachutes in case of an irrecoverable collapse," Richard added.

"And think of the gadgets. All those toys for boys," John said excitedly. "You can get really good radios, and variometers telling us our sink and rise rate, global positioning satellite systems, wind and ground speed indicators. We have multiple riser systems and speed bars. We can pull Big Ears, and B-line stalls to get out of trouble . . . "

"Okay, okay." I was getting confused.

"You should give it a go," Richard prompted.

"I don't know," I muttered hesitantly. "I'll have to retake my pilot examinations. It would take ages."

"No it wouldn't," John said. "You flew a lot before. It will come back really quickly, won't it Richard?"

"Sure." As a qualified instructor Richard knew what he was talking about. "You'll have to mug up a bit on some of the technical questions in the written exam but I'm sure you'll pass."

Within a few months I had retaken my pilot exams after flying a refresher course with Roger Shaw of Peak Paragliding. I was pleased to find that I had forgotten very little of my flying skills and had been enviously eyeing up the baffling variety of wings and harnesses now available on the market.

I ordered a canopy and from August to October I waited impatiently for it to arrive and tried to ignore my heavily damaged bank balance. A good harness with an air bag back protector, an emergency reserve parachute, radio, variometer, helmet, and flying suit had not left me with much change out of £4000 and the long wait made me wonder whether it would be worth it.

In the third week of October it finally arrived and I spent days reading manuals and trying to familiarize myself with the bewildering number of adjustment straps, speed bar connections, and sitting positions of the harness. It required hours of testing in the garage hanging in the harness from a beam trying to get everything to feel right. Given that I had no idea how it should feel, this was a tricky operation. Trying to understand the manual for the radio proved completely beyond me and the variometer had me equally baffled. I would have to find someone on the hill who might be able to set me right on their use.

The good flying weather of the summer had long gone and the cold gusty conditions of the autumn meant that I had a long wait. I had no intention of starting my first flight on a new wing in anything other than benign conditions.

GIVEN WINGS TO FLY

I WAS AT MY DESK SORTING THROUGH A CONFUSED jumble of photographs and boxes of slides when the phone rang.

"Joe? It's John."

"Hi, John. How's tricks?"

"Bad news," he said, sounding somber. It was a phrase I had heard all too often and at the tone of his voice my heart sank. Immediately I was trying to think who we knew who was away on climbing expeditions. *Tom Richardson? No. He's just got back. Anyway it's mid-October, everyone is at home right now.*

"How bad?" I asked warily.

"It's Tat," John said in a strained voice. "He's dead."

"Tat? Dead?" I couldn't understand it. *He wasn't climbing, maybe a car accident?*

"I've just heard from Peter Franks," John continued. "Geoff Birtles heard something on the radio so I rang Peter on his mobile. He's come off the hill and now he's at the police station giving a statement."

"Peter Franks? The pilot?"

"Yes, he was on the hill when it happened."

"What hill?"

"In Greece," John said and I remembered Tat and Peter had gone to Greece the previous Saturday for a one-week paragliding holiday at Tolo in the Peloponnese, south of Athens.

"They were flying on a site called Jesus," John added. It meant nothing to me. I couldn't think clearly and stared numbly at the boxes of slides on my desk. There was one marked "Bolivia—Tat." I looked at it blankly. *Not Tat. Please, please tell me it's not Tat.*

"Joe, are you there?"

"What? Yes . . . sorry John, I was just wondering . . . I mean, are you sure it's Tat?" I pleaded hopelessly. "Maybe you heard wrong . . . "

"No, it is Tat. I've just talked to Peter. He saw it happen. He's gone, Joe. Tat's gone." There was a catch in his voice. I could sense the tears, the disbelief, the incredulous grief.

"What happened?" I whispered, hardly wishing to hear it.

"Oh, God, I don't know. We can't understand it . . . "

"Did he have a big collapse?" I asked, thinking that Tat might have been caught in strong turbulence when the air comes vertically down onto the top of the wing, collapsing it completely. If he had been close to the ground he would have had no chance to reinflate the wing in time.

"No, he didn't seem to do anything wrong," John replied. "Peter said they took off together only about three hours ago. Jesus. They've carried him off the hill. They wrapped him in his wing . . . " I heard John hesitate as he struggled to come to terms with the awful facts. Although he knew them to be true the shocked incredulity in his words was from a man desperately trying not to believe them. He breathed in deeply, gathering himself.

"Peter took off and tracked to the right along the ridge. Tat went left. When Peter looked back he saw that Tat had found good lift and had climbed nearly 600 feet. Peter turned back towards Tat to try and join him in the climb and then he saw Tat's wing go into some sort of collapse that induced a fast spin. He didn't seem to do anything to stop the spin. It doesn't make sense."

"Did he throw his reserve?"

"No, he did nothing. Peter thought he might have passed out under the G-forces. At one point it looked as if it had sorted itself out and then the canopy went into a strange sort of parachutal stall, folding into a U-shape. Then he hit the ground."

"Who got to him first?"

"Peter did. He flew over and landed beside Tat. He said he knew it was serious because Tat just lay there motionless, wedged in the rocks. The rest of the group was running up from the take-off. Tat was unconscious, bleeding heavily, when Peter got to him. There was nothing they could do. Tat had massive head injuries. He never regained consciousness and died within fifteen minutes of Peter reaching him."

"Oh, God!" I could scarcely believe what John was telling me. Stupid thoughts ran through my mind. *Tat gave up climbing so this wouldn't happen any more. This isn't right.*

"At least he won't have known anything about it," John said. "No fear either. He would have been working hard to sort the problem out and then—bang, lights out. Wouldn't have felt a thing."

"I suppose that's something," I agreed. "How's Peter? He must be in a terrible state."

"He is," John agreed. "He feels awful that he couldn't save Tat. Keeps thinking there was something he should have been able to do."

"I can imagine." I thought of Peter standing there helplessly and then six of them carrying Tat slowly down the hill. "So Tat was just unlucky then?" I asked.

"Yeah, very," John said bitterly, "He just landed badly, rolled back, and hit his head. I mean, you could do that falling off a step-ladder."

"What about his helmet?"

"It was undamaged. The injury was low down below the back edge of the helmet. You know how they're made? They cut them high at the back so you can get a good field of vision." I knew exactly how they were made. The chances of being injured like that were always possible but very unlikely.

"Oh, Christ . . . not Tat . . . "

"I know," John agreed. "This is all wrong . . . "

"It's always fucking wrong," I said bitterly. I suddenly thought of Tat's wife and his two boys, Paul and Jamie. "What about Jane and the boys?" Tat doted on them. During every trip I had been on with him he had constantly referred to them. There was always a frantic last-minute effort to buy them the right presents; always models of racing cars, I remembered. He delighted in the way that as they had gotten older their relationship was maturing into a deep friendship rather than the roles of father and sons. "Does Jane know?" I asked and John paused.

"No, not yet." I could sense his hesitation. Who would have to be the one to tell her the dreadful news? I said nothing. I was still stunned.

"I'll do it," John said at last. "I'll give her a ring now. It's already out on the radio. I don't want her to hear like that."

"No, of course not," I agreed. "Actually it might be better if you rang Tat's colleague, the Irishman?"

"Oh, yes. Good idea," John said. "That way he could do it in person rather than over the phone."

"Who else have you told?"

"Just you at the moment," John replied. "I was going to ring Richard next and then all the pilots we know."

"Look, why don't I call all the climbers and you call the pilots?"

"Would you? That would help."

"Yeah, I'll ring Ray now," I said. "He'll be devastated. And Pat and Liz Duff, and Kate . . . Oh, God, and Andy Perkins as well. Jeez, this will be hard on him." Last time Andy and Kate and Tat and I had been together we had stood in a crowd of mourners by Mal Duff's grave as Tat had stood bareheaded and recited a poem hoping, as always, that this would be the last time. Some hope.

After innumerable phone calls all around the country listening to the stunned reaction to my news and the tears and the disbelief, I became hardened and detached as if I was telling some other news. I stood up, pushing the photos to the side of my desk, and turned to leave. There in the corner of my office lay my brand-new paraglider with all the gadgets strewn untidily on the floor. I looked at my helmet and I felt sick and empty inside and wondered if I would ever fly again. Then I walked downstairs and saw the lovely photograph of Alpamayo that Tat had taken in 1995 after we had climbed, laughing with joy, up the southwest face of what had been dubbed the most beautiful mountain in the world.

I remembered the rappel descent of the face when we had been bombarded by falling ice dislodged by two German climbers above us. I had been standing beside an old snow stake protruding from the ice tying a piece of tape through the eye in the stake. There was no ice screw to make myself safe and as Tat rappelled towards where I stood, I hurried to complete the fiddly knot so that I could clip myself in. Just as Tat arrived at my side a football-size lump of solid water ice hit him squarely on the helmet. As his head was inclined to the side he managed to expertly glance it off onto the back of my exposed neck as I bent over the snow stake. It struck me a stunning blow momentarily blocking the flow of blood on the side of my neck, and I found myself subsiding into unconsciousness. I came to seconds later to find Tat holding me up by the hood of my jacket as I tried to shake the dizziness from my mind.

"I think I just passed out, Tat," I said groggily.

"Oh, no doubt about it, kid," he replied cheerfully. "It made a hell of a thump on my helmet."

"Did it hit you first then?"

"Yes, right on the noggin, but hey, what a header. What skill, eh? They should have me on the England team, don't you think?"

"Some bloody doctor you are," I muttered grumpily and clipped myself to the snow stake.

"Why? How are you feeling? NTC?" he asked, using his familiar abbreviation for his favorite medical expression—"none too crisp."

"I'll survive."

"Of course you will." He had laughed and clapped me on the back. "You're good at that, kid." And on we went down, happy to be alive, elated to be there. I stood and stared at the photograph, seeing the faint line of our tracks leading up to the foot of the face that we had climbed the previous day. Now I would always notice those shadowy tracks from a delighted past etched on the photograph and know we had made them. They had been our footsteps into a special world. We had sat on a high col having a last lingering look at the mountain rising serenely into the morning sky when Tat had taken the photograph. We had sat quiet and reflective at the realization of how very lucky we were to be able to do and see such things. It had been a wonderful trip.

As I turned away I saw, in the periphery of my vision, a man's face etched into the snow. It appeared to be benevolently watching the two tiny figures as they followed our tracks to the start of the climb. A trick of the light, a fortunate coincidence of shadows and crevasses, had created a startlingly familiar face in the snowy flank of the mountain. I stared intently at the bearded face with the eyes and nostril picked out by the dark recesses of crevasses and the shadow thrown by an ice cliff. It had a familiar proud aquiline nose. I wondered why I had never seen it before. Why now, when he had left us? I went downstairs and poured a strong whiskey and cried.

That evening we gathered in the pub and drank too much beer and tried to work out how it had all come to this, and why he had died, why they had all gone. It still didn't make much sense. When Peter at last got back from Greece we did it again and were no more enlightened. Peter looked haunted and kept apologizing because, he said, we had known Tat for so much longer and it must be so much harder for us, which of course was not true.

Tat and Peter had been great friends, rivals in the air, and the quality of friendship is not judged on the length of time you have known each other but simply on what you know to be true. Friends do not care about how much you know, as long as they know about how much you care. It is as simple as that.

Peter said he had kept trying to do something but Tat was bleeding heavily and he couldn't stop it and then Tat was gone and it was over. We tried to reassure Peter that there was nothing he could have done but the bleakness of his gaze said that he did not believe us. He would come to terms with it in his own time.

Tat hadn't done anything daft or dangerously ill judged. He took off just exactly as every pilot does and worked his way up in a climb. It was commonplace and it killed him. As John said, it was as if someone had just gone on a lighthearted skiing holiday and been killed. These things don't happen. It wasn't supposed to be like that, he said, looking confused and angry.

I thought of the time when we had been rappelling off Alea Jacta Est and I was scared of the fragile knife-blade pegs pulling out so I had made some jocular remark about how rappel points had never pulled out on me. It was a feeble attempt to bolster my courage and Tat had looked at me.

"I have," he had said quietly. "Twice."

Later in the bar he told me the stories. Once, when rappelling off a winter climb in North Wales, his rappel peg had ripped out. Tat had gone first and his partner had stood on the ledge clipped to the same rappel peg as Tat slid 20 feet down the rope. Then he was gone, flipping over backwards, twisting around as he plunged downwards. In an instant he hit a small ice-covered ledge feet first, facing outwards, with his back to the cliff face. How he managed to spot the landing he never knew, but the moment his crampon points bit into the ice on the ledge he instinctively threw himself backwards and braced himself against the rock to regain his balance. Almost at the moment he let out a sigh of relief there was a rushing sound and the shadow of his partner flashed past. He had been pulled off as the peg pinged out and tightened instantly on the sling clipped to his harness. Tat was still holding the ropes running through his rappel device; he was locked into the system and there was no time to grab anything, not that there was anything to grab anyway. His partner thumped heavily onto the rope. Tat somehow held the fall standing on a two-foot-wide ledge with no belay, no anchors whatsoever.

The second fall came as he and a friend were descending from the summit of the Lotus Flower Tower, a stupendous 2000-foot pillar of rock in the Cirque of the Unconquerables in Canada. They had placed a rappel peg and Tat clipped into the ropes and stepped back off the edge. He had barely descended any distance when the peg flew out and once again Tat found himself airborne. After falling about 30 feet he hit a chockstone wedged in a vertiginous rock gully cutting down the pillar. Tat stopped dead, winded, but otherwise unhurt, perched above thousands of feet of space. Fortunately his partner had not been clipped to the peg.

I wondered at the probability of surviving two such catastrophic rappel failures. By comparison the slight impact of his paragliding accident should have left him unscathed. Perhaps he had simply run out of luck.

All the risks Tat had taken on mountains, ice climbs, and rock faces all over the world and got away with by skill or judgment or fortune had become meaningless in one bad landing on a hillside in Greece.

Tat had been a good friend, a wonderful, caring, life-loving man whom I wished I had known for so very much longer. I wished I had told him how much I admired him, how astounded I was at his climbing record, how proud I was that he was my friend. I wished that I had told him that just to see him walking towards me after a short absence filled me with happiness. His presence was a pleasure, a gift I treasured and had now lost forever. We all felt the same. It is difficult to articulate, hard to pin down the inexpressible emotion he generated. Perhaps it was just that when we met he made it so obvious that he liked you; that he was delighted to be with you. It made you feel special, content.

In many ways we were like chalk and cheese but somehow our

Joe cutting loose on Quietus *Stanage Edge, Derbyshire* (Photo by Jim Curran)

Ian Tattersall on the summit of Alpamayo. (Photo by Joe Simpson)

RIGHT: *A ghostly face in the ridge watches climbers following our tracks on Alpamayo.* (Photo by Ian Tattersall)

Given wings to fly: Joe launches on a 56-kilometer cross-country flight in Brazil. (Photos by Les Wright)

Joe guiding on Chaupi Orco
(Photo by Brian Mucci)

Joe climbing the crux pitch on Bridalveil Falls
(Photo by Ray Delaney)

Ray shortly before his fall on Bridalveil (Photo by Joe Simpson)

LEFT: *Ray starting the first pitch on Bridalveil Falls, Telluride, Colorado*
(Photo by Joe Simpson)

Joe on steep ice, Bridalveil Falls (Photo by Ray Delaney)

differences seemed to complement each other. I was short, stocky, and abrasive. Tat was tall, gangly, and laid-back. I could be argumentative and obdurately pig-headed. Tat hated confrontation. I drank too much and he drank too little. Once after an ice-climbing holiday he laughed and said that it had been the most intensive drinking session he'd had in years and yet I felt we had been verging on abstinence.

I was lazy. Tat was driven, impetuous, always wanting to be doing something, never able to settle if he had time on his hands. I had always regarded myself as an impatient individual but Tat made me seem like serenity incarnate. Sometimes, as on Alea Jacta Est, his driven impatience and my lazy acquiescence led to near disaster, but for most of the time we climbed well together and our differing strengths seemed well matched. His zest for adventure and his infectious enthusiasm for another good day out always prompted me into suggesting yet another trip. Whether it had been saving a dying baby in the Langtang or nightclubbing in Huaraz, succumbing to his own wrong prescriptions on Pumori or trying to kill me in La Grave, my overwhelming impressions had been Tat's irrepressible and unlimited humorous passion for life. For most of the trips I had been on in the last decade those with Tat had always seemed the most fun-filled and memorable.

I wished he was still here with his big enveloping one-armed hugs and his "Hiya, kid" greeting, and the look of delight in his eyes at the prospect of another adventure. Of course I never did express these simple honest thoughts to him; we just don't do that sort of thing. Who would hug us now, I wondered? There would never be another Tat.

Life didn't seem cruel at that moment but frighteningly transient. It sometimes seems that we are beyond the grasp of our consciousness, mute witnesses to something we cannot comprehend until death, at last, snuffs out the dilemma. We strive to make death a stranger, to live safe lives, to hope against our reason for immortality, and yet death is the one thing that defines us all. It is never far distant from life and the dead are never far from the living. The problem is that we shut death out of our lives and so our dead become strangers to us instead of the friends they once were.

Was Tat now to become a stranger as we lived on without him? I hoped not. I have always been astonished at how quickly time passes by after a loss and how soon our memories fade even to the point that within a few years we could scarcely remember when that death had occurred. I often wondered why we had chosen to play such risky games with our lives. The nearest explanation that I had for why we climbed was because it let us edge along that fine line between life and death, because for a brief moment it changed our perspectives on life. That chance encounter with the dark side made us realize quite how important it was simply to be alive; it made us live.

We did it because we loved it and for no other reason. We didn't philosophize our way up frozen waterfalls or ponder the great mysteries of life as we endured storms and hard times on the hills. We just took whatever enjoyment we could glean from the experience.

That was the point; it was a very simple game. We played it because it seemed the best way of living. John Huston, the film director, once wrote, "The most important thing about life is to avoid boredom at all costs. If you find that what you are doing is uninteresting, then you had better change your routine. I'm held together by things that fascinate me."

The hills had always fascinated us, held us in thrall so we went to them. Maybe that was all we had ever tried to do—played games on a dangerous stage to avoid boredom at all costs. I thought that I had no illusions about what we were doing, but I had been forced to realize that the man who says he has no illusions has at least that one.

I didn't fly for a long time after Tat's death. I was unnerved. Only when spring came round and the weather improved did I realize that either I had to sell all the brand-new flying gear or give it a try. The thought scared me deeply. John and Richard, Les and Peter were wonderful, encouraging me not to give up. They were right, I knew that instinctively, but Tat's death had shaken me to the core. They had a lot of flying under their belts. They had been in big thermals, flown through turbulent thermic winds, and had experienced the joy of long cross-country flights. They knew and understood why Tat had loved flying so much.

"Why don't you just wait until you've had one really good flight?" Richard suggested. "Something you've never done before, big thermals and a cross-country, say, and if after that you still don't like it, well then, go ahead and sell the gear."

"At least that way you'll be making a decision based on facts and not emotion," John added. "If you give up now you might regret it because you would never be certain whether you were right or not."

"Yeah, I suppose you're right," I agreed reluctantly.

When the good weather arrived I made a few tentative and very nervous attempts at flying and to tell the truth I was pretty disappointed. We didn't seem to do anything different from before. I popped the wing up and took off and flew around in circles ridge-soaring and landed on the top of the hill again. It wasn't the wonderfully exciting adventure that John had promised.

I knew that flying conditions in Britain were always much harder than in Europe so in the end I decided that the only thing to do was book a holiday in central Spain, based in Piedrahita, about two hours' drive north of Madrid. I was assured that it was one of the world's very best flying sites.

A few weeks before Richard, John, Les, and I were due to fly out to Spain John broke his ankle in a botched take-off on Mam Tor. I visited him in hospital the next day. He looked gray and sickly from the morphine and the pain and his yellow bruised foot with the livid scar and bristling stitches reminded me of all the operations I had undergone on my knee and ankles. Whatever frail confidence I had managed to regain evaporated at the sight of him lying in his hospital bed. I never wanted to go through that again. Consequently the holiday wasn't a great success. I was too worried to enjoy myself. The weather was indifferent and most of the flying was ridge-soaring but I did catch my first thermals and climbed up in the presence of two watchful hawks swinging in fast circles on the lifting air.

On our last day and last flight Richard had his best flight ever travelling over the pass en route to Avila and landing some 30 kilometers (19 miles) from our take-off point. I had dropped down to the valley in sinking air, watching in dismay as Richard disappeared into the far distance. When I landed I was absolutely livid. For a short period I was so frustrated and disappointed I stomped around the landing field furiously cursing the local wildlife. It was only when I calmed down that I realized I must be getting hooked on this flying game if it could mean so much to me to have failed. What would it have been like if I had succeeded and followed Richard over that distant pass?

A few months went by and John, recently out of plaster and annoyed at missing out on his Spanish flying holiday, suggested we go back to Piedrahita for another quick trip. This time the weather and the flying were superb. One day as I was sinking into the middle of the valley almost 3000 feet below my take-off point on the ridge overlooking Piedrahita I remembered something John had mentioned to me about "trigger points." These could be anything from a group of boulders, a tower on a ridge, the roof tiles of a village, or even different-colored fields. They acted as trigger points where thermals broke free of the earth and rose up in warm columns of air drifting back on the breeze. My variometer had been emitting a constant depressing drone indicating how fast I was sinking. As I neared the ground and began searching for a good landing field free from high-powered cables and tall trees I noticed a dark patch of ground, a sort of earthy hillock just to the right of the town's bullring. This had been one of the "trigger points" that John had pointed out to me. I turned towards it, flying to its downwind side, feeling dubious about the chances of getting a saving climb from this low in the valley.

Suddenly the leading edge of my canopy buckled on the left side and the wing tip momentarily tucked beneath itself. I kept pressure on the right brake handle to maintain my direction and watched as the wing tip popped out again. I had flown into a thermal. It was small, tight, and punchy and as I turned into its center and began to circle as tightly as I could, I was delighted to hear the variometer making a rapid high-pitched pipping noise. I did not need it to tell me I was climbing. It felt as if I had been sitting in the armchair comfort of my harness and suddenly a huge hand had reached down and hauled me bodily upwards. The initial violent lift had thrown me to one side and my heart was hammering as I shot skywards. I had never done anything like it before and was at once exhilarated and apprehensive. As I gained height the thermal became smoother and wider and easier to core. I glanced at my vario, which at times was showing a climbing rate of 1600 feet per minute. I looked around to see if there were any other canopies in the thermal but I was alone. I relaxed a little, glad to know I didn't have to contend with a gaggle of up to forty wings searching and circling above the take-off zone in a hectic, chaotic, multicolored mass where I would have been terrified of a midair collision. *I can enjoy this*, I thought, as I flew inexpertly out of the back of the thermal and felt the canopy bang over in a partial collapse as it was hit by the rapidly sinking air.

Soon I had climbed 3500 feet and could see that I was in the center of the wide valley leading towards the pass cutting through the hills to the west. I wondered whether I should head back for the comfort of the ridgeline and almost immediately bounced exuberantly into another powerful thermal and began to spin upwards. As I approached the pass I began to worry about whether I had the experience to be doing this sort of flying. I tried to remember how much height above take-off John had said I needed to clear the pass safely. If I crossed without enough height I would risk being caught by fast-sinking air and turbulent rotor on the other side. John had warned me that a pilot had broken his ankle in a hard landing doing just that the previous year. *What had he said?* I couldn't for the life of me remember. I was using all the concentration I could muster simply to keep flying. I began to feel stressed and anxious. *Three thousand feet above take-off. That was it. So where am I now?* I glanced at my vario. *Five hundred feet above take-off. It's not enough.* I had to find another climb. I hit sinking air and the vario began its depressing drone, then stopped: silence for a moment, then a pip, another pip, then another. *Come on, come on, catch me,* I muttered to the invisible thermal—and it did.

Swinging in wide climbing circles I watched two large birds of prey circling below me. Their wing-tip flight feathers moved imperceptibly as they rode the rising air. Suddenly I saw another paraglider sweeping in from my left. He had seen me catch the thermal and had glided straight for my position.

We hung opposite each other, exactly level, carving great sweeping circles through the sky. Sometimes it felt as if we were still and the world was spinning around us and I had to look away. I was laughing as we rose, then swearing as I fell out of the back of the thermal again and I had to scratch around the sky looking for lift. I was keenly aware of my incompetence, especially when I next looked for my companion, only to see him far to the west thousands of feet above the pass and heading for Avila.

I remember looking down between my legs at one point and suddenly being overwhelmed with a sense of vertigo. The unwelcome thought popped into my mind that I was sitting in a nylon seat hanging by silk-thin kevlar lines above 7000 feet of empty space. *What if they snapped?* For a moment I had this horrific image of plunging down to the valley floor before reason took over. *Of course they won't snap, you idiot! And even if they did you would just throw your reserve.* I immediately let go of my right brake toggle and reached back to the right side of my harness, searching for the reserve deployment handle. It came comfortingly into my hand and I mentally rehearsed what I would have to do. *Pull the strap out and forward and then swing it back and throw it vigorously behind me.* The packed circular emergency canopy would sail out and deploy almost instantly. *Or so the theory goes,* I cautioned myself.

I grabbed the right brake toggle and continued flying towards the pass. Glancing at my vario I could see I had reached an altitude of 10,500 feet. It meant I was at least 4000 feet above take-off and there was no good reason not to attempt the pass. I straightened my flight, lessened the pressure on the brakes, and pressed my feet against the speed bar in an effort to gain the best glide.

An hour later I found myself sinking steadily into the Avila valley. I had not only crossed the pass but flown a total of 30 kilometers (19 miles) from my take-off point. It was strange how the moment I had stopped thinking about trying to stay in the air I had immediately begun to sink. I had suddenly realized how drained I felt from the flight. All I had wanted to do was cross the pass and I had exceeded my hopes beyond all expectation. I knew an experienced pilot would have done it in half the time and would now be intent on reaching Avila, a further 20 kilometers (12 miles) up the long broad valley stretching to the west. I was content to fly gently down and land.

I came into a soft landing in a sandy ploughed field and was astounded at how weak and wobblylegged I felt the moment the stress of flying had gone. I hadn't appreciated how physically exhausting and mentally taxing flying could be. I was drenched in sweat and my neck ached from constantly craning it to the left. I shrugged the harness off my shoulders, unclipped the leg straps, and let it fall to the ground. I turned and looked back at the pass and it suddenly dawned on me what I had done. I had just had my first really good flight. I had never experienced anything like it in my life. There was a mixture of exultation and unsteady relief, of delight and fading fear. My legs were trembling and I felt shaky so I knelt in the soil.

I suddenly understood what Tat had been doing and why and it overwhelmed me for a moment. I did not know whether I was crying for Tat or at the wonder of what I had just experienced. I could fly. It seemed pretty damned special.

John had warned me that there were fighting bulls bred for the bullring in some fields and it was worth looking out for them. They were extremely dangerous. He had once landed in an apparently empty field and had almost packed up his wing when he saw a dark shape suddenly rise from a tree-shadowed corner of the field. The bull charged with furious speed and John had only just managed to throw his wing, harness, and himself over a dry-stone wall topped with barbed wire before the beast had reached him.

I was walking wearily towards the main road where I hoped to hitch a lift back to Piedrahita when I heard the sound of drumming hooves. I glanced wildly around but couldn't see anything. I was in a grassy field planted with an orchard of fruit trees. I ran towards the nearest tree hoping to be able to jump up and grab the lower branches. It wouldn't be easy with fifty pounds of paragliding equipment in a huge unwieldy rucksack on my back. As the hoof-beats became louder I knew I had no chance of reaching the tree. I spun round, flipping one shoulder strap free. I might be able to protect myself with the paraglider.

A foal and a gray horse galloped into the grove of trees in which I was cowering and wheeled round in an excited rush, whinnying and snorting and then galloping off through the trees. I sank to my knees and began to laugh.

As I sat in one hundred degrees of blazing sunshine watching Spanish motorists blithely ignoring both the speed limit and my outstretched thumb I thought about the flight and what I had done wrong and how I could improve.

There was so much to learn. I thought of Tat and all the fun we had enjoyed. He was gone. We could do nothing about it. It

was his time. I remembered the words of the Blessing for the Dead
that I must have learned as a child:

> Blessed are the dead
> for they have been given wings to fly
> and not dwell upon the earth.

Yes, I thought thinking of Tat, *that seems about right, kid.*

I remembered the first verse of Gerard Manley Hopkins's
poem "The Windhover." It seemed to evoke everything that was
wondrous and life enhancing about flying. Tat would have appreciated it:

> I caught this morning's minion, kingdom
> of daylight's dauphin, dapple-dawn-drawn Falcon, in
>   his riding
> Of the rolling level underneath him steady air, and striding
> High there, how he hung upon the rein of a wimpling wing
> In his ecstasy! Then off, off forth on swing,
> As a skate's heel sweeps smooth on a bow-bend: the hurl and
> Gliding
> Rebuffed the big wind. My heart in hiding
> Stirred for a bird,—the achieve of, the mastery of the thing!

THE COLDEST DANCE

THE PLANE WAS DESCENDING INTO NEWARK AIRPORT, New Jersey, on its final approach and I sat peering out of the window at the lights of the city and the last flare of the sun on a darkening horizon of gold-layered clouds. As the runway came into view and the airport lights sparkled against the night sky I braced myself for the landing. I had never been a particularly keen air traveler but in recent years I had been forced to do so much of it that now I only became fraught during take-off and landings. There was a hum of surprised conversation as we climbed back into the air and began a series of wide sweeping turns above and to the east of the airport. I assumed that we were in a stack of other aircraft queuing above the airport awaiting their landing windows. I presumed that our aborted landing was due to some shuffling in this queue allowing a flight with a fuel shortage to get in before us. It was a fairly common occurrence so for forty-five minutes I thought no more about it.

At last my hangover was beginning to recede and the liverish nausea induced by a night of tequila and beer was fading. I was thinking wistfully about the last week of lecturing and ice climbing in Colorado and planning a return visit to Boulder the following year with Ray and Tat when the pilot interrupted my thoughts.

"Good evening, ladies and gentleman, this is your captain speaking," he announced in a languid Texan drawl. "As some of you may have noticed we did pull out of a landing attempt and we are now running a little late this evening. I assure you there is nothing to worry about."

That made me sit bolt upright. When the captain of the plane who hasn't uttered a word in the entire flight from Denver International Airport suddenly announces that there is nothing to worry about it is usually time to get seriously worried.

"As we made our final approach, an undercarriage warning light was indicating a problem," he continued congenially. "It is not something to worry about. Just a slight technical hitch, probably a circuitry problem, that's all. We believe the wheels are down and locked but this little ole light keeps saying it ain't. So we're just being careful up here tonight, folks, and as you can see we are circling to bleed off fuel."

Oh, Jesus, Mary, and Joseph! I muttered. *You don't bleed off fuel unless you have got a problem worth worrying about.*

"So, ladies and gentleman, we are going to make a low pass across the tower so they can get a good look-see at our wheels. Don't be alarmed when we climb back up. This is not an attempt at landing. Relax and enjoy the ride and we apologize for the delay this has caused."

Relax! He must be barking mad! I glanced around the cabin and was not reassured. No one was looking especially relaxed, I noticed. There was a buzz of conversation and I saw people glancing around surreptitiously just as I was doing, trying to work out how relaxed they should really be. Not very, by the looks of it. I pulled my seat belt tighter and pressed my face to the window. We began a long gliding descent and I felt my stomach tighten.

I switched on my personal stereo. Bob Marley was singing "No Woman, No Cry."

My fear is my only courage
So I'm going to have to push on through . . .
Everything's go'n' to be all right, Everything's go'n' to be
    all right . . .

Is it buggery! I thought and turned the machine off. I tried to unworry myself by thinking of some utterly useless facts by way of a distraction. I had read somewhere that they had once used aircraft to try and prove Einstein's theory of relativity. Apparently in a transatlantic flight time warps by about forty-nine nanoseconds, whatever that was. This has been timed by flying atomic clocks around the world to prove that Einstein was correct. In effect his theory means that the faster you travel, the slower time moves. Is this why, when you are falling to your death, it seems to take a very long time? I tried to ignore this unwelcome diversion. To put it into perspective, if you live for one hundred years and spend your entire life flying around the world in an airliner then you can expect to be one 100,000th of a second younger. Wow! So that means if you live fast then you die older? And the whole notion of living fast and dying young is therefore completely wrong, in fact the whole thing is counterintuitive; it is not what we would think. Where does that get me?

We swooped across the airport and then rose smoothly into the sky again. Everyone waited expectantly for the captain's words of wisdom. He cheerfully came back on air.

"Well, folks, the good news is that the wheels are down." There was a general hubbub of exhaled breaths and excited comments. "However," he continued, silencing everyone instantly. "We still have this little ole light telling us the gear is not locked." There was an ominous silence from the cabin and the passengers generally shuffled around, fiddled with seat belts, put shoes on and then took them off again, peered out the windows, and avoided all and any eye contact.

I tried to get back to the "useless fact" distraction ploy. Most people would think that hard-core porn or a sadistic and violent video nasty would be the most common source of fantasy material for serial killers but no, it is the Bible. In fact, the Book of Revelations is a special favorite. Now who would have thought that and aren't some folks just plain weird?

I noticed that the plane seemed to be lining up with the airport. Did you know, I asked myself, distractedly, that basking sharks take about fifteen years to reach sexual maturity at which point they are just about the right size to be worth hunting? So just when they are looking forward to losing their virginity they get harpooned and turned into pet food. The liver oil of a basking shark is so fine that it is used in the lubrication of precise navigational instruments in modern jet airliners. *I wonder how many livers of horny basking sharks we are about to splatter over the runway?*

"Ladies and gentleman," the captain drawled in his relaxed and inanely cheerful manner. It was beginning to irritate me. "We are on our final approach now and should be on the ground in about ten minutes' time. There is nothing to worry about so if you'll just make sure that your seat belts are securely fastened I'd like to thank you for flying with us this evening and wish you a very pleasant onward journey."

Fat chance of that, I thought. *And why is he so damn cheerful?* Remember, when someone annoys you, it takes forty-two muscles in your face to frown but it only takes four muscles to extend your middle finger. I glanced hopefully down the aisle to see whether the pilot would make an appearance.

It occurred to me that he hadn't referred to the "little ole light" again, so maybe that meant it was all sorted out. But if it had been sorted out wouldn't he have told us, so we didn't have anything to worry about? Maybe he didn't mention it because it wasn't sorted out and we did have something to worry about but he didn't want us to do that so he didn't mention it? *God, I hate flying.*

The airport lights swung into view and as we lost altitude I noticed that we were not approaching the same runway as before. *So, that's your plan. You're keeping us away from airplanes full of people and fuel and concourses and hard things we don't want to go bumping into when our undercarriage collapses and the wings fall off, eh? Very clever. Then we turn into a giant fuel-filled tooth-paste tube and worrying will be the last thing on our minds. Stop thinking that way, idiot. Think of something else!*

Did you know that a pig's orgasm lasts for thirty minutes? In my next life I want to be a pig. Some lions mate over fifty times a day. If a pig did that it would need a twenty-five-hour day. I still want to be a pig.

The plane's engines rose in pitch as the pilot adjusted the approach speed to the runway. I gripped the armrest with tight, whitened knuckles.

The plane dipped slightly and ran parallel with the runway no more than 50 feet above the tarmac. I stopped trying to distract myself and peered fixedly out of the window. The pilots were bringing the plane in on a very long and shallow glide. *So they are worried about the wheels collapsing.* Even as the thought occurred to me I saw a fire engine flash past the window traveling at high speed along an adjacent runway, then another and another. I watched the flashing orange lights recede and counted another six emergency vehicles zip past the window. It was clear that somebody was doing a great deal of worrying about something.

I once learned that a cockroach can live for nine days without its head before it starves to death, which always seemed to be a bit pointless. It was even odder than the male praying mantis, which cannot copulate while its head is attached to its body. The female initiates sex by ripping his head off. It seemed nastily familiar. I made a mental note to troll back through some of my past relationships. *What the hell! If I die in this plane I'm definitely coming back as a pig.* I kept furiously thinking about pigs in the hope that it would favor my chances of reincarnation.

I breathed deeply and continued clutching the armrests in a viselike grip, waiting for the wheels to touch down. I glanced down the aisle and counted the seats to the nearest emergency exit. Three rows down there was the red exit sign above the oval door. The three seats beside this left-hand over-wing exit were unoccupied. I wished I had thought of it earlier and changed position. At least I knew what I was going to do if anything went wrong. *Get to that exit fast.* I had the strength and agility to open the door without any problems. I pulled out the emergency exits brochure from the seat back and tried to study it.

Then we were down with barely a bump and racing down the runway and slowing and the fire engines were catching us up and drawing alongside and I heard the relieved laughter in the cabin. It had all been for nothing. As I put the brochure back in its place and vowed to read them more often, I realized that my hangover had entirely disappeared.

One week later my slides of the Colorado trip arrived and I flipped through them on the projection monitor in my office. Despite having only four days to spare I had enjoyed the chance to climb ice with Jack Roberts, Clyde Soles, and Eric Coomer. The thrill of steep ice and sun-baked rock climbs still draws me back into the hills. It was mountaineering that I was abandoning. The attrition on the peaks had killed off my desire to climb them.

On the last day we had climbed a few minor ice lines in Vail and then top-roped Rigid Designator, a spectacular freestanding 150-foot pillar of ice. I felt a bit guilty about not leading it but owing to an urgent medical condition called cowardice I had been unable to resist the proffered rope.

Earlier Jack had demonstrated the fiendish art of "dry tooling." This mainly involved climbing mixed ice and rock using crampon and ice axe points to maintain adhesion on tiny edges and cracks. Mixed climbing was so called because although ice was generally present in some form on the route it was not in enough quantity to resemble a pure continuous waterfall type of ice climb. Sometimes it was dry rock, sometimes rock with a skim of ice covering the surface. Hooking the tips of ice axe picks delicately into wafer-thin ice, torquing the picks or even the shafts of axes in cracks, and teetering with mono-point crampons on fractional rock edges was the generally accepted form of progress. It was a lot harder than it looked, as Clyde and I found out by repeatedly falling off the bottom 10 feet of rock that Jack had just danced effortlessly up. His skill enabled him to cross otherwise blank sections of rock and reach the tenuous sanctuary of millimeter-thick ice weeps. Hopefully these led to a thickening ice formation and back onto good old plain ice climbing. It was strenuous, delicate, difficult to protect, and downright nerve-racking.

I had given a slide show to a packed audience in Gary Neptune's climbing shop in Boulder one evening. While waiting for people to arrive I had been flicking through books and magazines and had seen a stunning black-and-white photograph of Bridalveil Falls. I had heard of the route and the remarkable history of its first ascent but had no idea where it was. The photograph left an indelible mark on my mind. I had to climb it.

As always in climbing, some routes tend to capture my imagination in an immediate and distinctive way. It may simply be the aesthetic beauty of the line or its magnificent position; it may have a reputation as a classic hard and intimidating climb or it may simply have history. By which I mean the manner of its first ascent made it stand out as a famous landmark piece of climbing for its era. For that alone it would be coveted.

I remember as a young aspirant climber dreaming about routes such as Cenotaph Corner and Left Wall on the Cromlech, Point Five and Zero Gully on Ben Nevis, Right Unconquerable and Valkyrie on Derbyshire gritstone, and the great Alpine classics such as the Walker Spur on the Grandes Jorasses and the Central Pillar of Freney on the south side of Mont Blanc. In the end I had climbed them all, turning dreams into reality. What inspired me to try them was the fascinating history attached to the climbs as much as the technical difficulty and specific beauty of the routes. The true classic climbs combined all these elements and Bridalveil Falls was high on my list of eligible classics.

Climbing Bridalveil Falls had all of these attributes—beauty, legend, class, menace, and that essential ingredient, uncertainty. Its first ascent was way beyond its time. At a time when Point Five gully was regarded as an ambitious climber's dream, Jeff Lowe and Mike Weiss succeeded in climbing something that few people would have thought possible. Point Five has about 30 feet of seriously hard climbing in its entire length. Bridalveil Falls had 350 feet of sustained vertical and overhanging ice and was a good two grades harder. The hardest section of Point Five would be a short section of the easiest climbing on Bridalveil. When I had climbed Point Five I really had been naive enough to think I had succeeded on a classic hard route, and that was in the 1980s.

Lowe and Weiss made their extraordinary ascent of Bridalveil in 1974 using old bamboo-shafted Chouinard axes and ice screws that were notoriously difficult to use and not very reliable, yet they made a free ascent of the brittle bulges, insubstantial pillars, and numerous overhangs. They graded the route WI 6+. Twenty-five years later it remains a serious undertaking. In 1996 Jeff Lowe wrote, " . . . there are still very few climbs of greater difficulty, the top end of the scale is now only just WI 7 on pure ice."

There is a certain limitation on how hard pure ice can get from a technical point of view. Bridalveil Falls was originally graded as 6+. Today modern tools and techniques have lowered the grade to WI 5+ but in lean conditions it can easily be grade 6.

It was undoubtedly spectacular. Four hundred feet of narrow ice pillars, shrouds of cauliflower ice, and delicate fringes of chandelier icicles draped in a huge white veil down a rock face at the head of a box canyon. Great blossoms of icicles hung down like talons and billowing plumes of layered ice sprayed out in a spattered lacy filigree. In summer the waterfall thunders down in a continuous explosive roaring force and it is hard to imagine anything strong enough to still this awesome giant. A Telluride winter, however, is said to be cold enough to freeze hell over. "To-Hell-u-ride," as the old miners used to say of the place.

The technical ice climbing grades rate the single hardest pitch of a climb as well as factoring in its seriousness and the general nature of the ice—rock solid or honeycombed, rotten or hoarfrost. The medium is infinitely variable. Waterfall ice grades are designated by the acronym WI, which stands for "water ice" and generally goes from the easiest grade WI 1—easy walking on ice, almost impossible to fall on unless shot—to grade WI 6—unimaginably steep, exhausting, and frightening.

Some guidebooks include a grade WI 7 for pure ice and this involves climbing at the extreme limit of present-day difficulty, requiring immense physical prowess and a kamikaze-like sense of self-preservation that not many people possess. Only a handful of these routes exist and few have ever been repeated. If you find yourself on this stuff you are either irremediably stupid, have no imagination whatsoever, or are just very unlucky and probably soon to be communing with the angels.

Although a reasonably accurate grading system has been devised, ice is such a fickle medium and so dependent on seasonal and daily weather conditions that the climber cannot take them as read and the grade has to be assumed to be a consensus of opinion of what the climb is normally like. It might be more constructive to grade routes on the likely gamut of emotions the prospective climber is going to experience starting at the easiest grade and upwards—bored, intrigued, absorbed, alarmed, horrified, mentally certified, and dead.

A climb can be a grade easier than its given standard when it is in full, fat conditions or it can be a full grade harder in thin, lean conditions. Freestanding pillars of ice, often called "cigars," are notable for their unreliability. They can form in as short a period as a week and fall down without warning a few days later. If you happen to be attached to them at the time this can be very distressing. A certain degree of experience is needed to judge these variations. It can make the difference between enjoying yourself in a frightened sort of way or dying in a painful sort of way.

I've seen the waterfall ice grade 5 described as " . . . strenuous, sustained climbing on good ice, mostly vertical, with some resting places. Ice can be very thin and delicate. Protection may be reliable but require effort and ingenuity to create. There may be long run-outs between protection and belays may be exposed to ice fall."

The next stage up, WI 6, I have seen variously described in guidebooks as " . . . very steep, strenuous ice pitches that may be vertical the entire way, with overhanging sections, and very few resting places. Ice may not be of the best quality, can be rotten, cauliflowered, or chandeliered. Often thin and not protectable, or the protection may be very dubious. It can involve poorly welded pencil icicles and fractured chandelier-hung mushrooms requiring an open-minded exploratory attitude. It often entails hanging ice belays and a very high skill level is mandatory, as are a cool head for leading and following, and efficient and excellent climbing technique. Don't even think of falling off at this grade!" it adds helpfully.

Bridalveil Falls is about seven hours' drive away from Boulder, hanging above the town of Telluride in the San Juan Mountains, Colorado. I had been to the Mountain Film Festival in the town as a guest speaker a few years earlier and remembered it as a lively, picturesque, if somewhat expensive ski resort. It nestled at the end of a stunning box canyon and was overlooked by Mount Sneffels and the peaks of the Silverton west range of the San Juans. As Clyde enthused about the ice potential in Colorado he mentioned another famous route. The Ames Ice Hose was if anything technically harder and more committing than Bridalveil Falls and the two climbs were rightly regarded as megaclassic hard American ice routes.

As the evening drew to an end I decided that Bridalveil Falls would be our next winter adventure. Eric Coomer, a prolific climber of big walls who is happiest nailing his way up overhanging testpieces in his hunting ground of Yosemite, asked whether I fancied trying a big wall with him. Emboldened by an excess of alcohol, I forgot my long-held horror of jumaring up silk-thin ropes hanging over thousands of feet of emptiness and enthusiastically agreed that an adventure with Eric was just what I needed.

In truth I had always secretly harbored a desire to climb one of the classic big-wall routes on the granite of El Capitan. The

Nose, Salathe Wall, and the northwest face of Half Dome had always sung a siren call to me but to date I had never known anyone keen to join me. By the time I boarded the plane to Newark I had agreed to throw myself at two more classic climbs. I had thought long and hard about Tat's decision to quit mountaineering and, although tempted, I still felt there were a few climbs I needed to do. I was finding it very hard to let go. Privately I had been forming a tick list of classic routes in my mind. I knew I had to stop sometime—my legs gave me no choice—so rather than just cut and run I felt it better to wind down slowly with some memorable and very special routes.

Shortly after arriving home, I rang Ray in his climbing shop, "Kathmandu," in Utrecht, Holland.

"Listen, Ray," I said cheerfully. "I have this cunning plan . . . "

"Ah," he said warily.

"You'll love it."

"I've heard that before." He sighed. "Go on, what is it?"

"Bridalveil Falls," I said. "Colorado, next winter. What about it?"

"Bridalveil? I've heard of that. Didn't Jeff Lowe do it years ago?"

"Yeah, with Mike Weiss," I agreed. "They did it in 1974, for God's sake! Can you imagine climbing grade 6+ ice in those days with that sort of gear?"

"Six plus!" Ray yelped. "We can't climb 6-bloody-+. Are you mad?"

"Of course we can," I said, trying to hide my doubts. "Anyway, it won't be that hard. Not today with modern gear and not if it's in good nick."

"So, how hard is it in good nick?"

"Oh, 5+, maybe a little bit of 6 . . . "

"A little bit of 6! I don't want any 6. Six is overhanging. Six is frightening. Six is . . . "

"It looks bloody amazing! There's a photo of it in your copy of Jeff Lowe's *Ice World*. You've got it in the shop. Go take a look. It's on page 212." There was a prolonged silence and then the sound of pages being turned and the sudden hissing intake of breath.

"It looks good, doesn't it?" I guessed he was staring at the picture.

"I'm not sure good is the adjective I was looking for," Ray muttered darkly. "It gives it WI 6 here, you know?"

"Ah, well, yes, that's true, but it doesn't really mean anything . . . "

"It means it's grade 6 . . . "

"Yes, but it's a classic line. I mean, look at it. Just imagine being on that." I had the same book open on my desk and was staring at the stepped pillars of blue water ice and cauliflower mushrooms. "We've got to do it. Next winter. Okay?"

"Where is it?" Ray asked and I knew the hook had been set. He was tempted.

"Telluride," I answered. "Lovely place. We'll fly to Denver, hire a car, drive for seven hours, and throw ourselves at Bridalveil. If we do that we can try the Ames Ice Hose."

"What's that?" Ray asked suspiciously. "Another classic, I suppose."

"Well, yes it is, actually. It looks amazing. You'll love it."

"And how hard is that, then?"

"Well, grade 5 with a bit of 6, about the same as Bridalveil," I said and tried to hurry on and change the subject.

"You're kidding?"

"If we can climb Bridalveil we should be able to do Ames if it's the same grade."

"You don't sound so certain," Ray said accusingly.

"It's more serious . . . "

"Dangerous, you mean?"

"Sort of." I felt he was wavering. "But it's a megaclassic."

"They tend to be megaclassics because they are megadesperate," Ray pointed out succinctly. "What does the guidebook say?"

"Right, well it grades it WI 5/6, 200 meters (656 feet) high and it says . . . 'bring along Spectres, ice screws, and slings. Better to bring mostly skill, courage, and cunning rather than thinking that any gear placed on the first pitch could possibly be substantial enough to hold a fall. Usually the first pitch cannot be protected and screws are only useful for the last two . . . ' I stopped reading as Ray was snorting with laughter. "Come on," I coaxed him. "It'll be great fun and it'll be a change from La Grave."

"Yes, that's a point," Ray agreed.

"Okay, in principle I take it that you are keen on the idea?"

"Sort of," Ray said cautiously. "I'm just not sure we're up to that sort of climbing. I mean it looks horrifying."

"Of course we are," I said airily. "It's just an ice climb. We just do what we know and that's it. No problems. Anyway, we can always run away."

"Yes, we're good at that," Ray laughed.

One year later, in January 1999, Ray and I found ourselves standing beneath Bridalveil Falls peering up with cricks in our necks and wondering whether we might not have bitten off more than we could chew. We had walked up to the foot of the route to check on the condition of the ice. Secretly I think we were both hoping that it would be falling down, thus giving us an honorable excuse for running away. Unfortunately it looked in perfect nick and we had no excuses.

We had hoped to have Tat with us but sadly our plans to avoid scaring ourselves rigid on Bridalveil Falls by relying on Tat's renowned prowess had gone by the wayside. Tat had died three months earlier. We stood beneath the ice cascade feeling a little stupid and rather alarmed at our ambition. We made a few half-hearted jokes about Tat's final cunning plan to avoid having to climb it and then trooped wearily down towards the lights of Telluride.

Waterfall ice climbing is a strangely addictive pastime. It arouses in me a host of conflicting emotions giving rise to questions to which I have no answer. The most prominent of these is, *What are you doing, you idiot?*

This panicked thought normally howls through my mind as I reach a horrifying point of no return on some monstrous icy crumbling edifice. Unfortunately, having survived such an experience, the mind seems to be able to perform a bizarre sort of memory dump and as you sit in the bar supping a much-needed beer the nightmare climb gradually becomes a memory of ecstatic delight, an ascent of such aesthetic beauty it will live with you forever, an experience so deeply life-enhancing that from then on you are a changed person. Hence, the moment your climbing partner thrusts a guidebook under your nose and points excitedly at an even bigger and more perilous icicle you do not leap to your feet and rush screaming from the bar. No, you grin with measured insanity and say, "Hey, that looks brilliant. Let's do it." If you are wise and experienced you then head to the bar and order a large whiskey chaser, just to ensure that your dementia remains pleasantly stable.

Climbing frozen waterfalls appears to the uninformed observer to be a complicated if somewhat novel form of suicide. Quite often this very same thought is worming uneasily through the mind of the hapless climber.

Modern ice tools now come branded with fiendishly exciting and aggressive names. Rambos, Footfangs, and Terminators are, in fact, crampons. Black Prophets, Aliens, and Cobras are ice axes, previously known as alpenstocks. These are names to conjure up visions of mythic battles to be won fearlessly against all the odds. They also happen to appeal to the helplessly gullible and slightly desperate ice climbers looking for an edge in their war with icy wet verticality. If you don't feel brave waving these things around then you never will. I strap on a pair of Terminator crampons and leash my wrists to Cobra ice axes and I know I could whip Dante's demons if I so chose—until, that is, I leave the ground. Then I just feel scared and a little silly.

When previously the only protection came from hammering

smooth iron spikes into the ice or screwing in glorified corkscrews that had as much chance of holding your fall as a wet cigarette, today we have super-sharp ice screws that cut into hard ice with ease. Unlike their predecessors they can hold quite substantial falls, if the ice is good, and they no longer require enough energy expenditure to light up a small city when you place them.

One would have thought that these welcome developments would have made the sport considerably safer. Unfortunately climbers now throw themselves onto ice climbs that would have been unheard-of only a decade ago.

My first car, a rust bucket of a Mini, could, if pushed, go alarmingly fast and seemed to stick to corners like glue. It also had appalling brakes, the steering wheel vibrated like a washing machine on full spin cycle, and the size of the vehicle left you with no illusions as to what a small cube of twisted metal it could instantly become if you hit anything. Consequently I drove with a modicum of caution.

A recent report from the Automobile Association revealed that an alarming number of fatalities were being caused by the fact that the modern car with its near silent running, smooth suspension, antilock brakes, side-impact bars, air bags, and deceptively powerful acceleration lulled drivers into a false sense of security. Quite frequently it lulled the drivers into a sleep from which they never awoke.

These safety measures introduced to make motoring survivable have made people drive faster and more dangerously. I've always agreed that the most effective safety device would be a viciously sharp spike protruding from the center of the steering wheel to a point some ten inches from the driver's chest. No seat belts allowed.

The same seems to have occurred in ice climbing. Advances in equipment design have combined to make climbers attempt harder and more dangerous routes. It is a vicious circle and quite an amusing one if you do not happen to be a climber.

Yet, remarkably, fatalities are not that common in waterfall ice climbing. Of course some poor individuals do get swept away by avalanches, sometimes columns of ice collapse squashing the unfortunate parties attached to them, and some take short falls that inexplicably become very long ones abruptly interrupted by the ground—but that is only to be expected.

Such falls have acquired an imaginative series of descriptions. A "peeler," or a "lob," suggests a scary but survivable short fall. A "zipper," when all your gear rips out, and the aptly named "screamer," are altogether more serious, and if you are unfortunate enough to "crater" or "Desmond Decker" as a consequence, then your ice climbing adventures tend to be abruptly terminated.

So "bombing off," an uncontrolled free fall, can rapidly escalate into a "screamer," particularly if zipping occurs. In the worst-case scenario it may become a "birdman," a prolonged free fall with much flapping of arms and wild ice-tool spinning, before the inevitable "crater" and early retirement.

A stranger first viewing waterfall ice climbing could hardly be blamed for thinking the death rate must be somewhere in the region of 90 percent of all participants. Yet because it is such a bizarre-looking sport, because the dangers are so manifestly obvious even to someone whose testosterone level far exceeds his intelligence, only a handful of people are dumb enough to try it. And when they do, they are very, very careful.

Climbing vertical ice cascades the size of skyscrapers requires a certain lack of imagination. It can be physically exhausting, technically extremely difficult, demanding of immense concentration and coolheaded decision making, at the same time as being mind-numbingly frightening. It is an idiotic thing to do and therein lies the fascination. It can also be an exhilarating and absorbing experience. It is a paradox. It can be at once idiotic to the point of insanity and one of the coolest, calmest, most lucidly controlled, and vivid things you will ever do. It is so stupid as to be wonderful.

Jon Krakauer in his hilarious book *Eiger Dreams: Ventures*

Among Men and Mountains described an ascent of the crux ice pillar on Love's Way, a 360-foot-high waterfall in Alaska:

> *. . . no matter how carefully I swung my axes, every so often a shard of ice—some weighing twenty or thirty pounds—would break off beneath my blows, brush past my head, accelerate earthwards with a low whistle, and smash into the slope twenty stories below as I looked on, transfixed . . . Because the ice was overhanging, my arms were called upon to support approximately eighty percent of my bodyweight for most of the thirty or forty minutes it took to ascend the pillar. The physical effort was roughly comparable to doing pull-ups from a chinning bar for half an hour straight, pausing at the top of each pull-up to hang from one arm and swing a two-pound hammer a couple of times with the other.*

Doesn't that just sound great? When you also consider that the ice climber is bedecked with a wicked array of razor-sharp screws, crampons, and assorted spikes, falling off doesn't bear thinking of. Axes are attached to the climber's wrists with leashes so in the event of a fall they tend to have the disconcerting habit of spinning wildly through the air from the falling climber's semaphoring arms. Most of the time falling is not the problem. Hitting the ground is. Hitting the ground feet first with crampons on your boots tends to splinter leg bones with alarming efficiency. I know. I've done it twice now. This is painful enough without then having to contend with disemboweling yourself with the very tools and screws that are supposed to save your life.

Friedrich Nietzsche once cheerfully wrote, "If you gaze for long into an abyss, the abyss gazes also into you." He certainly had a point but it should be noted that he also once stated, "The secret of reaping the greatest fruitfulness and the greatest enjoyment from life is to *live dangerously.*" He might have thought twice about that one if he had been handed a pair of ice tools and pushed in the general direction of Bridalveil Falls.

Our first attempt on the Falls ended in ignominious defeat. When we arrived at the base of the route we were disappointed to find two parties on the ice. One pair was established on the left flank of the Falls and were climbing with shocking speed and ease.

However we had been told that the easiest line followed a steep ice pillar on the right flank of the Falls rising above the cone of shingled 80-degree ice at the foot of the climb. After this long pitch the two lines merged in the center of the Falls and the way ahead followed a column of ice to an alarmingly overhanging section of cauliflower ice. This is so named because of its peculiar formation of curled downward-facing plates of ice looking like serried clumps of huge upside-down artichokes. Once past this crux section of the route a vertical fluted pillar led up into a ramp of smooth water ice to a sheltered cave bivouac. From there a short 50-foot wall led to the top of the climb. The middle pitch was the longest and hardest section of the route.

We haggled over who would start first. Normally, keen and ambitious climbers are furious lead hogs determined to claim the hardest climbing for themselves. Owing to a highly developed sense of cowardice Ray and I tended to do quite the opposite and the argument was bitter and brief. Ray announced that the first pitch was his and promptly stomped off in the direction of the right-hand line where a party was ensconced on the first pitch. I had been lumped with the crux middle pitch, which I examined with mounting horror. I wasn't entirely convinced about my ability to climb overhanging cauliflower ice.

We watched as the lead climber struggled for a long time on this pillar and couldn't work out why he was taking so long until it was our turn to climb, an hour and a half later. Water was pouring down from the tips of some icicles hanging hundreds of feet above the pillar. The shower of freezing meltwater hadn't been visible when we had watched the wretched man's struggles and now with the water flow dramatically increased as the icy early-morning frost had dissipated, we found it impossible to make any progress. Apart from getting soaking wet it was almost impossible to look up into the deluge to see where to place our axes. We abandoned the attempt and walked down to the bars of Telluride.

As we stomped up the path to the foot of the route for the second attempt we were disappointed to notice tracks in the fresh snow that had fallen overnight. Despite our early start there were people ahead of us. Although it was freezing hard we were surprised to see that water was still pouring down the right-hand line. Since there was also a pair of climbers gearing up at the foot of the line we had no choice but to try the harder left-hand pillar. I was delighted to find that Ray's attempt to grab the easiest start had backfired so spectacularly. He looked glum at the prospect.

"At least you won't get wet this time," I laughed as he peered morosely at the ice rearing above him.

"Hi, guys. Come to do Bridalveil, eh?" A cheerful red-bearded man called out as he walked over to us from where he had been gearing up on the right. Ray and I looked expectantly around, wondering what on earth else he thought we might be planning on doing standing there as we were, armed to the teeth with ice climbing gear.

"Yeah, seemed like a good idea," I replied.

"Where are you boys from?"

"England."

"Brits, eh. Cool." He spoke with what I took to be a languid Texan drawl. "I've done it a couple of times now. It's different every time."

"You've done it before?" Ray asked incredulously. He clearly thought that if you got up the route once, the best thing to do was sell your ice gear and never step foot in America again.

"Oh, jeez, yeah, man. It's a cool route."

"Cool? Right." Ray muttered and fiddled with his harness.

"It's wild, man. Some years there are two sets of overhangs on it. Then it's solid 6."

"Two overhangs? Oh, Jesus!"

"Enjoy," Ray said to me in a mock American accent.

"What is that odd-looking ice like?" I was staring at the band of overhanging leaves of ice sprouting from the center of the Falls.

"The cauliflower ice. Hey, it's weird, man!" our companion enthused. "You can do some wild moves—hooking, stemming, chicken-winging . . . "

"Chicken-winging? What the hell is that?" I asked warily.

"It's crazy." The man demonstrated, holding his axe handle with his elbow bent at a right angle parallel with his body. "You get a good pick placement like this, right?" I nodded. "Lift your elbow and hook it behind the leaves. Do it with both arms." He made the same movement with his other arm. "And, hey man, you're chicken-winging, man! Outrageous moves, dude. You'll dig 'em." He flapped his elbows and chuckled happily. I looked at him as if he was out of his mind. He wished us luck and stomped happily back to his companions.

"Chicken-winging?" I said and stared at Ray. "He's barking mad."

"Yeah, and it's all on the second pitch that you're leading," Ray said cheerfully and marched off to the foot of the left-hand ice pillar.

Ray climbed the initial cone of shingled ice and then moved left onto a steep column of ice. Halfway up this he noticed a small cave formed between the edge of the column and the rock wall. Traversing awkwardly left off the column and into the cave he fixed an ice screw into the back of the cave and then had second thoughts about trying the airy and exposed moves swinging back right onto the vertical pillar of ice. I watched as he started to bridge with his legs stemmed wide apart, one cramponed boot scratching on the rock wall and the other dug into the ice. I could see the fringe of arm-length icicles that guarded the lip of the cave. The exit directly upwards from the cave would lead him back onto the ice but it looked extremely difficult. I wanted to shout a warning but I knew it would be useless. Fifty feet to my left a geyser of water was pounding down into the plunge pool at the foot of the falls drowning out all communication between us. I hoped the ice screw was good because if the screw ripped out he would fall nearly a hundred feet.

As the thought occurred to me I saw Ray reach up and swing his axe at the ice above the cave roof. Then he was off, falling backwards in a welter of arms and legs, as a large block of ice sheared away from his axe blow. I rushed backwards down the avalanche cone in the hope of pulling in as much slack rope as possible to lessen the length of his fall. I braced myself for the impact but nothing happened. Ray had disappeared. I saw a yellow ice axe arcing through the sky in a graceful parabola before it disappeared into the avalanche cone close to the edge of the plunge pool. A few minutes passed and I began to worry that Ray had hurt himself. *Where had he gone? Was he jammed head down between the ice and the rock?*

Just as I was getting seriously worried, Ray's head appeared level with the foot of the cave. He slowly got to his feet, shaking his head groggily from side to side. After a short pause he pulled up some rope and tied himself into the ice screw then waved for me to come up to him.

I noticed the spray of blood on the ice as I neared the edge of the cave.

"Are you okay, kid?" I looked up and Ray's head suddenly popped out of the cave. He had a sheepish grin on his face and a smear of blood on his chin and neck.

"Got a bang in the face," he said. "Did you see the size of that ice block?"

"I saw something big."

"Yeah, well it smacked me in the face. Knocked me clean off."

"I noticed."

"I seem to be bleeding." He touched the side of his face and looked at the blood on his glove. "Oh, and I dropped my axe."

"Yeah, I noticed that too," I said. "You idiot!"

He grinned happily at me and as he did so I noticed the hole in his cheek. It was about an inch and a half long and bleeding steadily.

"Well, that showed them what us Brits can do," he said and I watched fascinated as the hole, like a minimouth, mimicked the movements of his lips.

"They didn't see the fall. They're already on the second pitch chicken-winging like crazy, no doubt."

"I don't fancy doing any more leading," Ray said, looking a little shaken. "Thought I was going for a screamer but I just landed in the cave."

"I think it might be a good idea to rappel down and go and get that stitched up." I nodded at his face and he touched the hole again.

"It doesn't hurt; just feels a bit numb." The hole opened and closed obscenely and blood bubbled out as he spoke. I leaned forward and examined the wound. Pushing his cheek gently opened it out and I saw the gleam of his teeth.

"Good thing, then," I replied cheerfully. "Because it's gone right through. Must have been the ice. It's so clean it could have been done with a scalpel."

"Really?" He probed experimentally with his tongue.

"Don't do that," I said. "It looks horrible enough as it is without you sticking your tongue through it. Come on, let's get down." I handed him the axe that I had retrieved from the avalanche cone and then began sorting out the rappel ropes.

We trudged disconsolately back down the track to Telluride. I left Ray in the medical center demonstrating to the receptionist the various different shapes he could achieve with his wound by puffing his cheeks out, talking ,and pushing at it with his tongue.

"That's gross. Stop it!" she squealed and Ray grinned happily.

He was led off by the young and serious-looking doctor who had been called to check on the wound.

"That needs stitching," she said sternly and led him away by the elbow.

"Will it affect my modeling career?" he asked as she pushed him into a cubicle.

"I'll see you in the bar, Ray." I called after him and then smiled at the receptionist. "He's very, very stupid, I'm afraid," I said loud enough for Ray to hear. "It's congenital, you see," I added and she smiled at me warily.

He appeared at the bar an hour later proudly displaying the bristling line of stitches in his cheek.

"It cost four hundred bloody dollars," he complained bitterly.

"That's American health care for you." I peered at the stitches. "Looks like they've done a good job. You'll hardly see the scar in a year or so."

"Listen, I've been thinking," Ray said. "Maybe we should try another route. Get a bit more ice climbed before we go back to Bridalveil."

"Oh, good," I brightened up. "I was worried that you might have been put off it altogether."

"No way," Ray said sharply. "I've got a bone to pick with that bugger now."

The following day we climbed the Ames Ice Hose. The last pitch was melting furiously. Of the six ice screws I placed on lead all but the last one had melted out by the time I had reached the top and Ray had only to pluck them from the ice with his fingers.

The Ames Ice Hose proved to be one of the finest ice climbs I had ever enjoyed—varied, sustained, and challenging. Indeed we climbed it in such fine style that our confidence came surging back after our setbacks on Bridalveil Falls.

Early the following morning, nursing Ames Ice Hose celebration hangovers, we tramped wearily back up to the Falls. A light snow was dusting the air and it was freezing hard. For once there were no other parties on the climb. We could now make idiots of ourselves in peace.

Ray climbed swiftly back to the blood-spattered cave and set up a solid belay from which I led up a steep ice pillar to a solid belay on ice screws and threaded icicles just to the left of the central overhanging band of cauliflower ice. "Don't worry, I'm right behind you," he said with a grin as I made the first tentative swings of my ice axes. After about 15 feet I found myself braced across a groove between two vertical ice pillars with my arms tiring rapidly. Ray was out of sight hidden safely beneath the overhanging start to the pitch. My breathing became a little ragged as I struggled to place an ice screw in an awkward spot between two hollow icicles. An awkward swing to the right around the pillar led into a confused area of bulging leaves of ice. It pushed me off balance, forcing me to hang free on my arms from my axes as I tried to work out the best way forward.

A solid axe placement high and to my right enabled me to pull myself up to a point where I could lock my right elbow. I instinctively pushed the elbow out to my right. In an instant it had slid behind an adjacent leaf of ice and by pressing outwards I found that I could hold myself easily in balance. When I made the same move with my left arm I found myself perched on the overhanging ice with both elbows shoulder-high at right angles to my body jammed behind convenient slivers of ice. *Good God!* I thought. *I'm chicken-winging. So that's what the guy was on about.* It was an astonishingly stable and restful stance despite the spectacular position in which I was poised. I let out a whoop of glee and Ray called up to ask me if I was okay.

"Fantastic," I yelled. "Bloody superb." I looked above me and was disappointed that there was not the second band of overhangs that form in some years. Until that point the very prospect of such an increase in difficulty had filled me with dread. I knew that having overcome the first band of overhangs it would be extremely difficult if not impossible for me to retreat. Yet now I was looking forward to finding the way ahead blocked by another seemingly insuperable barrier. I knew I would be able to climb it with ease.

So long as it was water ice, I felt sure I could climb 6+, even grade 7. It wasn't vain boastful pride; it was simply true. I had learned that I was better than I had thought, at least on that day and at that time, and it made me feel wonderful. I knew then that we were going to succeed.

It was not about being a "hard" climber, not a challenge to prove to others how good we were, but a pure and simple test of ourselves. That moment when I knew I was strong enough and powerful enough, mentally and physically, to overcome the obstacles in front of me came as a rushing exultation, a joyous realization that this was why I was here. George Mallory once wrote after succeeding on a climb, "We're not exultant: but delighted, joyful: soberly astonished . . . Have we vanquished an enemy? None but ourselves . . ." I was meant to be there. *This is who you are; why you do this,* I thought, and grinned broadly all the way to the top of the pitch, delighting in the intricate mixture of power and subtlety, the delicate balance between gymnastic dance and thuggish strength. I became entranced, absorbed in the game of reading the ice. The feeling of invincibility was infused with the wondrous irrationality of what I was doing—immutable, anarchic living, the essence of climbing, of simply being.

Whether it was on a towering granite headwall, a Himalayan behemoth, an Alpine north wall, or a fragile lacy confection of towering water ice, the feeling was the same.

All my depressed thoughts had become meaningless. There was only one reason for my being there—to climb into the unknown, pushing my limits to discover how far I could go. I knew it would fade rapidly once the climb was done, and I wanted to luxuriate in the feeling. I hadn't felt like that for a long time. I had missed it.

The outcome needed to be uncertain, the prospect frightening, the potential for injury high, otherwise there would be nothing learned and nothing proved. I didn't want to die but if death hadn't been ever-present then I doubt I would have been there. It set the parameters of the game. What we stood to lose was everything. We were fugitives from reality and yet things never seemed so real, so clear and sharp and right.

When I reached the belay cave near the top of the Falls I fixed three solid ice screws and shouted down to Ray that I was fine and he could come up. I leaned back on the slings and looked out over the plunge of the frozen ice falls. The snow had cleared from the air. Telluride lay huddled in the valley far below. The air had a bright translucent quality, a tangy, crisp perfection, cool on the lungs. The clean, gin-clear winter sky had an almost solid feel to it, like a polished wineglass that you could reach out and ping with your finger. I pulled hard on the ropes as Ray began to move, slow and stiff from his long wait beneath the icy overhangs.

I looked at the main stream of the waterfall plunging into space in a rushing white stream, ice crystals glinting in the afternoon sunlight and clouds of steamy vapor blowing back into the sky. I listened to the calculated dissonance of the thundering water as it rose and fell in swells of sound like a heavy symphonic weltering sea, so resonant that the crashing of the water in the plunge pool was a memory of the oceans with the surf calling its crying song. I wondered why we had ever been menaced by the sight of it and not transfixed, mesmerized by its beauty as I was now. Part of me knew that I was seeing with exultant eyes deceived by the chemical rush of excitement. But it was true for the moment and I would happily accept it as such.

Soaking up the spectacle, enjoying the experience of being there, happy and alive, reading it in my mind in a tumble of breathless metaphors, I tried to capture it in my memory forever. I knew it would fade. It always did and the thought saddened me. What a strange, inexplicable misfortune it is, to come to this edge of perfection and then let it slip through your fingers.

I wanted to hold the moment for as long as possible before the inevitable lurch back to gray reality. The French have an expression for feelings such as these, *le petit mort,* the little death. The postcoital depression, the fleeting saddening loss when it is over. It seemed about right to me then. The bittersweet, heady ache of ecstasy and loss. The half-lost, half-won game of life that we could never quite finish. It seemed, sometimes, fleetingly, you could come close to the ineffable edge of perfection when it all goes to glory for the briefest of moments, an inarticulate moment, that leaves you with a vulnerable shattered sense of wonderment. It was life enhancing: pure emotion.

The ropes jerked tight in my hands. Ray had fallen off. I glanced down and saw him swing out from the overhangs with an expression of alarm and irritation on his face. The ropes slackened. He was climbing again. I was laughing at the fun of it all and the memory of his surprised dismay. He had been rushing the pitch, hooking his axe picks into air bubbles rather then smashing them forcefully into the ice.

Again the ropes went tight as one of his lightly hooked picks popped out of the ice, and I heard a stream of curses above the roar of the falls. He swung out into space in a gentle pendulum and his oaths swung out on the wind with him. I laughed again and shouted friendly insults into the winter sky.

Ray arrived in the cave breathless and smiling broadly. I knew how he felt. I clapped him on the back, and squeezed his shoulder and grinned happily at him but we did not hug. That was what Tat had been good at.

As we stumbled down the path in the gathering dusk we chatted excitedly about the climb, wondering at the audacity and skill of Jeff Lowe and Mike Weiss in attempting the climb nearly a quarter of a century earlier.

"You know your idea about tick lists?" Ray asked as we trudged down towards the car. "What do you have in mind?"

"I'm not sure really. It was just an idea I had. You know, do a few classic lines, fill in the holes in my climbing CV before giving it all up."

"Do you still want to do that?" Ray asked. "After this?"

"Yeah, I think so," I replied and stopped to look at Bridalveil rearing up at the head of the canyon. "It was good, wasn't it?"

"Superb," Ray said quietly.

"It would be nice to leave it like that, wouldn't it?"

"Yeah. I suppose it would," he agreed. "But it would be nice to keep doing it."

"I know, but it has to end some time," I said. "And I'd like it to be on my terms."

"Like Tat, you mean?" Ray said and laughed softly.

"Yeah, like Tat," I said quietly. "He was right, you know. He just got unlucky."

"Okay, so what about this tick list then? Any more cunning plans up your sleeve?"

"Maybe The Nose or Salathe?"

"Yes, that would be good," Ray said. "I've never been to Yosemite. And it would be warm . . . "

"I suppose so," I said. "Still we'll never stop if we don't get a final short list. And I mean short."

"Okay, so Bridalveil was one of them. The ice climb. Salathe or The Nose would be the rock climb on the list. We need a mountain route. A real classic. What do you think?"

"A new route somewhere, perhaps," I said doubtfully. "I'll think on it."

"Yeah, me too," Ray said as we reached the car. "Come on, let's go drink beer. We deserve it."

RITE OF PASSAGE

ON MY RETURN HOME I FOUND MYSELF AT A BIT OF A LOOSE END. I had recently moved into a new house in Sheffield. Well, new is an exaggeration. It was two hundred and fifty years old. It was an old farm laborer's cottage with three-foot-thick walls, not a single doorway square or a wall straight, ancient stonework with lime and horsehair mortar making hanging a picture a DIY nightmare. I loved it. It had character and individuality and a sense of the countless generations that had passed their lives beneath its roof. It had a garden, something I had always promised Muttley, my faithful bearded collie cross, and he peed all over it with delighted territorial abandon.

The bidding and eventual signing of contracts was the usual nightmare that British house conveyancing has always been; probably the most idiotic and stressful way to try to part company with a great deal of money that has ever been devised.

Some months earlier I had begun writing my second novel without a contract or an advance. I had assured my agent, Vivienne Schuster, that I didn't need one and it would help keep away the pressure of a deadline.

"But that's the only way you write, Joe," she said. "You come over all lapsed Catholic and guilty because you have signed the deal and that gives you the discipline to finish it."

"Well, yes, that was true in the past," I agreed. "But this time it will be different."

"A likely story," she said, accurately discounting any chance of

seeing a manuscript within her lifetime. I vowed to prove her wrong
and enthusiastically began tapping at my keyboard. I had completed twenty-five thousand words, only to find that I had written
myself into a cul-de-sac. There were only two characters in the
novel and I discovered to my incredulous dismay that I had killed
off both of them. This was a fairly major plotting error.

The house move conveniently provided me with a mass of
work-avoidance excuses, something that I have managed to
become very good at. The kitchen floor had to be tiled, a wood-
burning stove installed, and the chimneys relined. The office in
the attic needed two skylight windows to let in more light, and
planning permission for a summerhouse extension on the back had
to be applied for. Far from being irritated by these inconvenient
and expensive tasks I was elated at the chance to escape from my
keyboard.

A glance at the overgrown garden confirmed that major work
was urgently needed. Fences had to be repaired or replaced, the
lawn dug up and relaid, borders torn up and replanted. The 50-foot
eucalyptus that some previous horticultural lunatic had planted
close to the house had to be cut down before it crashed through
the roof in the autumn gales.

Within a year Bruce French, former Nottingham and England
wicket keeper, passionate climber, and expert builder, had reduced
my new home to a building site. What he was eventually to build in
its place was a superb testament to his building skill. Writing
ground to an inevitable halt.

There were other reasons for the disruption to my writing
schedule. A chance connection with Marek Kriwald, who ran a
corporate speaking bureau called Parliament Communications,
had led to a suddenly burgeoning speaking career. Although I had
given slide presentations all over the world it had primarily been
to climbing audiences and those many nonclimbers who had read
Touching the Void. Through Marek and Parliament I suddenly
found myself giving what were called motivational or inspirational

corporate presentations. In truth all I did was tell the story of *Touching the Void*.

I suppose it is inspirational in many ways, but to Simon and me it was only a reality and because we had experienced it, it never really had much shock value. As climbers we were a fairly pragmatic bunch and to some extent we regarded what had happened in Peru as an almighty cock-up from which we were both very lucky to survive. The fact that we had an accident came as no huge surprise, simply the fact that we had survived. We had already lost a number of friends in mountaineering accidents and had few illusions about the risks we were taking.

I found it very intimidating to stand in front of large groups of successful, highly motivated businesspeople and tell them what a mess we had made of our first mountaineering expedition. I found talking to chief executive officers of huge multinational companies every bit as challenging as climbing grade 6 frozen waterfalls. To my delight the talks did seem to hit some sort of inspirational or motivational button to which I was never privy and demand for more engagements quickly increased. I had never realized quite how many company conferences are being staged on a daily basis worldwide and how huge was the demand for corporate speakers. It was a new, exciting, and intimidating venture and, fortunately, also quite lucrative. Most of the fees earned seemed to be disappearing straight into Bruce's back pocket as the hole he was digging at the back of the house gradually became bigger and bigger in direct proportion to the hole appearing in my bank account. My writing plans were now seriously stalled.

Early in 1998 a phone call from Jonathan Sissons, the head of rights at Jonathan Cape, came as an incredible surprise. A production company based in Los Angeles was making inquiries about the film rights for *Touching the Void*. Jonathan had been trying to sell the rights for a movie for the best part of ten years with mixed results.

I was dubious about whether a film of the book could ever be made. In the late 1980s I had visited Fred Zinneman, the renowned Hollywood film director and producer. As a child in the Austrian Alps he had been a keen hill walker and mountaineer and had never lost touch with events in the mountaineering world.

Fred Zinneman had long since retired by the time he had invited me for coffee in his house in London and I was curious to know why he was interested. Expecting to see the walls of his room adorned with photographs of famous stars and legendary movies I was quite taken aback to see a predominance of mountain views of the Alps. We talked about the possibilities of making *Void* into a film. Zinneman pointed out that the story was very similar to Hemingway's *The Old Man and the Sea,* which I thought was quite a stunning compliment until he quickly made it clear that he wasn't talking about the literary value of the work. He had been the director charged with making Hemingway's great Nobel Prize-winning novel into a movie and, as he explained, they soon ran into major difficulties.

"The Old Man and the Sea makes a wonderful read but in movie terms it is extremely difficult to evoke the immense power of Hemingway's writing," he said. "After all, what have you got? One old man and a big fish. Everything in the book happens through the eyes and thoughts of the old man and to portray this in the film was an almost impossible problem. Then we had the fish. Our great big mechanical rubber thing kept sinking and refusing to look anything like a marlin. I gave up in the end and John Huston took over the project."

"I've never seen the film," I said. "But I loved the book. I always wondered whether it was what killed him in the end. He must have known that having written something so brilliantly, not a word wasted, a perfectly crafted story that was unsurpassable, he would never be able to write anything better. It must have eaten away at him."

"Perhaps," Fred agreed. "And from the point of view of a film you have the same problem. In your story there is only you and

Simon. Very soon the rope is cut and you are separated and from then on everything is seen through either your thoughts or his. How do you film that?"

So I was skeptical about the chances of a movie ever being made and was astounded when Jonathan Sissons rang and told me that Fogwood Films were interested in the rights. Fogwood was the production company of Sally Field, the multiple-Oscar-winning actress.

"They're serious," Jonathan said. "They have gotten together with the Cruise-Wagner production company."

"Who are they?"

"Cruise. Tom Cruise. The actor. It's his production company. He's read the book and wants to star in the film."

I burst out laughing. "Bloody Nora." I put the phone down and wondered what other strange paths this book was going to lead me down. Tom Cruise, the highest-paid male actor in the world, was going to play me. In some bemusement I tottered downstairs and poured myself a very strong gin.

I was flown first class to Los Angeles. A limousine dropped me outside the Beverly Wilshire Hotel and I was checked into a suite that was bigger than my house.

Sally Field proved to be a delightful woman, charming, genuine, and completely unpretentious; not my idea of a film star at all. We signed the deal at Paramount Studios. The famous Hollywood-based entertainment paper *Variety* had a photograph of Cruise on the cover with the headline "Cruise into the Void," and a statement from Martin Shafer of Castle Rock Entertainment announced that Tom Cruise would be the lead actor. It was a strangely disorientating experience, leaving me in a state of surprised disbelief and with the nagging worry that I was once again out of control.

I had never set out to be an author and the idea of a movie being made about me was even more bizarre. The great success of the book had left me feeling oddly insecure. As a climber I had always judged myself against my peers and those heroes of mine that I, secretly and vainly, hoped to emulate. In doing so I had always looked up at the climbers so much better than me and judged my worth by their standards. I never once thought to judge myself by how much better than others I might be. I was keenly aware that I was well known within the climbing world and yet, seen in terms of my own climbing prowess, I deserved none of it. I understood that it was my writing that was being appreciated, but the problem was that I saw myself as a mountaineer.

At home I was surrounded by climbers of world class. The achievements of rock climbers like Jerry Moffat, Ben Moon, Paul Pritchard, and Johnny Dawes and mountaineers such as Al Rouse, Rab Carrington, Jon Tinker, Mick Fowler, and Brendan Murphy soon put anything that I had managed to climb into a clear perspective. At trade shows or film festivals I met some of the world's most talented climbers and it only served to deepen the feeling that I was an impostor. Signing the film deal compounded these confused emotions. Having said that, I signed the contract with alacrity.

I spent three days in Los Angeles with the screenwriter and by the time I flew home I had considerable doubts about what sort of film was going to be produced. The screenwriter didn't seem to have a sense of the essence of the story, the psychological trauma of two people alone in a remote wilderness. His grasp of mountaineering techniques seemed even more tenuous, despite our visits to various climbing shops and my patient explanation of how crampons, axes, and ropes were used. I did mention the core problem that Zinneman had pointed out and was rather taken aback when his solution was to provide Simon and me with radios. I thought he was missing the point somewhat.

It was made abundantly clear that the film was seen as a star vehicle for Cruise and this left me in little doubt that any attempt to remain faithful to the story would be short-lived. With a few rare exceptions most of the major movies produced in Hollywood in recent years seemed to have little or no character development, vague and often pointless plotting, and were driven solely by action, with quality writing rarely evident. Truth and the facts of history were routinely treated with cavalier contempt. The few Hollywood climbing movies that I had seen had done nothing to boost my confidence. *K2* was stereotyped, overemotional pap. Sylvester Stallone's action climbing thriller, *Cliff Hanger,* was hilarious idiocy. Hollywood's most recent offering, the improbable stunt-driven movie *Vertical Limits* was such embarrassingly nationalistic schmaltz that I walked out. It wasn't even laughable.

Perhaps I should have been more principled about the deal and ignored the large sums of money on offer. I tend to think that the people who accuse others of "selling out" are usually the ones who have never themselves been offered guaranteed financial security. Flying home in a preoccupied state of mind I thought of Groucho Marx. "These are my principles," he said. "If you don't like them I have others."

For the next nine hours I tried to drink the first-class galley dry and speculated on who would play Simon—Nicole Kidman, probably.

The film deal, moving house, and the new challenge of corporate speaking had marked something of a turning point in my life. I should have been very happy. I had the freedom to climb water ice and rock faces and mountain walls whenever I chose and somehow make a living out of it. I did far more now than I ever used to do. I enjoyed paragliding in the Peak District hills fifteen minutes from my home and planned to fly on sites all around the world. I nursed plans to climb on the towering granite walls of El Capitan in Yosemite and to paraglide in Nepal with the white sails of Annapurna and Dhaulagiri as a backdrop.

Because of climbing, writing, and speaking I had a life full of adventure and travel and excitement. In the course of these ventures I have met wonderful people of all races and creeds and colors and had my mind broadened and my sense of the world changed utterly. Above all I have made many friends all over the world and experienced things with them that have changed my life immeasurably. I have seen how strong we can be, and how frail. I have watched friends put their lives on the line to save mine and it has humbled me and left me forever in their debt.

I enjoy the anxious jeopardy of public speaking and it was flattering as well as humbling to realize that some people at least seemed to derive pleasure and inspiration from what I said. It put a lot of things into perspective. There had always been a sense that I was out of control, that I had just rolled along life's road and got lucky breaks all the way along. I had never planned any of it.

My unease started in the winter of 1998. I had returned from a holiday climbing on the overhanging rock walls of stalactite-draped limestone islands in Koh Phi Phi, a rock island in the Andaman Sea in southern Thailand. As usual there was a mass of letters and junk mail on the front-room floor and I bundled it together and put it on the kitchen table. The return journey had been complicated by tension with Iraq and I felt tired and jet-lagged from the seventeen-hour flight back from Thailand. I blearily sorted through the envelopes as I drank a strong black coffee. A letter stood out from the pile, marked as it was by the red stamp of "Curtis Brown." I knew that it was from Vivienne and quickly slit open the envelope, wondering what it might be about.

When I placed the letter slowly back on the table a few minutes later something had irrevocably changed in my life. Ma had died while I had been away. No one had been able to contact me. In desperation my sister, Sarah, had asked Vivienne if she knew how to reach me and told her the news about Ma. Unaware that no one had managed to tell me Vivienne had written a beautiful, gentle, caring letter of condolence. I was in shock. I knew that Ma had been ill. She had been going into hospital for a routine investigation and she had assured me it was not serious and that there was no need to cancel the Thailand holiday. I suspected she had known far more than she was telling me.

I stood up and fetched the phone through and rang Sarah,

hoping there had been some sort of communication breakdown.

"Yes, it's true," Sarah said softly and went on to explain what had happened and I sat there numb and mute. "We've all been waiting for you," she added. "We didn't know where you were so everything has been delayed."

I felt terrible and guilty—it was bad enough that I hadn't been there with Ma when she died. "The funeral? When is it?"

"Tuesday. Four days' time. Come home soon, Joe, we'd love to see you." And that was it. Ma was gone.

Ma was an extraordinarily devout woman. She was born in Listowel, Kerry, Ireland and her Catholic faith was the linchpin of her life. She was also a very strong and determined fighter. She had put down her surviving throat cancer in the mid-1970s, when everyone had felt sure she was dying, to her faith in God. She had told me that one day when she was very bad an Irish nurse in the Royal Marsden Hospital in London had rebuked her for giving up. As a good Catholic she was not allowed to relinquish life: that was God's choice and Ma should start praying. Ma prayed and she lived. It was clear-cut to her. The prayers had been answered. Privately I thought it was because she was tenacious and stubborn, but she wouldn't have it.

So, when I was sixteen, I found it very difficult to tell Ma that I no longer believed in God. It was harder still to be convinced that I was right. I wasn't certain that in the face of death I would be steadfast in my atheism. In Peru in 1985, when I knew that the game was up and I was dying and it led to nothing, no paradise, just eternal emptiness, I never once thought to turn back to the God of my childhood. If for one moment I had thought that some omniscient being might be looking down upon me and offer a helping hand I would have stopped moving instantly, gotten rid of the pain and the effort, and waited to be helped. And I would have died. In fact it was probably one of the most powerful and saddest things that I learned in those awful days in Peru. For me there was no God.

I respected Ma's faith immensely. Indeed, I was jealous of it. I wished I had something that strong. Although I no longer believed, it had been a source of quiet comfort to know that Ma was praying for me. I would take all the help I could get. And then she was gone. I wondered how things would be from now on.

Sometimes, as in Bolivia after surviving the avalanche, I look at the stars and I wonder whether she is wandering among them. Had she found the place that she had prayed so hard for? Just as mountains can make you feel insignificant and vulnerable, the stars, so vividly clear at high altitude, can make you realize how inconsequential your existence is. On some nights it can unnerve me looking up at myriad diamonds in a velvet black sky. The whole set of beliefs, the philosophy by which I try to live my life and understand my world, begins to fall apart.

I wonder about the probability of surviving in the mountains and then I look at the stars, at an infinity of other worlds, and I realize that it really doesn't matter that much. There are more stars in the known universe than there are grains of sand on all the world's beaches. We are unimaginably ignorant and in the context of space and time we are an utter irrelevance. It is a chilling thought if you have no God to prop you up, to offer something other than this bleak enormity, to explain the meaninglessness. We are no more than the blinking of an eye between two eternities.

Without the comfort of a religion to fall back on I'm left grasping at vague ideas of what I am, and why I am here, and whatever set of beliefs I cobble together I never seem to be quite as secure as I once was.

It seemed to me that if I could escape the need to know the future and free myself from the constraints of the past, acting in and only for the present, then I could achieve an absolute freedom. It seemed most true in those strange, ghostly moments on mountains when I edged along the slender line between life and death. It made a sort of sense; it amounted to a fragile, almost comprehensible, rationale.

I no longer hold to a religion, a theology, or any system by which I can understand my world. Without beliefs I try simply to accept a spiritual sense of the world as life passes by. It is an overwhelming combination of all that I've experienced, felt, seen, and cannot explain. It stays with me and refuses to depart, and it drives me again and again back to a place in which I am never certain; a place that is alluring because it will not be defined. It is intangible and must simply be lived. Perhaps that is why I loved the mountains. They allowed me, however briefly, to escape, to act without the need to ask questions.

I once read that for a mountaineer " . . . hardship and great effort hardly matters since the life of a mountain climber is an introduction to death, and when death comes or is about to come, the climber is at least partially satisfied." Then again, I don't recall satisfaction being my reaction to lying in the bottom of a crevasse with a shattered knee.

The paradox and incongruity lie in the fact that we willingly choose such risks when we so much want to stay alive. Why? Perhaps it all boils down to sensation—what we feel is all we really know; all we can accurately say we are. Yet others may not feel the same way. This isolates us. We hope that others also experience the same things because it keeps us sane and allows us to build a construct within which to live.

Whatever ideas or beliefs I had collected together in my life were shattered when Ma died. Did I love her? I never thought of her as being any more than my mother. She was Ma. Like the foundation of a house she was always there, always the same—and I did not have to think of her until she was gone and there were so many questions unanswered.

When Vivienne had said in her letter that losing a parent was a "rite of passage" I didn't really understand what she meant—it irked me. I felt she was right but I did not know how. As the years have passed I get a sense of it now. Leaving on my own journey, alone, an adult drifting through the last half of his life, it begins to dawn on me, this sense of life closing in. Ma had said I was selfish in her last letter and how right she was. It came after a classic family row, like so many others in the past, when passions had risen too high and words were spoken that shouldn't even have been thought. Like so many rifts it would be short-lived and soon forgiven, and it was—just in time—but it was her last letter to me and left an indelibly sad impression. I had replied angrily, for we had argued bitterly that last Christmas, but my anger was because she was right, as always, and it cut me to the quick. We made up with flowers but I will regret it forever, that and the fact that I was not there when she died.

As I stood at the front pew of the church I felt dislocated and disorientated looking down on Ma's coffin as the priest gave the blessing for the dead in words that seemed pointless and inane to me. As I bent with my brothers to lift her onto our shoulders tears splashed onto the polished wooden lid and I kept my head down and slightly bowed, hoping that I would regain some self-control. As we stepped into the sunlight I was amazed at how immensely heavy she seemed to be for such a slight old lady.

BECAUSE IT'S THERE

THE FOLLOWING SPRING I WAS AT MY DESK WORKING on a review of Peter and Leni Gillman's biography of George Mallory. I remembered the news flash on the radio announcing that an expedition had found Mallory's body high on the north side of Everest. It had been exciting and intriguing news. Later I would see the published photographs and feel dismayed and disgusted. I was already fairly sickened at the knowledge of recent appalling behavior on Everest.

When the gruesome photographs of Mallory's frozen body were sold around the world something inside me became hardened and cynical and died; a passion was extinguished. Climbing wasn't the same any more and it never would be. I felt betrayed.

When Conrad Anker found George Mallory's body frozen into the scree at 27,000 feet on Everest's north face on May 1, 1999, it was an extraordinary discovery. The search expedition had hoped to solve the mystery of Mallory and Irvine. Had they reached the summit? Was there photographic proof frozen within the Kodak vest-pocket camera that Mallory or Irvine had been carrying? It must have been an intensely moving moment to be sitting there beside the body of one of the most famous mountaineers in history, on the verge of solving one of the great mysteries of mountaineering.

A careful and respectful search of the body was all that was required. Unfortunately, there was no camera. From the position of the body, the injuries revealed, and the snapped rope at Mallory's waist it was now pretty safe to conclude that the two men didn't reach the summit but died in a fall while retreating in the dark. That was all we needed to know. We didn't need the photographs or the tasteless descriptions of what the birds had done to his body. I wondered if the searchers had ever stopped to think for a moment about what they were actually doing as they went through his belongings and then buried the body under a cairn of rocks and read a prayer over the fresh grave.

Conrad Anker had lost close friends in the mountains, as we all have. Some could fairly be regarded as the finest climbers of their generation, modern Mallorys in effect. I imagine Conrad Anker would be appalled if, in years to come, the frozen, battered bodies of his friends were found and picked over, photographed, and had their possessions removed.

In 1997 Paul Nunn was part of a British expedition to the west face of Latok II in the Karakoram. One of their team, Don Morrison, was killed falling unroped into a crevasse. Some ten years later Paul Nunn returned to the region on another expedition to Latok. At the edge of the glacier expedition members were surprised to find the remains of their friend, Don Morrison, extruded from the glacier. They were confident that the shattered body parts were those of their friend because they had managed to identify his harness. Carefully collecting as much as they could, they chose a site safe from further movements of the glacier and buried him with a sense of sadness at renewed memories and pleasure that they had been able to do this last dignified service for their friend. They didn't take photographs of him.

An Ecuadorian friend of mine lost his brother in an avalanche on Antisana. He knew the glacier was fast-moving and when his estimated time elapsed he returned repeatedly and searched the glacier edge for several years until at last he found his brother. They collected the pitiful remains and buried them in a poignant, dignified service. I came across this man's carefully tended gravesite on the high open paramo near the edge of the glacier.

White stones formed a star shape around the grave, wild plants flowered beautifully around the simple headstone, and looming into the sky above the grave were the striking ice-laced slopes of Antisana. It was a moment for quiet reflection and respect; a time for a private admonishment that it could so very easily have been me.

I glanced at the book on my desk. There was a photograph on the back cover of Mallory in army uniform, no doubt on leave from the trenches of the Western Front. His pencil-thin moustache contrasted oddly with his smooth, childlike skin. His eyes stared directly from the photograph, clear, bright, questing. In the background his wife, Ruth, looked out from the page with the same startlingly open gaze as her beloved husband.

I looked at the photograph and all I could see was that awful image of his body, with the alabaster white back, and the broken leg and hobnail boot. I thought of what the goraks, the Nepalese ravens, had done to him and wished the expedition had never published the cursed photograph. It hadn't just been offensive and tasteless. It had ruined a memory.

I looked again at the photograph of Mallory's face staring out from the past. Thom Pollard and Andy Politz had come back for a second look armed with a metal detector to see what artifacts they had missed. They set to digging him out of the grave of stones that had been placed over his body, disregarding the prayers that had already been uttered in reverential farewell. A scan with the metal detector revealed a broken wristwatch in his trouser pocket. They then pulled free a loose section of the weathered rope tied around his waist, snapping it with ease. They promptly removed the hobnailed boot from Mallory's broken right leg, thus adding three more artifacts from the body that they could claim would be of significant research value. No doubt these will be a great help in solving the mystery of whether the two men actually reached the summit.

They now wanted to see his face. They managed to overcome whatever restraint the initial searchers experienced and started chipping away at the ice locking Mallory's head into the stones of the mountain. Eventually they prized his face free from the hard grasp of the ice and they could turn him over and look directly at it. It was "in perfect condition . . . His eyes were closed. I could still see whiskers on his chin." They found a head wound sustained in his violent fall that may or may not have caused his death. At least it presented them with an excuse for so heartlessly prizing him from the ice. They then buried him a second time so that he wouldn't be disturbed and one of them read Psalm 103. I wonder whether that was for the benefit of Mallory's soul or theirs?

Whether the immense potential financial value of these pathetic remains ever occurred to them I do not know. Maybe it was done purely in the interests of historic research. Otherwise they might as well have stripped him naked. The aim of the expedition was to find either Mallory or Irvine and solve the mystery of whether either or both of them had reached the summit or not. In my opinion they plundered a corpse.

When I interviewed Sir Edmund Hillary in front of a thousand-strong audience at the Hay Literary Festival in 1999 the question of Mallory inevitably arose. Somewhat wearily, since he must have been asked it countless times, Hillary explained his view of recent events surrounding the discovery of Mallory's body. It had not solved anything, he said, and without photographic proof, it never would.

"I may say," he added, "that I was absolutely disgusted when in all the media they had these photographs of Mallory lying there on the rocks. To me Mallory had been an heroic figure. He was the man who had inspired my interest in Mount Everest . . . and for this heroic figure to have all these terrible photographs of him there on the rock, bare back, broken-legged . . . I thought was appalling." The applause was thunderous, sustained, and heartfelt.

Photographs, like paintings, of people from the past have an ethereal connective effect on the viewer. I looked again at the portrait of Mallory staring out from the back cover of the book. He was a handsome man in the prime of his life and his eyes seemed to fix on mine, leading me on through this window into his life.

In his biography of George Mallory, David Robertson described him as an "ever-young and singularly lovable" man. He is "Mallory of Everest" now, but we should never forget that he was also a father, a husband, a loyal friend, a man of honor and elegance. I would far rather think of him as Wilfrid Noyce did on the successful 1953 Everest expedition. Looking up at where Mallory had been the first person to discover the Western Cwm route in July 1921, Noyce wrote that " . . . the Western Cwm conjured up for us the figure of Mallory, peering from the col between Lingtrem and Pumori"—an heroic figure from the past looking down in ghostly approval of that then-successful expedition.

His grief-stricken friends " . . . could hardly bring themselves to understand that George would not again be seen moving with ineffable grace on the mountains, or heard speaking in his unforgettable voice about beautiful things and right actions." The great alpinist Geoffrey Winthrop Young described Mallory as "the magical and adventurous spirit of youth personified . . . Neither time nor his own disregard could age or alter the impression that the presence of his flamelike vitality produced. There are natures whose best expression is movement. Mallory could make no movement that was not in itself beautiful. Inevitably he was a mountaineer, since climbing is the supreme opportunity for perfect motion . . . " Today some fellow climbers have no such considerations: to some he is simply a commodity.

The discovery of his body generated a frisson of excitement— and not only within the mountaineering world. The mystery of what happened to Mallory and Irvine has gripped the imagination of people all over the world. What we have learned from these recent findings has solved little of the mystery. Yet there is an ethical dilemma thrown up by how the discoverers have behaved.

The two climbers may have reached the summit twenty-nine years before Hillary and Tenzing but unless a camera is found and photographs produced we will never know. Does it matter? They died. They failed. Most mountaineers would say that one cannot claim a successful ascent if one has died on the descent. Sir Edmund Hillary said as much, as have Mallory's son and grandson. Clare Millikan, Mallory's daughter, has said that she has changed her mind now that her father's body has been discovered and believes he did reach the summit. She adds, however, "I don't think it really counts unless you come back alive." From the outset there was never any real risk that Hillary and Tenzing's success in 1953 was going to be usurped by revealed history.

We now know something of how Mallory and Irvine died. They were not separated. The theory that Mallory, the more experienced climber, may have gone on alone on a solo summit bid has been disabused. They probably fell whilst descending. Possibly the rope snapped and Irvine fell further down the mountain. It would appear that after a long fall Mallory survived, although with a double fracture of his leg. It seems from his body position that he may have attempted to crawl to a place of shelter and died in the process. It is enough for us to imagine what happened, and for a mountaineer the image is all too grim.

This is all we have learned. Finding Irvine's body may or may not resolve the summit issue but no more.

Why did the expedition members feel that they had to publish photographs of the frozen flesh of Mallory's corpse? We do not need to see the photographs to accept that Mallory has been found. We can take their word on the matter and the proof can remain in archives in case it is ever questioned.

In his book *The Lost Explorer* Conrad Anker gave a graphically tasteless description of how Mallory's body " . . . had been hollowed out," by the goraks, "almost like a pumpkin." I wondered how this description furthered our knowledge of Mallory and Irvine's attempt on the summit. He went on to describe how he cut a one-and-a-half-inch square of skin from Mallory's right forearm. Apparently it was not easy. Using the serrated blade of a utility knife he described cutting into Mallory's flesh as "like cutting saddle leather, cured and hard." Did we really need that?

Why on earth did they still feel it necessary to take a flesh sample from his forearm for DNA testing? If you find a corpse dressed in hobnail boots and tweeds high on the slopes of Everest with G. Mallory tags stitched into his shirt collars and a letter from his wife in his breast pocket, who on earth do you think you might have found?

Some of the relatives may have approved DNA samples being taken but surely only in the event of the remains being unidentifiable? Both his son and grandson have said that they are appalled at the publication of the photographs. Julia Irvine, Andrew Irvine's niece, has said that she hopes her Uncle "Sandy" is never found for fear that he will, like Mallory, suffer the same fate. She was quoted in the Sunday Times saying, "Surely these two incredibly brave men deserve to be remembered for achieving so much with so little rather than as exhibits in a freak show?"

How long must you be dead before your body becomes no more than an archaeological relic? Some would say forever. Does the degree of fame attributed to you decide how much respect and dignity is shown to your remains?

If so, and if it were practicable, would it be acceptable, today, to go and find the frozen bodies of Captain Scott, Wilson, and Bowers? Would the interest generated be excuse enough to photograph their remains, take as many artifacts thought suitable for a display, film the bodies freely for a full-blown documentary about their rediscovery, do whatever it takes to make it a sellable event? Of course not, but if this were done, despite the furor, everyone would look at the photographs and gawp at the film. We are helplessly curious. Responsibility for feeding that curiosity lies primarily with the photographers and secondly with the press and media.

On Everest there is already a grisly record of the many dead left unburied on the slopes of the mountain. As recently as 1996 climbers were routinely walking past the frozen and tattered remains of one of their own in the Western Cwm. Sadly, photographs in Anatoli Boukreev's book *The Climb* show the remains to be no more than 20 yards from where hundreds of climbers trudged up the Cwm towards Camp III at the foot of the Lhotse face. For reasons I find quite inexplicable no one thought it might be common human decency to go over and bury the unfortunate souls in a nearby crevasse. The truth is they simply did not care enough. They had paid a lot of money to be guided up Everest and this wasn't part of what they had paid for.

In 1996 during their summit bid two Japanese climbers passed three Indian climbers in varying stages of collapse high on the mountain. They made no effort to offer them succor, food, water, oxygen, or simply a consoling hand. They avoided eye contact and went on to their eventual triumph on the summit. They passed the still-living Indians on their way down to the high camp. There was nothing that they could have done to rescue the Indians but they could have displayed a shred of compassion. On reaching base camp Eisuke Shiqekawa announced " . . . above 8000 meters is not a place where people can afford morality." If that were true, no one should go there.

If climbers on Everest really "cannot afford morality," and ethical behavior becomes too expensive, then has the sport been prostituted? When did the means ever justify the end in mountaineering? We know beyond doubt that Shipton, Tilman, or Whymper would never have behaved in this manner towards their fellow mountaineers.

I think that most climbers believe that style, ethics, and morality are fundamental to the future of our sport. I wonder what non-climbers make of us when they hear of these incidents occurring on Everest and believe that this is what mountaineering is really about.

One simple fact remains true whatever other debates may have been stimulated by this sort of behavior. Climbers would not like their own corpses, or those of their father, son, wife, brother, or lover, to be treated in such a manner, so they have absolutely no right to treat George Mallory in this way. To me, it amounted to little more than modern-day grave robbing.

The feelings this behavior evoked in me—a mixture of revulsion and sadness—seemed to compound my already uncertain emotions about climbing. Tat's death in Greece five months later was the final straw. Ray and I would climb the few routes on our private tick list and be done with it.

I looked again at the handsome photograph of Mallory and thought of him moving with ineffable grace, thought of his flame-like vitality making no movements that were not in themselves beautiful. That was how I would remember him.

THE STRETCHED DREAM

I WAS IDLY FLICKING THROUGH A DICTIONARY OF QUOTATIONS looking for inspiration when my eyes were drawn to the section on youth and old age.

> *Youth is not a time of life . . . it is a state of mind. It is not a matter of ripe cheeks, red lips and supple knees . . . it is a temper of the will, a quality of the imagination, a vigor of the emotions . . . it is a freshness of the deep springs of life.*
> — Unknown

"Oh really?" I thought, as I examined a furry tongue and the glazed eyes of a post-fortieth-birthday morning. My cheeks, far from being ripe, seemed unduly fevered and as for supple knees, mine creak. Forty. Today I am forty. God's teeth! Who would ever have thought it? Time for the bag over the head and the slow slide into decrepitude.

People chatter on about how life begins at forty and I mutter that only people over forty would ever utter such tosh. Of course life does not begin at forty—it just begins to show. At forty you are halfway towards the grave; some beginning! Life changes at forty. I'll give you that.

What is it that is better after turning forty? For the life of me I cannot say: a belly heading inexorably towards my toes; hairy nostrils and tufty ears; aching injuries and gray hairs.

What about the thinking parts—the insidious slide towards

totally reactionary thought without any apparent reason, shouting at news commentators and journalists' scribbles in outrage when for the past four decades I never gave a damn. My passions were once fuelled by the irrational escapist stunts of carefree youth but now I am reduced to muttering incomprehensibly at the television, aroused and irate but too apathetic to do anything about it.

Why spend the first part of one's life living on the edge of everything, having those brilliant ideas that spring to mind soon after eating the worm at the bottom of the tequila bottle, rocking the Casbah and trying to sink the boat, and then spend the second half too stressed to change your toothpaste? Where did it all go?

As a callow youth all my illnesses were self-inflicted and worth it—to a degree, I suppose. A year and a half on crutches, nine operations, all those scars and stitches, pins, plates, wires, and nails—no, they were not much fun or worth much at all. Nor the morphine and the sweet stench of anesthetic gas as I wheezed into a conscious agony, or the sour smell of old plaster casts and the wire-taut pain of physiotherapy. But hell, think of the *craic* we had, the tales we told, laughing all the way to the operating table. It was grand—sure it was—and I miss it.

I miss the idiocy of it all. I dread the day I can't drink five pints and not sleep through the night. How long will it be before bladder control is just a distant fantasy; before the tufts in my ears try to entwine with the hairs in my nostrils? Why don't I look forward to the same things? Once doing things to excess was more than enough for me. My body was my target and my temple was the pub.

I never used to think twice about climbing up into the third-floor bathroom window, seven pints of Old Roger to the bad—or not, that is, until John fell legs astride a brick wall from 40 feet, shattering his pelvis in five places and acquiring an impressive set of testicles the size of grapefruits.

We would gamble on anything: play three-card brag until dawn, going to the edge of fiscal sanity, playing blind and winning with a five high and not a fear in the world, laughing fit to bust on the adrenalin of it all.

Age is said to bring wisdom, prudence, and the comfort of experience but if I could find it I'd trade it all in just to do something utterly daft without thinking, for the chance to make idiotic mistakes and not give a damn. How could I ever think that getting out of my head and tobogganing off a skijump could be anything other than fun?

I swallowed two aspirins and a glass of Alka-Seltzer and hobbled down to the kitchen. As I waited for the kettle to boil I perused Mr. Unknown's ditty with a jaundiced eye.

> *Nobody grows old living a number of years, people grow old only by deserting their ideals. Years wrinkle the skin, but to give up enthusiasm wrinkles the soul. Worry, doubt, distrust, fear and despair . . . these are the long, long years that bow the head and turn the growing spirit back to dust. Whether seventy or sixteen, there is in every being's heart the love of wonder, the sweet amazement of the stars and star-like things and thoughts, the undaunted challenge of events, the unfailing child-like appetite for what is next, and the joy and game of life.*

I was contemplating my own unfailing childlike appetite when the phone rang and John asked if I was going flying. I said no, I had work to do and replaced the receiver. Then I looked at the blue sky and the clouds and thought of wafting through them, rising effortlessly in their swirling cores, heart jumping at the sudden partial collapse of the canopy, and I looked at my computer screen and the book I was reviewing and thought, *Sod it, I'll get old some other day.* I grabbed my paraglider and headed for the door.

When I returned there was a light blinking on my answer machine and I pressed the button to hear Ray Delaney tell me he had an idea and that I should ring him at once. I rang him in Holland and he answered first time and said he had a cunning plan. My heart sank.

"Is that so?" I said in a wary voice. "Okay, what is it this time?"

"Ah ha, you'll love this. We need to talk," he said.

"We are talking. Come on, spit it out."

"Right, well, you know your idea about having a tick list?"

"Yes . . . "

"Well, I was just thinking . . . "

"Not always a good thing as I recall . . . "

"We've done a classic ice route: Bridalveil. Okay? We want to do something on El Cap or Lotus Flower Tower or both, so that's a rock route . . . " He paused. "But we haven't really got a mountain route, have we?"

"Well, I thought that was because we wanted to give up mountaineering," I said patiently.

"No, no, we're going to do that after we've completed the tick list."

"We're going to try that huge ice cascade in Nepal. What's that if it's not mountaineering?"

"It's an ice line. It starts twenty minutes' walk from a bar and ends with a walk down to a village."

"Exactly. The perfect mountain route."

"It's not a mountain. It's just a bloody hillside. It's an ice climb. Anyway, that's not the point. I was looking at this video the other day and I thought that's it, we'll go and do the 1938 route on the north face of the Eiger."

"What? Are you mad?"

"No, listen. I'll send you this video. It was filmed live over three days last September when two Swiss parties climbed the face. They had helmet cameras and some fixed camera positions and it looked brilliant. More than that, it didn't look hard at all."

"That's because you were sitting in your living room drinking beer," I suggested.

"Come on, Joe. You always said you wanted to do it. Remember on Ama Dablam, ten years ago, we said we were going to do it."

"Sort of . . ."

"You said it was the greatest route in the world. You said you would regret it if you never even tried it, never even walked to the foot of it and had a sniff . . ."

"I must have been drunk. It's that Nepalese whiskey . . ."

"You were walking down the track to Lukla, sober as a judge."

"Ray, we're forty, fat, and fearful."

"We can do it. If we get good conditions and the weather is fine, I know we can do it. If the rock is dry it's not technically hard . . ."

"There seem to be an awful lot of 'ifs' around all of a sudden," I said.

"Now you're just being negative . . ."

"I thought I was being sensible."

"Listen, just think about it, okay? I'll send you the video, have a look, and think about it."

"Nothing to think about, kid," I muttered. "The tick list was about having fun, about doing them and walking away. The Eiger isn't fun."

"It could be. The video is in the post, give me a ring," Ray said and promptly put the phone down. *The scheming little bugger!* I thought and wandered up to the office, trying not to think about it. A copy of Peter and Leni Gillman's superb biography of George Mallory, *The Wildest Dream,* still lay on my desk. I had finished writing a piece for the back cover having struggled to find the words that would do justice to this considerable and thought-provoking book that told so much more about the man than a history of his Everest expeditions would ever tell.

> *A finely wrought and meticulously detailed biography of Mallory that seeks to answer far more questions than whether he reached the summit of Everest. It is at once*

*compelling and evocative, resonant of a bygone era when
dreams went unsullied by the pressures of modern life.
The Wildest Dream reveals a passionate man who climbed
from the heart. It is rare indeed to find someone like
Mallory, who so wholeheartedly believed there was no
dream that must not be dared and whose life stretched to
the very end.*

I saved the writing and e-mailed it to Peter Gillman. I added a
note congratulating him and Leni on such a fine work and said I
felt sure it deserved to win the Boardman Tasker Prize. As I was
about to place the book on my bookshelf I saw a copy of Heinrich
Harrer's *The White Spider.* Beside it was Dougal Haston's autobiography, *In High Places.* There was an extensive account of his
ascent of the direct Harlin Route on the north face of the Eiger
during which John Harlin had died. I recalled that Peter Gillman
and Chris Bonington had been covering the story of the climb for
the *Daily Telegraph.* Chris climbed on the face as the climbing
photographer and Peter wrote the story. He later collaborated with
Haston to write *Eiger Direct,* a thrilling account of the ascent of
the Harlin Route. I spotted it sandwiched between Harrer's and
Haston's books on the shelf. I have hundreds of mountaineering
books stuffed haphazardly onto bookshelves ringing my attic
office. The chaos of moving house had meant that none of the
books had been shelved in any particular order or arranged by
subject, author name, or title. So it was with some surprise that I
saw that there were twelve books stacked side by side, all either
histories of the Eiger or with a direct account of an Eiger climb or
epic struggle prominent in their contents. I thought of what Ray
had said on the phone that afternoon.

"Come on, Joe. You always said you wanted to do it."

And he was right, of course. It had always been one of my most
cherished dreams. The Eiger, its literature, and its history had always been at the heart of why I had started climbing and what I

thought climbing should be: bold, committing, and inspirational. It wasn't the hardest or the highest. It was simply "The Eiger." The very mention of the name made my heart beat faster. The seminal mountain, a metaphorical mountain that represented everything that defines mountaineering—a route I had dreamed of climbing for my entire adult life.

I used to daydream about the great climbs through university lectures and seminars, hacking my way up ice fields and climbing boldly over roofs of granite thousands of feet above pristine glaciers. Then came the day when I was sitting on the summits of these dreams and they had become real, ordinary—evaporating like dew in the sun, never to be recalled in quite the same addictive, compulsive way again. If I ever climbed the Eiger then my greatest dream would evaporate too. *No,* I told myself, *don't crush the dream. It's safer that way.*

I have always been a poor liar and the lie did not sit comfortably. I should have admitted that I was not good enough. I should have said I was scared of it, but I never did—even though there was an element of truth in both thoughts. Now as I looked at the group of Eiger books I wondered whether I had subconsciously stacked them like that because I knew that one day I might need to read them again.

There was a passage in Peter and Leni Gillman's book in which they quoted Mallory's article for the *Alpine Journal* describing his ascent of Mont Blanc:

> *As they toiled up the final snowfield to the summit, Mallory was afraid of an anticlimax, but then he was suffused with an uplifting awareness that even this most arduous stretch was part of the whole experience.* "The dream stretched to the very end." *Once again Mallory had invoked the idea of the dream to describe his aims and goals. He ended with a passage using the construct of the dream.*

"One must conquer, achieve, get to the top: one must know the end to be convinced that one can win the end— to know there's no dream that mustn't be dared . . . Is this the summit, crowning the day? How cool and how quiet! We're not exultant: but delighted, joyful: soberly astonished . . . Have we vanquished an enemy? None but ourselves . . . "

I was struck by the familiarity of his ideas, remembering a time as a young, egotistic, and overly ambitious alpinist when I had thought in similar terms. It often seemed, on later reflection, that I had spent so many hours and days dreaming about these gilded climbs that when the eventual summit was attained, the route ticked off in the guidebook, it was as if I had subconsciously willed it to happen. On some ascents I would find myself privately asking, *Am I really doing this?* as I looked at a friend struggle up a strenuous golden granite finger crack. Sometimes I would come across a soaring bookend corner or a steep icy overhang and be surprised to find that it looked so familiar and so exactly right. It was not a sense of déjà vu but rather an uncanny feeling that I had been led to this place, to this uplifting experience. That this was what I was meant to do. It felt right.

After years of reading guidebooks and the exploits of my heroes I found myself delighted and awestruck to be cautiously following in their ghostly footsteps, sharing the same storm-swept bivouac ledges, fighting up ice-filled finger cracks, perched over the same airy, sweeping ice fields and all the while intently conscious of how much greater they were than I could ever be. It happened by accident, not design, and I am keenly aware that I have no right to stand anywhere close to the memory of these pioneers who were my true inspiration.

It was the words of my heroes that inspired me to climb. Hermann Buhl's *Nanga Parbat Pilgrimage*, Riccardo Cassin's *Fifty Years of Alpinism*, Walter Bonatti's *The Great Days*, Lionel Terray's superbly titled *Conquistadors of the Useless,* and Kurt Diemberger's evocative *Summits and Secrets* were my bibles. These were their memorials and my motivation. Head and shoulders above them all stood Heinrich Harrer's *The White Spider*—not because it was a particularly masterful piece of literature but because it was a story so fearful that when I finished it at the age of fourteen I sat and wondered at the awful experiences these men had put themselves through. I vowed then and there that I would never be a climber.

I often wondered if these heroes of mine ever climbed with quite such a baggage of fears and dark terrors as I did. I was convinced that heroes do not feel such emotions. I, on the other hand, seem beset with nightmare thoughts of how it will all end. It is as if some dark, hooded crow squats on my quaking shoulders muttering dire warnings of calamities to come. I never asked if any of my climbing companions ever felt the same way. Shame at my weakness and fear of their scorn were deterrent enough. There were moments, often in the fraught hours of a stormy bivouac, when my nemesis, the crow, wafted in with an icy beat of its wings and bent its beak to my ear. *You shouldn't be here, boy, this is not your place, tell him now, go on, tell him that you want to go down.*

And I would shiver on through the long dark bivouac hours waiting for the edge of dawn to creep up and make black-humored jokes to my companion in a pathetic attempt at bravado. I never once suspected that he might have been thinking exactly the same things. I would never have dreamed of asking.

Then a burning sun rose through a morning sky and we climbed on and up, dancing over sun-heated golden granite, tiptoeing along the filigreed ribbon of a knife-edged ridge of snow towards a distant summit, and I wondered why I had ever thought to ask such foolish questions. I watched Alpine choughs playing acrobatic games dancing on the thermal winds, and entirely forgot the foul crow.

I shook my head and tried to stop thinking about the Eiger. *Damn Ray!* I leaned forward to place the Mallory book on the bookshelf and spotted a copy of Daniel Anker's *Eiger: The Vertical Arena*. On impulse I pulled it out and flicked through the pages of text and photographs. It was an updated history of the mountain with a wealth of old and new photographs. Part of the book was divided into a blow-by-blow description of the salient features on the north face: the Difficult Crack, the Hinterstoisser Traverse, the Swallow's Nest bivouac site on the edge of the First Ice Field; the Ice Hose and the great sweep of the Second Ice Field leading up to the Flat Iron; and then the forebodingly named Death Bivouac. Then came the Third Ice Field, the Ramp, the Traverse of the Gods, the White Spider itself, and the fearsome Exit Cracks. Wonderful, evocative names drenched in the history of tragic accidents and bold fighting victories.

At the start of each section there was a page of text opposite a full-color photograph of the salient features. The book fell open to a photograph of the face during a storm with the great buttress of the Röte Fluh, a thousand feet high and yet lost within the immensity of the vast amphitheatre of rock buttresses and stonefall-blackened ice. Huge waterfalls were coursing down the face, leaping into space in bursting geysers from the edges of the ice fields. It was an impressive photograph. I could imagine how unpredictable a monster the mountain could be. The face was streaming with water but it didn't take much imagination to see the infernal fusillades of rocks that would be whistling down flushed loose by the thunderstorm, avalanches spewing out of gullies, as if the mountain was self-destructing.

I turned the page and there was the chilling photograph of Toni Kurz hanging in space, slumped from the waist, frozen to death. On the opposite page there was a photograph of him taken just before the ascent—young, happy, smiling. Again I was reminded of the photograph of Mallory and the clear direct gaze of his eyes staring out from the past. I looked at Toni Kurz sitting amid alpine flowers smiling at the camera with the unruly curls of dark hair framing his boyish face.

The faces in the photographs, particularly the eyes, seem to reach out from the past as if trying to pull you into their lives. Looking out from that moment in an alpine meadow sixty-four years ago oblivious of his impending fate the youthful Toni Kurz seemed to be speaking to me. "I am gone but I pass on to you my liveliness and my life, for you too will be taken, as once I was, and you will be as still and content as am I, for whom centuries are not even seconds." Now immortalized in mountaineering history, he lived on frozen in two moments within the pages of a book: alive on the left-hand page, dead on the right.

As I flicked idly through the book from the grisly photograph of Edi Rainer's body crushed into the screes at the foot of the mountain to the dark cleft of the Ramp I was enticed and intimidated in equal measure. One moment I stared in dread, the next I leaned forward fascinated, wondering how hard it might be. Could I climb it?

The phone rang and I placed both books on the shelf and picked up the receiver.

"Have you been thinking about it?" Ray asked conspiratorially.

"About what?" I blustered.

"About the 1938 route on the Eiger . . . "

"Don't mention the bloody Eiger."

"Well, have you?"

"No, of course I haven't," I lied. "You only told me a few hours ago . . . "

"I've been looking at the videos again," he said.

"I've been working," I replied defensively.

"It looked dead easy, you know."

"I think the 'dead' bit is the pertinent part," I complained, remembering the photographs I had just been looking at.

"No, I mean really easy, flat almost," and before I could interject he rushed on. "I've sent you the videos. They should be there on Wednesday. There's five of them."

"Five?"

"Well, they are German, very long-winded you know." He laughed and I heard the suppressed excitement in his voice. "They made a live outside broadcast with film crews all over the place, and helmet cameras and palmcorders, the lot. You get a really clear sense of what the face is like and I thought, hey we can do that."

"We?"

"Why not? You always said you had wanted to do it and here's our chance."

"Ray," I said patiently, "you seem to have forgotten a few salient points here. I grant you, it can be easy in perfect, dry, and cold conditions, which presumably it was when they made this film."

"Oh yeah, it looked immaculate. No verglas, and I can't remember hearing any rockfall. It was in September, which probably took advantage of the colder nights . . . "

"So what happens if we don't get these perfect conditions?"

"No problem," he announced confidently. "We'll run away. Just like we always do."

"Not so easy if we're stuck in a Föhn storm halfway up the Exit Cracks. They come screaming in with winds strong enough to destroy tents down in Alpiglen. These then turn the face into a moving mass of avalanches and waterfalls. When it's over it freezes, hard . . . "

"Ah," he said, less exultantly, "not good, then."

"And now you're trying to climb Scottish grade 5 or 6 mixed climbing with no protection and nonexistent belays to boot."

"Right, that wouldn't be good news."

"Quite. Remember Brendan and Rob? Remember what happened?" There was a pregnant silence from the receiver. Ray was remembering the time when Rob Durran and Brendan Murphy had been pinned down in the Exit Cracks in a winter storm, fighting for their lives. Rob had been leading, unable to find any protection when he fell. He knew that Brendan had no belay to speak of and in that instant he knew he was about to fall the length of the 6000-foot face beneath him. As his axes skittered down the icy rocks they suddenly held and he stopped, poised above the abyss as he scrabbled to set his crampon points. The terror of the moment had made him void his bowels.

"But that was in winter," Ray protested.

"Yeah and don't forget that Brendan had made the first winter ascent of Divine Providence on the Eckfeiler," I said. "At the time it was one of the hardest routes in the Alps. They were that good and the Exit Cracks nearly killed them," I said pointedly.

"Right, good point . . . " Ray muttered.

"How do you fancy leading the Exit Cracks in those conditions?"

"Ah, well, you see this is where the cunning part of my plan comes in," he said, cheering up. "I thought you might like to lead that bit." And with a slightly deranged note in his laugh he put the phone down.

I let out a long sigh and tried not to think about it. But the worm was in and turning frantically. The Eiger. Just the word got my heart pounding. All these years I had dismissed it and here it was back again and the hooded black crow was flapping in towards my shoulder with a sibilant rush of wind. *Do you want to die then, kid? Do you really?*

"Bugger off!" I muttered and stood up, wandered downstairs, and ran a bath. Settling back into the warm water, luxuriating in the heat soothing the aches in my injured knee and ankle, I read a magazine on fly-fishing and fly-tying, thought about taking up golf, and tried to forget I had ever heard of the Eiger. It didn't work. The clever part of Ray's plan lay simply in the fact that he had suggested the idea. As the words came out the plan emerged fully formed and undeniable.

The phone rang. It was Ray again.

"One last thing," he said abruptly. "Just remember that you'd really kick yourself, Joe, if you looked back from a grand old age and realized that you had never even just gone and had a look at it. I mean, if we at least get onto the lower face and decide for whatever reasons . . . "

"Cowardice," I interjected.

"Yes, I'll accept that, cowardice is good with me. But if we then decide we want to back away, well, at least we'll have the satisfaction of knowing that we tried. We got close up and personal and then made our own decisions. We won't regret the fact that we just went and looked. How about we just go and take a wee look? Better by far than never to have even dared to try, eh?"

"Quite," I thought as I lay in the bath, "and very cunning, Ray."

Despite my misgivings I kept thinking of reasons why his plan was less stupid than I had first thought. When Simon and I had returned from Peru, Simon went to the Alps and climbed the Eiger whilst I went to hospital. After six operations on my smashed knee the doctors told me that I would never walk without a limp and most certainly never climb again. I ignored them and after years of physiotherapy, aided by falling downstairs when drunk, I eventually managed to get considerably more flexion. It forced me to become a better climber. I had to think of my footwork far more than I used to and consequently became technically superior. Years of using crutches had increased my upper body strength and with the advent of the development of indoor climbing walls I found that I could climb at grades far higher than I had ever attained before.

The physical struggle to fitness was simply a matter of hard work and stubbornness. Psychologically, however, the accident in Peru had left me deeply traumatized. A great deal of success in climbing is down to confidence, mental commitment, and motivation. For a long time I was happy to bumble around on fairly easy routes well within my ability but I was not prepared to commit myself to a technically hard and potentially dangerous climb. In the back of my mind there were shadows of doubt and fear that I never seemed to be able to shake off.

In the ensuing fifteen years of painful and often depressing attempts to regain my fitness I eventually climbed in Nepal, Peru, Pakistan, Africa, India, Bolivia, and Ecuador. I even managed to climb a couple of first ascents alpine-style in Peru and Nepal, but never at the extreme level of difficulty that we had committed to on the west face of Siula Grande. However, I hadn't realized as the years had passed how much better a climber I had actually become. It was a gradual progress judged most often by the standards of other friends who climbed at far higher standards and because of that I hadn't really been aware of how much I had improved.

When Ray suggested we try the Eiger my first thought was whether I was technically capable of climbing such a route, especially if conditions turned bad. I had no intention of starting up the face blindly, hoping that the weather would stay fine and relying on the rescue services if things became too difficult. I would only consider an attempt if I felt sure I was up to the challenge.

I thought about the standards that I had been climbing at in the 1980s just prior to going to Peru. To be able to climb at an E 1, the lowest of the extreme rock grades, wearing big mountaineering boots and carrying a rucksack was pretty good going at the beginning of the 1980s. I had climbed grade 5 water ice in Scotland and made ascents of complex and objectively serious routes in the Alps. I was confident climbing Extréme Difficile (denoted ED in the alpine grading system), and at the time this was the hardest grade of alpine routes.

By the time we set off for Siula Grande I was an experienced mountaineer, whether it was on technical rock routes in the Dolomites or big mixed north walls in the French and Swiss Alps. Ascents of the difficult mixed climbing on the Dru Couloir above the Chamonix valley or the harsh conditions found on the north face of Les Droites in winter had given me the confidence to believe that I could attempt a hard first ascent in the greater ranges.

Today I was climbing at far harder grades than in 1985 when we had made the first ascent of Siula Grande's west face. I had led rock routes four or five grades harder than anything I had attempted in the early 1980s and my ice climbing had come on apace. Attempting something like Bridalveil Falls in 1980 would certainly have led to an early death for me. It was simply beyond anything I could have climbed at the time.

In many ways the terrible experience on Siula Grande had made both Simon and me better climbers. It was a steep learning curve, but we made mistakes that we would never make again.

I looked after myself more carefully, I was a better judge of my abilities, and possessed a far more experienced eye for the objective dangers and technical challenges that mountaineering presented. I had no problems with retreating from a route if I wasn't entirely happy about how things were going. The more I thought about it the more tempting the idea of climbing the Eiger became.

My mind turned to what I had written about Mallory, who so wholeheartedly believed there was no dream that must not be dared and whose life stretched to the very end. It might be good to stretch our dreams a little. I had always longed to climb the north face of the Eiger. So perhaps the time had come to dare the dream.

THE EIGERWAND

THE GREAT BLACK AMPHITHEATER OF THE NORTH FACE of the Eiger rises for over a vertical mile straight out of the sunlit meadows of Alpiglen. The face is the biggest continuously steep mountain wall in Europe. For most of this century it has been the climb that has defined extreme mountaineering. It remains a lonely and unrivalled peak, widely regarded with awe and respect by all aspiring alpine climbers. It is a place of shattered rock and polished ice fields. To date, sixty climbers have died attempting to climb the face. Its history is one of bleak tragedies played out in the full gaze of an uncomprehending public. It is a horribly public place to die.

The somber northern wall of the Eiger has an intimidating and brooding menace. Few approaching the foot of the face would do so without an aching sense of dread. For over sixty years it has killed some of the finest climbers of their generation. For those brave enough to attempt the face there is the added weight of its tragic history. This brings to bear upon the climber such psychological stress that many have failed before even laying hand on the lower rocks. The intricate line of the classic first ascent route involves 13,000 feet of climbing—almost two miles uphill on hands and knees—over some of the most inhospitable terrain imaginable.

The Eiger is part of the northern bulwark of the Alps that is prone to sudden savage storms, frequently generated by the powerful warm Föhn winds, often prolonged and lethal. In an instant the face becomes a maelstrom of avalanches, waterfalls, and falling rocks, cutting off all hope of retreat for anyone trapped high. Water that has cascaded down the black limestone walls in the relative warmth of the storm freezes solid in the cold front that always follows. Previously dry rock becomes glazed with verglas, a glassy sheen of hard water ice, filling the cracks and fissures and covering all protection points. The rock itself is layered in a distinctive downward strata so that all holds are now sloping, ice coated, and lethally treacherous.

The concave shape of the vast wall seems to generate its own distinct weather systems so that while a ferocious storm lashes the wall the meadows below bask in sunshine. Far below, yet less than an hour's walk from the foot of the face, tourists crowd the terraces of the hotels and peer morbidly through binoculars and telescopes at the life-and-death struggles being enacted on the wall above them.

The Eiger has a well-earned reputation as a killer. At one point the north face became so notorious that the Swiss government banned all climbing on the wall, something unheard of in the history of alpine climbing—but still climbers came and men died. Since then the fearsome reputation of the mountain has grown. Despite the huge advance in climbing standards, the Eiger north face remains the preeminent alpine route coveted by aspiring alpinists. For those given the grace to succeed, it is an achievement for which they are forever grateful and that they will never forget.

The first ascent in 1938 was one of the great landmarks of modern mountaineering, comparable with the ascents of Nanga Parbat, Annapurna, and later Everest in the way in which it advanced the standards. The great climbers of the 1930s, 1940s, and 1950s—Kasparek and Harrer, Herman Bühl and Diemberger, Cassin and Bonatti, Lachenal and Terray—became my inspirational heroes. It was their standards, ethics, and traditions that guided me in the formative years of my climbing life. Now, in my fortieth year, there was still one thing missing from my climbing career: the north face of the Eiger. For years I had shied away from its imposing shadow, persuading myself that I didn't really want to attempt the face. I knew all along that this was a thinly disguised lie.

Eleven years after reading Heinrich Harrer's *The White Spider* I was to find myself hanging helplessly on a single strand of rope in a storming, freezing Andean night waiting to die. It had eerie and disturbing parallels with the death of Toni Kurz on the Eiger in 1937. That experience convinced me that I would never climb the north face of the Eiger.

Yet, as I watched the videos that Ray had sent me I found myself studying the terrain, judging the technical difficulty of the climb. With mounting excitement I began to realize that his idea was not quite as half-witted as I had first thought.

I was now vastly more experienced as a mountaineer. I was no longer the driven, ambitious, and obsessed climber of my youth, and although caution and a highly attuned sense of mortality may well have held me back on some occasions it had also meant that I was still alive. The boldness and confidence of youth can lead to striking success or tragic failure. The wariness of age and experience can be just as paralyzing. It can be a very fine line to tread and I felt we had the balance about right.

It was a neat little rationale that I found myself warming to as I watched the climbers making their way steadily up the north face. When they finally reached the summit ridge I knew with growing excitement that Ray was right. We had at least to make an attempt on the route. We would regret it for the rest of our lives if we never even went up to the bottom of the face and had, as he put it, "a wee look." If either of us didn't like what we saw we would just walk away.

I went up to my office, turned on my computer, and sat down to read my e-mails. There were some routine messages and then a surprise greeting from Mick Fowler.

He and Simon Yates had returned for an attempt on Siula Grande's satellite peak, Siula Chico. They had wanted to try a steep

ice line that Simon and I had coveted back in 1985. To their astonishment they had found that the intervening years of high average
temperatures had reduced the glacier by almost two-thirds of its
original size and the ice line on Chico no longer existed. Fowler
also noted the terrible state of the moraines and screes leading up
to the glacier that I had crawled down fifteen years earlier. With
typical Fowler humor he wrote, "If I haven't said so before I must
congratulate you on such a fine crawl. The ground you covered is
unbelievably horrible . . . full of razor-sharp boulders that keep
toppling over."

It was strange to be reminded of this. It had suddenly made
the whole experience real again, hitting home with some force.
Over the years I had told and retold the story so many times that it
had become slightly unreal to me. In fact, psychologists treating
victims of stress and trauma frequently make them tell the story of
what happened over and over again until the reality becomes a
fiction and they can move forward, away from that destructive and
traumatic event. I had given so many slide shows and presentations
over the years that I began to wonder whether my memory was
betraying me. Perhaps it hadn't been so bad; maybe any good
crawler worth his salt would have covered the distance in half the
time without so much as a wince to betray the perfection of his stiff
upper lip.

I had frequently been asked how far the crawl was and I could
never remember. I didn't think in those terms. The crawling just
went on and on and it was hard. So it came as some surprise when
I read Mick's e-mail.

"I would say that you would be well impressed with yourself if
you went back. I'd guess it's about six miles: perhaps one and a half
miles on the glacier, one mile on shit-awful moraines, one mile in
the V-shaped bowling alley, and about two and a half miles on
easier ground back to camp. Wild!"

Yeah, that sounds about right, I thought. *And it was hard and
it bloody hurt.*

". . . the beckoning silence of great height," Eiger north face, September 2000
(Photo by Joe Simpson)

Anderl and Trudl Heckmair with Joe and Ray. Kleine Scheidegg,
September 2000 (Photo by Joe Simpson)

Max Sedlmayr and
Karl Mehringer's names
in the Hôtel des Alpes
register, Grindelwald
(Photo by Joe Simpson)

Joe, Anna Jossi,
and Alice Steuri
with the register,
Grindelwald
(Photo by
Joe Simpson)

Joe beneath a sunset-washed Eigerwand
(Photo by Ray Delaney)

BELOW: *A somber Ray packs for the climb*
(Photo by Joe Simpson)

BELOW RIGHT: *A sobering reminder of previous attempts*
(Photo by Joe Simpson)

Joe climbing the Difficult Crack (Photo by Ray Delaney)

RIGHT: *The face turns into a deadly trap after a violent storm*
(Photo by Andrea Forlini; reproduced in *Eiger: The Vertical Arena*, ed. Daniel Anker)

Joe crossing the Hinterstoisser Traverse during the storm
(Photo by Ray Delaney)

RIGHT: *Ray at the Swallow's Nest*
(Photo by Joe Simpson)

LEFT: *Ray belaying as the storm sweeps in*
(Photo by Joe Simpson)

Ray dodging stonefall while retreating across the Hinterstoisser Traverse
(Photo by Joe Simpson)

BELOW: *Alpenglow over the Scheidegg Wetterhorn*
(Photo by Joe Simpson)

The message, however, had prompted me into a decision. I picked the phone up and rang Holland.

"Ray?" I asked when he answered the phone. "When do you want to do it?"

"What? The Eiger?"

"What else?"

"Good God! I was half hoping you'd say no."

"Well, if it all goes belly-up I can blame you. It was your idea."

"Thanks." There was a pause. "Winter or summer?" he asked.

"Summer," I said firmly.

Friends had suggested that winter—although far more serious—would be the best time to attempt the face. The threat of stone-fall would be nullified by the freezing temperatures but heavy powder snow conditions, especially on the lower part of the face, could make it an exhausting ascent taking as long as six or seven days. Everyone I had talked to who had climbed the face in winter had mentioned the fact that the rock was invariably dry and nowhere had they encountered verglas. This was due to the continuously icy temperatures. Whatever verglas had formed at the end of autumn had sublimated away by the middle of January, evaporated by the arid harshness of winter conditions. This meant that the rock climbing in the Ramp and the Exit Cracks would not be coated in a treacherous skim of ice.

On the other hand it was likely that they would be covered in a mantle of powder snow hiding all the possible in-situ protection points such as bolts and pitons. Although the weather tended to be more stable in winter and we could hope for as many as ten days of clear skies the predicament of being trapped high on the face in a prolonged winter storm was not something I relished. I had always thought that my winter alpine routes had been some of the most serious climbing I had ever done.

"Let's go in September," I added. "There's a good chance of cold nights later in the month that might help cut down on the stonefall. Can you spare the entire month?" I asked, aware of how busy Ray was with "Kathmandu," his flourishing climbing shop in Utrecht.

"Yeah, probably, but I won't be very popular. We're opening a second shop on September the first."

"It's your call," I said. "September is best for me."

There was a long pause.

"Hell, why not?" Ray said and I could hear the enthusiasm in his voice. "Do you really think we can do it?"

"If we get the weather I'm certain of it," I said. "I reckon that once we are on the face all that baggage of fear will disappear and it will just become another climb, another set of problems to solve."

"It had better do, otherwise we'll be a pair of gibbering idiots," Ray laughed. "By the way, did you see the latest issue of *Climbing* magazine?"

"No. What about it?"

"Some Americans have repeated your route on Siula Grande. Hang on, I've got it here." I waited as he flicked through the magazine. "Carlos Buhler and Mark Price . . ."

"Carlos Buhler?" I demanded. "*The* Carlos Buhler?" He was one of America's leading climbers with an impressive list of hard ascents to his name as well as vast experience on some of the highest mountains in the world.

"Yup, the very one," Ray said. "Here, you'll like this," he said and read out the report on the expedition:

> Made famous by Joe Simpson in his epic tale of survival, Touching the Void, *the west face of Siula Grande had its second ascent this June. Carlos Buhler and Mark Price decided to take on the ghosts of Simpson and Yates's venture of 1985. Buhler writing in his diary before embarking: "I sure hope we can avoid the touch." Their 3300-foot route differed from the original taking off left up an ice gully at half height. Very technical: twenty-four*

*pitches of constant steepness with some of the finest alpine
ice Buhler (one of America's most accomplished mountaineers) has seen, and also some of the scariest.*

"I can believe that," I said fervently.
"It goes on," Ray said.

*. . . Buhler was leading on the second day when one of his
ice picks broke in the hard ice . . . climbing on he looked
up to see giant chunks of cornice thundering down directly
at him . . . "I closed my eyes and prayed," wrote Buhler. "I
kept waiting for the big thud that would break my neck or
smash me. But it never came." He was forty feet above a
runner at the time. There is no easy way off the mountain
and after bivvying one night on the north ridge the pair
chose to make 20 committing rappels, the first from a pair
of knife blades on a rare section of exposed rock along
the heavily corniced ridge and then 18 rappels from ice
V-threads.*

"Ah ha, so they wimped out of the ridge did they?" I chuckled.
"I don't blame them. I'm glad they thought it was so serious."
"Yeah, it goes on to say . . . ."

*On the lower part of the face the dangers from falling
debris were great enough for Buhler to write . . . "I felt
like it had to be the last time I put myself at such risk."*

"Clever boy," I muttered.
"You'll like this last bit," Ray said, before continuing:

*In 1936 two Germans, Schneider, and Awerzger, climbed
the north ridge of Siula Grande, although the mountain is
remote and high enough, 20,800 feet, even their route is*

rarely climbed. As for Joe Simpson and Simon Yates's
route on the west face, most people were too spooked by
the subsequent Void *account to consider trying it. Buhler*
commented, "I have a tremendous amount of respect for
Joe and Simon for their boldness. Siula is a wilderness
climb that doesn't in any way finish on the summit. That's
what makes it so serious."

"They called their variation on your route 'Avoiding the
Touch.' How about that then, kid?" Ray asked. I felt stunned.

"Bloody hell! That's great," I said at last.

I had always felt that we had done a very serious route but it
had been overshadowed by the accident. It was sometimes a little
irksome to think that I would be known as the climber who fell off
a hill and crawled home. "But we probably did bite off more than
we could chew," I added.

"Yeah, but you climbed it in style, youth. That was your first
experience of high-altitude climbing and you did the route in less
time than Buhler and Price and think of the experience those
guys have."

"That's probably why we screwed up. We didn't have their experience. We were running on empty, completely overstretched . . . "

"Don't be so hard on yourself. They damn near killed themselves
as well."

I felt quite emotional at the news. In a way it was a great vindi-
cation for Simon and me as climbers to be praised by one of our
peers.

"Well done, mate, you deserve it," Ray said. "It's some compliment, isn't it?"

"Absolutely brilliant," I said. "Funny, isn't it? I was just thinking
about Siula Grande, trying to convince myself that the Eiger was a
good idea and now you tell me about Buhler."

"That settles it, then," Ray said confidently.

"You know, we might be climbing well," I added, "but there is no way either of us are as fit as we used to be or will need to be for the Eiger."

"Better get training, then," Ray said confidently. "How long have we got? Five months. We'll be fine, kid. You keep looking at those videos, familiarize yourself with the face," he added.

"Listen, I've read so many books on the bloody Eiger I think I know it like the back of my hand now. Whenever you see a mention of the Eiger in any climbing books there is always some epic story involved."

"Stands to reason," Ray replied. "What's the point of writing about a perfectly successful but uneventful climb? This sort of thing is self-perpetuating. The rat needs feeding."

"You mean like a self-fulfilling prophecy?"

"Yeah, that sort of thing. As if people are so conscious of the history of the place that they inevitably start making it themselves."

"No, I don't buy that," I said. "It is just a mountain in the end. Strip away the history and it is just another hill."

"Do you believe that?" Ray exclaimed and burst out laughing.

"Not really," I muttered sheepishly. "But if you think about it, when we went to Siula Grande it was just a mountain. When we came back it suddenly had some pretty serious history and now Buhler has just added to it. But the mountain itself hasn't changed at all, has it? I mean, we didn't think twice about attempting the west face. It was just a series of problems. There was no psychological baggage at all. All we have to do on the Eiger is see through all the tragedies . . . "

I put the phone down and thought about our decision to climb the Eiger. I felt the fear but it was overwhelmed by a keen sense of anticipation. Ray was right. It was where we should be, win or lose. And thinking about it, failure is never quite so frightening as regret.

AGAINST THE DYING OF THE LIGHT

AS I DROVE SLOWLY UP THE WINDING ROAD twisting through a forest of pine trees I thought about what we had come to do. *You're here now, kid. No turning back,* I thought and I was surprised at how calm I felt. I looked at the picturesque town of Interlaken built on the banks of the lake and surrounded by meadows and woodland. The landscape was astoundingly beautiful, almost unreal, since it was the sort of thing you saw on a chocolate box and never expected to see in reality.

I knew that soon the valley would open outwards as we approached the small hamlet of Grindelwald and there looming above it would be the immense north face of the Eiger. Friends had told me what an imposing and intimidating sight this was and how its vast dark shadowed wall could deter a previously enthusiastic north-wall climber into wary submissiveness. I thought of all the Eiger books I had read over the summer, absorbing the countless photographs and the list of tragedies played out in full view of the watching tourists. I had constantly asked myself whether I wanted to be doing this and every time the answer came back, stronger and more positive with each time of asking. *Yes, I really do. I want to follow in the footsteps of those climbers.* It is how I had always climbed in the Alps, paying homage to the heroes I had read about by climbing their routes.

Reading the books had been my way of breaking down the psychological baggage associated with the wall. From every implacable story there was a lesson to be learned—when to turn back, where the dangers lay, what decisions to make—and I began to feel as if I knew the face intimately. I imagined all the things that could go wrong and then tried to decide what my best decisions would be—retreat or push on, sit out the storm or risk the stone-fall and avalanches of a descent. Sometimes I gleaned a little extra information that I knew might be vitally important and I stored it away in my memory for just such a moment.

I remembered reading Chris Bonington's accounts of his early attempts on the face in his autobiography, *I Chose to Climb*. Chris and the legendary Don Whillans had turned back from one attempt on the north face when they had reached the Second Ice Field. They had sensed that the weather was changing and realized that they still could safely make a rappel retreat down the Ice Hose and the First Ice Field to the shelter of the Swallow's Nest. This 18-inch-wide bivouac ledge sheltered by an overhang was perched spectacularly on the edge of a huge rock band. From there they could use the old fixed ropes, now routinely left in place, to reverse the Hinterstoisser Traverse and make their way slowly down the remaining 2500 feet of broken walls and ledges to the foot of the face.

It was from this point that Toni Kurz's fateful party had struggled desperately to reverse the Hinterstoisser Traverse in 1936. The four-man party had reached the Death Bivouac, Max Sedlmayr and Karl Mehringer's high point of the previous year—so-called because it was here that Sedlmayr and Mehringer had frozen to death. On the first day of their climb Andreas Hinterstoisser had discovered what was to be the key to the climb and had brilliantly unlocked this crux rock barrier that gave them access to the heart of the face. When he and his three companions—Willy Angerer, Edi Rainer, and Toni Kurz—had safely followed him across the glistening shield of slabby rock they retrieved the traversing rope that Hinterstoisser had so expertly fixed in place. From that point onwards the door back to safety was now locked behind them.

Despite desperate efforts Hinterstoisser couldn't climb back across the traverse when they were forced to retreat, nursing Angerer who had suffered head injuries from a rock-strike. Hinterstoisser spent hours in frustrating and exhausting attempts to climb sideways across the glassy shield of rock that was now coated with a hard film of verglas.

The weather worsened and the rockfall began spitting down accompanied by avalanches and waterfalls. Watchers at the telescopes in Alpiglen and Kleine Scheidegg could sense that a tragedy was beginning to unfold. The men were trapped. From the lower lip of the First Ice Field, adjacent to the Swallow's Nest ledge, they attempted to rappel directly down the great rock barrier that lay between them and the easier ground of the lower face. This vertical rock face dropped beneath them occasionally jutting out in overhangs and roofs. The line of descent also lay in the path of torrents of rocks and avalanches, sweeping from the rim of the First Ice Field above them. Somewhere down on the icy rock wall lay the gallery windows—the great open holes tunneled from the rock by the builders of the Jungfrau railway. This railway had been carved through the heart of the mountain to carry tourists up to the Jungfrau Joch, the col between the summits of the Monch and the Jungfrau. The gallery windows were positioned in the center of the face and had been created primarily to dump rock spoil down the face from the excavations after 4 kilometers (2.49 miles) of tunneling. Once the tunnel had been completed the gaping holes were developed into spectacular viewing windows for the hordes of tourists eager to look down the forbidding, ice-plastered precipices of the north face.

In 1936 the beleaguered party had tried to rappel directly down to a ledge that ran across the wall and that would with luck lead them to the safety of the Stollenloch, a small workers' access window. They almost made it.

It was a bold decision in the days when rappelling was fraught with danger. Modern braking devices had not been invented and traditional friction rappels were used, winding the heavy, wet ropes across the back of the shoulders, around the chest, and down between the legs to brake the speed of descent. It was precariously difficult to control. As Hinterstoisser and his three companions slid down through the tumult of avalanches and whistling stones Von Altmen, the sector guard stationed at the gallery windows, opened the huge wooden doors and looked out into the storm, searching for any sign of the retreating party. He was delighted to hear a cheery yodel. All was well despite the severe conditions. He ducked back inside to make a warming pot of tea for the young climbers who must have been exhausted after four days on the face.

Two hours later when no one had arrived he looked out of the window again. Conditions were more ghastly than ever, with mists rising from the abyss below as stones and slides of snow rushed down from the black emptiness above. This time there was no cheery acknowledgement to his shout, only the despairing cries of one man—Toni Kurz—shouting for his life. His companions were dead and he was hanging helplessly on the rope, spinning in space. Some dreadful calamity had caused Andreas Hinterstoisser to be swept from his rappel stance—a direct blow from stonefall or an especially heavy rush of avalanching snow. Hinterstoisser had fallen the entire length of the face. Rainer had been dragged up by the weight of Kurz and Angerer, who had been swept from their stance. Rainer, pulled tight against his carabiner clipped to the rappel piton, had frozen to death, unable to free himself. Below Kurz the lifeless body of Angerer swayed in the wind, strangled by his own rope.

A hurriedly organized party of rescuers managed to climb from the Stollenloch up 300 feet of iced rock slabs to a point 300 feet below where Kurz dangled. As night came on apace the rescuers realized that it would be impossible to climb up to the stricken climber directly. They told him to stick it out for the night despite his despairing pleas. It was an awful decision since they knew he would not survive the night unprotected from the savagery of the storm. In the dark, on that face, there was no one capable of the climbing feats required to reach Kurz. Not even the brilliant Hinterstoisser, one of the best climbers of his day, could have made such a climb.

Toni Kurz endured a long despairing night. For me, this was all that was hard, uncompromising, stern, and nightmarish about mountaineering. It was a freezing, lonely night as he swayed on a slender rope, swinging backwards and forwards as the stones sang by and the icy gale lashed at him, bleeding the warmth from his body. Above him the rope played across the frozen corpse of his friend while beneath the wire-tight rope trembled as the wind swung Angerer's corpse from side to side. All Kurz could do was endure. When at last morning broke the guides were astonished to find that the young Berchtesgaden guide was still alive and calling down to them in a strong, clear voice.

The long, cold hanging had ravaged his body. Ice plated his jacket and trousers. His left hand, exposed when he lost his mitt in the terrifying fall, had been quickly frozen. By morning his entire left arm was grotesquely congealed into a solid, immovable claw. His core temperature was critically low, yet he had stoically hung on, waiting for the faint glimmer of dawn, praying for the sound of friendly voices.

Despite the benefit of daylight the guides attempting the rescue could climb no nearer than 130 feet from where Kurz hung out over the abyss—a single rope-length from rescue. The cliff was so overhanging that they could not see Toni Kurz swinging freely in the wind. Attempts to fire a rope up to him using rockets failed as they whizzed futilely into space. Kurz was weakening fast. The guides insisted that he try to descend the rope beneath him as far as possible and cut away Angerer's body. Then he had to climb back up and cut free some of the loose rope connecting him to Rainer's contorted, lifeless form.

Despite a useless, frozen arm Kurz completed this exhausting maneuver, clinging tenuously to the rope with the hook of his frozen limb, as he cut the rope with his axe. He expected to see his friend's body wheel down into the chasm. Angerer didn't fall. During the night his body had swung against the wall and become frozen to the rock. When Kurz gathered the freed rope he painstakingly untwisted the triple hawser-laid strands and knotted them together. It took five hours of unbelievably frustrating toil as Kurz struggled to untwist the stiff, wire-like rope with an incapacitated arm and numb, blackened, and swollen fingers. He tugged desperately with his teeth and fought to knot the stiffened rope into sections of cord. Eventually he had a thin cord just long enough to reach the arms of his dispirited rescuers.

As the hours passed Kurz's strength was ebbing fast. By the time the fragile cord came snaking down the guides knew there was very little time left.

He had displayed phenomenal endurance, strength, and mental stamina in his struggle to live. That was all it had become—a lone figure fighting for his life, able to draw on nothing but his willpower.

An avalanche thundered down, battering Kurz's decrepit body and almost sweeping the waiting guides to their death as they attempted to fasten a climbing rope and a sling equipped with carabiners, pitons, and a hammer to the cord. Suddenly a boulder spun down through the air, almost decapitating one of the rescuers. Then came the frightful rushing noise of a body plunging towards them. Angerer's body—torn free from the grip of the ice—plummeted to the foot of the wall.

Kurz barely had the strength to haul up the heavy rope with the hardware swinging and clattering against the rock wall. Still the rope was not long enough. The guides spliced on another rope and at last they could see that Kurz would be able to reach them. Unfortunately the knot joining the two ropes together hung in space just out of their reach. Somehow Kurz would have to bypass the blockage. They said nothing.

Kurz's body appeared over the rim of the impending wall, legs dangling and spinning in the air as he slid painfully down the rope. Slowly, he inched down towards the knot joining the two ropes. He had threaded his rappel rope through a carabiner clipped into his waist belt to increase the friction on the thin rope. Gripping it with one glacial, insensate hand must have been appallingly difficult yet he managed to creep down towards his rescuers. Inch by inch the tortured figure came swinging down until the knot came up against the viselike grip of his frozen hand and then caught against the carabiner. It would not pass through the snap link. He was hanging in space, unable to get his weight off the rope, and it was now impossible for him to unclip the carabiner. He was locked into the system.

He thumped helplessly at the hardened knot, uttering pitiable groans of agony. He bent forward in a pathetic attempt to bite the knot down to size as his grotesque left arm pointed sticklike into the sky. He mumbled incomprehensibly through bleeding lips, his face blotched purple from frostbite and emotion. The guides strained to hear him.

Then in a firm, lucid voice he spoke aloud. "I'm finished," he said and lolled forward, his body tipping so that he hung from the waist, arms dangling by his legs, swinging gently in the breeze. He had died at the very point of rescue, almost within arm's reach of the guides. The piteous photograph of his corpse hanging in space with icicles growing from his fingers and the points of his crampons will remain in my mind forever. Days later, the guides used a knife tied to a long pole to cut him free.

Rainer had been prophetically quoted in the press before the ascent saying, "We don't want to die, we're still young and want to live. We always leave our way down open. We know that it takes luck and we have to count on that." Then he added ominously, "If it is possible to do the Wall we'll do it—if not, we'll stay up there."

His luck ran out. Rainer's body was found crumpled on the screes at the foot of the face, melded into stones as if he had become assimilated into the very fabric of the mountain. He was carried home to be buried in Salzburg. During the search for their bodies the guides found Max Sedlmayr, who had died the previous year. His companion, Karl Mehringer, frozen into the ice at the edge of the Second Ice Field, would not be found for another twenty-seven years.

A month after the tragedy Kurz's twisted body was eventually found in the icy depths of a bergschrund at the base of the wall, extracted, wrapped in a tarpaulin, and carried down to Grindelwald. The following year Hinterstoisser's body was found by Matthias Rebitsch and Ludvig Vorg during their first unsuccessful attempt on the wall. So ended one of the most powerful and poignant episodes ever to be enacted on the Eiger.

From the mumbled, fragmentary, and incoherent sentences that Kurz had uttered, the guides managed to piece together what had happened to the retreating party. Hinterstoisser was off the rope when hit by stonefall, perhaps because as the best climber he was trying to fix a secure piton placement for the next rappel, and he fell the length of the face. A second volley of rocks then knocked the remaining three men from their stance, trapping Rainer and strangling Angerer. Tattered scraps of bandage found wrapped around Angerer's skull proved that he had suffered a serious head injury.

For the helpless guides it was a terrible experience. When Sedlmayr and Mehringer had died the previous year they had done so alone, hidden within the maelstrom of the storm that had pinned them down in the center of the wall. Toni Kurz, however, died in the full pitying gaze of his fellow guides. Arnold Glatthard, one of the guides, said, "It was the saddest moment of my life." I have always been haunted by the story of this brave young man's vain but heroic fight for life. As Heinrich Harrer wrote in *The White Spider:*

> . . . *it was one of the grimmest tricks of fate that left Toni Kurz uninjured at the outset, so that he was forced to*

endure his agony to its uttermost end. He was like some
messenger from the beyond, finding his way back to earth
simply because he loved life so well.

Thirty years later, when Chris Bonington and Don Whillans were struggling to retreat down the face when rescuing a dazed Brian Nally, Don Whillans remembered the fateful lessons of the Kurz party.

Brian Nally and his partner Barry Brewster had reached the far left upper edge of the Second Ice Field. Brewster was climbing the difficult rock pitch that led up from the ice onto the distinct triangular rock buttress called the Flat Iron when he was struck by a fusillade of rocks. He fell 200 feet and the impact bent Nally's belay piton to the point of breaking. Nally attempted to help his paralyzed friend lying exposed on the ice field. He dug a ledge in the ice for Brewster to lie on secured to one of the ropes, despite continuous rockfall.

Early the following morning Brewster died of his injuries as Whillans and Bonington were climbing across the ice field towards the distant figures. Suddenly another barrage of rocks swept Brewster from his perch on the ice. Whillans and Bonington watched mesmerized as the body flew clear of the Second Ice Field and plunged 5000 feet to the foot of the wall. "It was like being hit hard in the stomach," Bonington later wrote. "I just hugged the ice and swore over and over again."

When Nally, Whillans, and Bonington reached the foot of the Ice Hose at the top of the First Ice Field Don Whillans displayed his genius as a mountaineer. He noticed a stream of meltwater washing down to the right of the Ice Hose to plunge over the overhanging walls of the Röte Fluh. From his previous knowledge of the face Whillans knew that this plume of water often flowed from the rock wall above the start of the Hinterstoisser Traverse. Instead of descending to the First Ice Field, as countless retreating parties had done before, he led down to the right as a deluge of hailstones and rocks clattered down the wall. He followed the stream to a point where he could hammer in a secure rappel piton. In one rappel the three men found themselves at the start of the Hinterstoisser Traverse. Whillans's brilliance as a mountaineer had saved them the effort of having to reverse the Hinterstoisser Traverse. If only Toni Kurz and his party had known this they could have retreated safely instead of being forced to make the intimidating and critical decision to rappel the rock band beneath the First Ice Field.

These were lessons to be learned and easily remembered because of their grisly nature. Ignorance is the greatest source of fear. With foresight and common sense we could reduce the face to a set of distinct climbing problems routinely overcome.

"Bloody hell!" Ray blurted out and I glanced over at him. He was staring through the windows, eyes wide in astonishment. I looked forward and there it was. The Eiger. My heart leaped. I was transfixed.

"Watch the bloody road," Ray yelped and I hauled on the steering wheel and swerved to avoid an oncoming lorry. "Jesus, I'm scared enough as it is without you killing us both."

"I'm not scared, you know?" I said and looked again at the Eiger as a sweeping corner brought us up into the open meadowland surrounding Grindelwald. "I'm excited, mate. Thanks."

"Thanks?" Ray asked, looking puzzled. "What for?"

"For suggesting that we have a go at it," I said. "You were right. I feel great about it."

"Not scared, then?"

"No, not really. Nervous anticipation, maybe . . . " I trailed off, lost for words. "I haven't been back to the Alps for fifteen years." I grinned at Ray. "This is where it all began for me. Not just the Alps but the Eiger. The first route I ever heard of, the one I always dreamed about. Maybe the dream will come true."

"Well, if it all goes belly up it just goes to prove what I've always thought."

"What's that?"

"Our sole purpose in life is simply to serve as a warning to others. Whoa!"

I laughed and swerved the car quickly out of the way of an oncoming bus.

"Stop staring at that bloody hill," Ray shouted and grabbed at the dashboard as the bus passed by.

"Look, we're going to have to stop for a beer and have a good look at her or I'm going to crash this damn car. I can't take my eyes off her." I swerved again and a Landcruiser towing a caravan beeped its horn angrily as it swept past. I smiled at the irony of being killed in a traffic accident just outside Grindelwald. *That would be just typical.*

"There! On the right," Ray said, pointing at a classic Swiss chalet-style restaurant. There was a wooden balcony at the side with tables set and the Eiger loomed up in the background.

"Have you got your binoculars there?" I asked as we closed the car doors. Ray held them up.

We sat on the terrace drinking beer and eating goulash soup. The sun was shining from a clear blue sky and the green meadows in the sweeping valley below Grindelwald were dotted with picturesque chalets set amidst manicured grasslands. Cowbells clanged lugubriously in the distance.

"It's plastered," Ray said as he peered at the Eiger.

"Yeah, it does look rather white," I agreed. "Maybe it's just powder snow?"

"Could be," Ray muttered. "But the upper face looks bad. The Ramp is crested with what looks like ice. I can't even make out the line of the Exit Cracks."

"I wonder how fast it clears," I said.

"Here, take a look," Ray said, handing me the binoculars. The face suddenly reared into view and I jerked back. Binoculars gave a very distorted image. Everything seemed plumb vertical and all sense of scale disintegrated. "Jesus!" I gasped and heard Ray laughing. At first I was completely lost as the eyepieces seemed filled with immense rock bands, sweeping ice fields, columns of hanging icicles, and vast yellow overhanging walls of limestone.

I gazed at the Eiger. *How would it change me?* Past experiences had shaken me to the core, storms both real and metaphorical had raged through me, leaving an indelible sense of vulnerable fragility. Afterwards I was filled with a strength I had never experienced before, an exultant confidence born from standing unharmed within the tempest. I had lived through it. When the fear ebbed it was replaced with a mounting wonder at the beauty I had witnessed. The mountains were contradictory, in equal measure. I could remember their beauty, yet could never fully recall the fear. Perhaps that was because you could see beauty while fear crept in unseen. It was easier to recall the aesthetic that had been so fiercely photographed onto my mind.

I remembered a time trapped on the south face of Les Drus. We had crept past the summit, feeling our hair rising in static on the backs of our necks as the air grew tight and we sensed the awful dread that it was going to explode at any moment and we would be in the center of it all. In near panic we had scuttled blindly out onto the face away from the ridgelines and the twin-pointed summit. The storm, like a living thing, surged against the ramparts of the peaks eating inexorably into the fabric of the mountains. The tension in the air increased to a pressing, ominous urgency. There was a fizzing crackling feel in the air around us as we pulled frantically on the ropes and our jackets rustled in the electric atmosphere. It became unendurable. I felt like weeping, scared and frustrated at our helplessness. Then it was upon us in a colossal explosion of thunder. The pressure released around us. We stared in mute amazement.

Ostentatious lightning, the color of burnished gold, burst in white-bright flashes flaming along the crenellated ridges. Thundercracks colliding in sheets of sound rattled the air and trembled the dark underbelly of the storm as fire lit the menacing skeins of racing clouds. The wind rose to a shrieking venomous pitch in its furious battle with the mountains, bursting through the passes like floodwater through bridge arches so constricted that it roared in furious retaliation, harrying the nervous clouds, pressing them forward until they convulsed skywards into the angry blue, black, and purple of the storm wall. The dying sun flashed bright and quick from the boiling thunderheads. The storm pounded against the flanks of the mountains, tearing at their obdurate solidity.

Then the sky ignited in a painful, killing flash leaving sudden blackness on my quickly shuttered eyes followed by the crimson intensity of blood seen pulsing through my closed lids. Ragged breaths rasped through my gritted teeth and my fingers trembled in the staccato light. I clenched a fist to hide my fear. The storm hammered at us for an age and the air stank of shattered stone and the ammoniac reek of sweated fear.

We stood cowering in the heart of this cataclysm with fire and light and flame all around. Yet I felt blessed. We were mute spectators, impotent and awed. The world exploded around us and we stood still and quiet until it seemed we too were spinning wildly in the storm, twirling helplessly in space, no longer human, nonsentient, absorbed by the tempest, elemental. I gazed spellbound as the tremendous forces erupted around us: I was in the midst of an exploding shell watching as white-hot shrapnel rent the air. Somehow I knew without question that I would not be harmed; as if I had earned the right to witness this moment, to live it to the end. Boulders blasted skywards by bolts of flame seemed to slow-tumble darkly against the searing light. The crashing roar of thunder, like the storm surf of some titanic sea breaking on a stony beach, muffled the cracking reports of shattering rocks.

Hail washed over us in waves of stinging needles. Ice formed on the narrow rocky shelf where we stood, crunching under our feet as we winced and slipped on the sliver-thin shards of raw glass. Ice water slid down my neck in rivulets, frigid veins lancing across the warmth of my back.

Then it was silent and the storm passed into the horizon, bickering and snapping angrily as butter-colored lightning stabbed in exasperation and I smiled, released to life. A tranquil rain flooded away the storm, cleansing the sky as thunder rumbled in muted barrages like heavy guns on a distant half-remembered battlefield. The light died softly and the passing violence left the air ice-bright, and a wonderment, sharp as crystal, remained in my memory. The setting sun painted the emptied clouds with glowing pastels. The storm was over. Night followed, swiftly dark, and I took a final refreshment from the light then drank in the glory of emerging stars scattered like carelessly discarded gems across a velvet black sky.

I stood up and braced my shoulders, straightening the cower from my spine. I blew a long exhalation of breath in a plumed smoky vapor. I felt wondrously alive. I thought I should be dead and shivered. My memories may have changed the reality of that storm but it is all I have and I must believe it. I remember the beauty and the awe. I do not recall the terror.

"Penny for your thoughts?" Ray asked, disturbing my reverie.

"Oh, nothing," I said. "I was thinking about bad weather."

"Yeah, we could do without it," he replied.

I put the binoculars on the table and glanced over at Ray who sipped reflectively at his beer and gazed fixedly at the Eiger. I wondered what we would find up there.

HEROES *11* AND FOOLS

I ROLLED ONTO MY SIDE AND GLANCED OUT of the door of the bivi tent. There was a slithering sound and a handful of wet snow slid from the angled roof of the tent and struck the back of my neck. I swore and tried to flick it off before it melted and dribbled down my back. Snow clung to the rocky buttresses and rubble-covered ledges outside the tent. In the swirling gray clouds darker shadows were occasionally visible, a few rock walls soaring skywards would coyly reveal themselves and then the mist would wrap them from view. I knew it was the imposing flank of the Röte Fluh, a 1000-foot-high overhanging limestone wall that reared up out of the north face to the edge of the west ridge of the Eiger.

For acclimatization and the chance to get a view of the face we had climbed tiredly up to the west flank the previous afternoon. I had quickly regretted the decision to walk all the way from Grindelwald and avoid the comfort of the train ride to Kleine Scheidegg. It would get us fit, I had announced confidently, and three hours later I had felt half-dead as I staggered into the station bar at the end of the line.

As we had climbed up the initial ledges and scree slopes of the west flank the weather had steadily worsened. By nightfall it had begun snowing heavily. Our plan to leave the tent and make a fast ascent of the west flank the following morning was quickly abandoned. We had hoped to learn the descent route down the west flank that we knew could present tricky routefinding problems in poor conditions, particularly after an ascent of the north face. It would have the added advantage of getting us fit at the same time and perhaps we could look across the Second Ice Field and into the Ramp from the top of the Röte Fluh, giving us a clearer idea of the conditions on the upper part of the face.

"What's it like?" Ray asked from the depths of his sleeping bag.

"Not too crisp," I said and wiped the cold wetness from my neck. "No point continuing," I added.

"Oh, I thought we were going to check out the descent route."

"We'd be lucky to find the bloody thing in this stuff," I said as I placed a pan of half-frozen water on the stove and lit the gas. It purred comfortingly. "It's a total white-out, snow everywhere. May as well have a brew and bugger off," I suggested. "Did you sleep okay?" I asked as I handed a brew of tea to Ray.

"When you weren't snoring, yes." He sipped at the tea. "Is this the first time you've been to Grindelwald?"

"Yeah, I nearly came here twenty years ago but it all went belly up."

"How come?"

"Oh, it was my second season, a good one mind, and I was stupid enough to think I could climb the face. My partner said otherwise." I drank my tea and told Ray how Dave Page, my climbing partner at the time, had decided at the very last minute that I wasn't experienced enough to try the Eiger and how disappointed and humiliated I had been.

We had climbed the Walker Spur together on my twenty-first birthday and of course I had immediately thought of the Eiger. We had heard that the conditions on the face were good that summer and when Dave had mentioned it to me a surge of excitement and dread rushed through me. I could scarcely believe that I had already succeeded on the Walker Spur, one of my most coveted routes. To do the Eiger as well in only my second alpine season seemed too good to be true.

Unfortunately, I had sat in a tent in Snell's Field in Chamonix and listened despondently as Dave Page patiently explained why he thought I was too inexperienced to attempt the Eiger. We argued long and loud and I felt humiliated to be pleading with him so audibly to everyone else on the campsite. I remembered the sense of bitter disappointment when he elected to climb with a complete stranger and set off for the Swiss Oberland.

In a fit of pique I teamed up with a Canadian climber, Doug Pratt Johnson, and headed for Zermatt, praying that Dave would return after an ignominious failure on the Eiger. Doug and I climbed the heavily snowed-up Schmidt Route on the north face of the Matterhorn, enduring a freezing bivouac without sleeping bags 200 feet below the summit. One of the two pegs holding us in place on the steeply angled slab we had bivouacked upon fell out during the night. Luckily the second peg, the one I thought to be the weaker of the two, held our combined shivering weight for the rest of the night.

On the train returning to Chamonix I was torn with guilty thoughts about Dave's attempt on the Eiger. I didn't want him to die but a temporarily incapacitating stonefall injury would have been useful. In truth I wished him no harm but prayed that he would have failed, fallen out with his companion, or been driven back by storms. He just might, I reasoned, decide on a second attempt with me now that I had proved my competence on the Matterhorn. To my utter despair he was waiting in his tent in Snell's Field beaming broadly. He congratulated me on my success and then told me how well it had gone on the Eiger.

He and his companion had joined forces with a pair of climbers from Newcastle at half height on the route and completed the climb without incident and in good weather throughout. He actually mentioned that the climbing wasn't as hard as he had expected and I had to restrain myself from throttling him. He said that he almost regretted that they had not been through the classic epic battle of an Eiger storm. I wanted to yell at him to shut up. Instead I murmured reluctant congratulations and thought bitterly of what could have been—three of the six classic north faces in only my second alpine season.

Calmly, Dave described how the four-man team had been tentatively descending the west flank of the Eiger. At no point was it especially difficult but it could prove deceptively treacherous. The descent route wove a complicated line down the west ridge in places straying out onto the broad west flank. The four climbers moved down confidently, unroped, making the occasional rappel on the steep upper section of the ridge. Horrified, Dave watched as one of his newfound friends lost his balance, slipping to his death from the top edge of a short rubble-strewn wall. It was a sobering moment, the first of many deaths I was to be told about in the following decades. I thought about the Eiger and decided then and there to cut my losses and head for home.

Gaston Rebuffat in his book *Starlight and Storm* had named the six classic great north faces of the Alps: the Eiger, the Grandes Jorasses, and the Matterhorn were the hardest to climb, followed by Les Drus, the Piz Badile, and Cima Grande. There were many other routes in the Alps that were just as imposing, often considerably more difficult and very committing. Rebuffat's choice, however, was based on a period in alpine mountaineering that could justifiably be regarded as its Golden Age; an era when the sport came of age and that signaled the birth of extreme mountaineering.

These ascents were at the forefront of what was deemed possible at the time. They were achieved using rudimentary equipment—weak hemp ropes, inadequate clothing and bivouac equipment, and exceedingly heavy hardware. Ice screws were crude and unreliable. They had no harnesses, rappel devices, metal wedges, or chockstones. They didn't even use helmets. Torches and stoves were bulky and liable to fail. They had little to rely upon other than their astonishing fitness and strength of will boosted by sausage, bread, coffee, and cigarettes. The famous "heart pills" consumed by Heckmair on the Exit Cracks, most likely a form of amphetamine, were a rarity. A Dr. Belart of Grindelwald had pressed Heckmair to take them on the climb, saying, "If Toni Kurz had only had them along, he might even have survived his ordeal." Dr. Belart had counseled that the little vial of "heart drops" were only to be used in *direst need*. At the time, in the midst of a vicious storm, Heckmair had just fallen off the Exit Cracks, ripping his protection pitons out. His fall had been held by Wiggerl Vorg's outstretched palm—punctured by Heckmair's crampons in the process—and the heavy impact ripped out their belay pitons. They fell 4 feet below their stance only to stop miraculously on steep ice perched over a 5000-foot abyss. Having got much closer to their Maker than they had planned they decided that "direst need" had been reached. Heckmair studied the label on the bottle with the careful and precise instructions recommending a maximum dose of only a few drops:

> *I simply poured half of it into Wiggerl's mouth and drank the rest, as I happened to be thirsty. We followed it with a couple of glucose lozenges and were soon in proper order again.*

These brave pioneers were my heroes, even though I am sure they would have hated such an emotive sobriquet. The *Oxford English Dictionary* defines the essence of heroism as:

> *A man who exhibits extraordinary bravery, firmness, fortitude, or greatness of soul in any action, or in connection with any pursuit, work, or enterprize; a man admired or venerated for his achievements and noble qualities.*

I have always nurtured heroes in my soul and been challenged and inspired by their deeds. The great American mountaineer Thomas Hornbein answered the question of "who needs heroes" with admirable insight:

Who needs heroes? . . . I think we all do . . . Where do heroes fit in? In a way they are the stuff of dreams. For me, they occupy a special summit a bit less accessible, a mountain peak that in my mind's eye has grand walls of rock and brilliant ice, clouds veiling an elusive, lonely summit. It is not a mountain I can climb, and never will, but one I nonetheless dream I might.

I was an unashamed hero-worshipper and I still am. The great pioneers of the 1930s and the early postwar years inspired me with their style and boldness. I had been fascinated by the exploits of men such as Comici, Cassin, and later the likes of Hermann Buhl and Walter Bonatti.

Much to my astonishment I managed to climb the classic Comici Route on the north face of the Cima Grande in the Dolomites in my first alpine season. I had never been on anything so huge and intimidating—1600 feet of overhanging and vertical limestone. The scale of the wall was overwhelming. We had only climbed a few short multipitched routes in Britain. The thought of being trapped on that immense wall with no hope of retreat or rescue quite unnerved us. We climbed the route slowly and incompetently, stunned by our audacity.

The Comici line on Cima Grande had gained its classic status after its ascent in 1933 by Emilio Comici. It was Comici, considered the ultimate stylist, who had taken the Dolomites by storm in the early 1930s. The great Riccardo Cassin, first ascensionist of the northeast face of the Piz Badile and the Walker Spur on the Grandes Jorasses, was happy to be led and influenced by this maestro of Italian climbing.

Comici regarded climbing as a form of art and compared its harmonies with those of a piece of music. The rhythms and movements of the climber had to be elegantly adapted to the nature and texture of the rock he was climbing. He thought the aesthetic qualities of the chosen line to be as important as the climb itself.

This was epitomized by his famous dictum:

I wish someday to make a route and from the summit
let fall a drop of water and this is where my route will
have gone.

The thought of attempting one of his routes terrified me. When we crept insectlike up that yellow wall I fervently hoped that I wasn't about to become one of Comici's falling drops of water.

Riccardo Cassin's ascent of the northeast face of the Piz Badile in 1937 quickly became one of the classic north faces. During the stormy descent from the summit two of Cassin's companions, Giuseppe Valsecchi and Mario Molteni, collapsed and died of hypothermia and exhaustion. Today it can be climbed in half a day with lightweight rock-climbing gear, but that in no way detracts from the boldness of its first ascent.

The Allain and Leininger Route on the north face of the Drus, climbed in 1935, also gained classic status with the boldness of its line and difficult climbing in ice-choked jamming cracks on the summit headwall. The Schmidt Route on the north face of the Matterhorn, the first of the great north faces climbed in 1931, was praised at the time as the hardest and most serious face ever climbed in the European Alps. It was eclipsed by the ascents of the Eiger and the Grandes Jorasses in 1938. Indeed, all these north faces were regarded as the hardest climbs of their day and all were put up in the 1930s—the true Golden Age, the birth of extreme alpine mountaineering.

Riccardo Cassin, Walter Bonatti, and Hermann Buhl were my all-time heroes of the alpine world. Cassin, not content with being the first to climb two of the north faces, had actually turned up in Kleine Scheidegg with Gino Esposito and Ugo Tizzoni to attempt the Eigerwand in July 1938, only to find Heckmair, Vorg, Kasparek, and Harrer already fighting for their lives during their epic first ascent of the face. The disconsolate Italians promptly took the train back to Italy and headed directly for the Grandes Jorasses. Despite having never climbed in the Mont Blanc range they immediately put up the wildly elegant *direttissima* on the Walker Spur.

It became an instant classic and the ascent of this magnificent bastion of ice-sheathed rock is one of the most beautiful lines ever climbed on a mountain. Bradford Washburn's stunning photograph of the moon rising over the great north wall of the Jorasses hangs above my fireplace. Its detail is so fine that I can see the cracks we climbed and the bivouac ledge we slept on twenty years ago.

After Dave Page's success on the Eiger in 1981 I decided it was best to err on the side of safety. I vowed to come back the following summer and head directly for Grindelwald. I never did and as each year passed it seemed increasingly unlikely that I would ever attempt the Eiger. After the accident in Peru in 1985 I went to hospital and Simon Yates went to the Alps and climbed the Eigerwand. I remembered hearing the news as I lay recuperating in a hospital bed after they had rebroken my knee for the third time. There was a pang of regret at the thought of what I had missed, quickly quashed by a private admonishment that I would now never be up to such a climb again.

Every doctor I talked to said as much. Lead a sedentary life, they said. What the hell did they know? But by then the damage had been done and I had convinced myself that the Eiger was beyond me.

"So, if we climb the Eiger," Ray said, "you'll only have to pop over to the Bregalia and climb the Piz Badile to get the six classics done."

"I hadn't thought about that," I said. "But I thought we were giving up mountaineering after the Eiger?"

"Well, yes, we are, but it would be a shame not to do the Cassin Route on the Badile, wouldn't it?"

"Is it hard?"

"No, not especially," Ray said. "We did it in rock shoes in four or five hours. Great climbing on superb granite and the Bregalia is beautiful. You'd love it."

"Come on, let's get out of here before you come up with any other cunning plans." I threw the dregs of my tea out of the door and began to lace my boots, thinking about warm sunny days on the granite of the Bregalia.

"We should be down in an hour if we get a move on," I said as we packed away the bivi tent and shouldered our rucksacks. "The north face will be plastered for days now."

"I know, and the Mittellegi Ridge," Ray agreed morosely. We had hoped to traverse the Mittellegi over the summit of the Eiger and down the west ridge as part of our training regime. The bad weather was throwing these careful plans into disarray and we were running out of time.

"Better get some rock climbing done in the meantime, then," I suggested. "We should go up to the Hintisberg. It's south-facing, overhanging, and over 700 feet high in places."

"Great," Ray said with a distinct lack of enthusiasm. "Over-hanging rock, my favorite."

"Come on, we need to get some hard rock routes under our belts. It will do our confidence a load of good. We could even practice climbing with rucksacks and big boots on if you like."

"Get out of here." Ray gave me a playful shove and I struggled to maintain balance on icy rock. "It's bad enough climbing over-hanging rock without these bloody things on," he complained as he pulled the laces tight on his clumsy plastic double boots.

Ray seemed strangely nervous as he sorted out the carabiners and hardware on his harness. I leaned back on the sling I had clipped to a shiny new bolt at the foot of the route and peered up at the stepped roofs on the wall above us. It was warm in the afternoon sun and the white limestone wall reflected a glaringly harsh light into my eyes. As my gaze travelled up the wall I spotted two tiny figures perched on a great prow of rock hundreds of feet above me.

Their ropes hung free in space, twirling in the breeze. Further to the right I saw another climber pulling over the lip of an enormous horizontal roof. He moved with controlled precision, exuding an effortless grace as he flowed upwards with the poise of a dancer and the power of a gymnast. There was no sense of the immense strength he was using to remain in such an exposed and airy position. A flurry of black shapes swung beneath him as a flock of birds wheeled around on the rising air.

I looked down at the meadows perched in the valley below. An ancient farm building with shingled roof and heavy beams stood picturesquely by a group of pine trees. I looked across at the Eiger dominating the head of the valley.

"Are you right, then?" I asked Ray as he tied the rope into his harness.

"Yeah, suppose so," he said grudgingly and glanced up at the climber clinging to the roof far above him. "Bloody hell! Are we going up there?"

"It's a bit uphill, isn't it?" I said and laughed at his expression of dismay.

"God, I hate this sort of limestone climbing," Ray said fervently. "It's so in-your-face, so damned steep."

"You'll be fine," I reassured him. "There's loads of bolts. They're all brand-new. You could hang a truck off them."

"Maybe." Ray chalked his fingers and looked anxiously at the first pitch.

"I'll be right behind you." I patted his shoulder and he moved reluctantly up the initial easy moves towards where the rock began to overhang, pushing him off balance. The ropes dropped straight down into my hands and I watched as he carefully clipped the blue rope through the first bolt.

"Okay, I've got you, kid!" I shouted. "Go for it."

"Go for what?" Ray said irritably as he gazed at the impending wall and the small roof jutting from its upper end. His hands flitted around the rock, searching for a comfortingly large handhold.

What followed was a display of such staggeringly inept climbing that I was left lost for words. I had climbed with Ray all over the world from the Himalayas to the sea cliffs of Pembroke, on rock towers in Sardinia and the frozen waterfalls of Colorado. I had never seen him climb so badly and I couldn't understand why.

He swarmed up until he was clinging tenuously to the leaning wall. Then he came to an abrupt halt. Occasionally a hand fluttered above his head, blindly searching for holds. One foot began to vibrate as if working a sewing machine. Then his other foot began shaking. I tried not to snigger.

"You are now below all major difficulties," I shouted encouragingly. He grunted an irritated reply.

After what seemed an age he crept up to the roof and pawed at it frantically. The wild vibrations of his feet were beginning to set up a sympathetic motion in his upper legs, then his shoulders. He seemed to be getting a little blurred. Cocking one leg out to the side, he began waving his right arm above the roof like a drowning swimmer trying to attract attention. He was breathing hard, gasping with the effort of remaining attached to the rock. Gravity was creeping in, dragging him downwards. A few frantic arm movements suddenly became a bold and dynamic lunge upwards. He had spotted a "Thank God" hold above the roof. I smiled in approval of his confident solution to the problem.

There was a squeal of alarm as his fingers closed around a smooth nipple of rounded rock and began to slip. Unable to retreat and now vibrating uncontrollably he slapped his hand desperately to the right and grabbed a thin sharp edge. The lactic acid coursing through his forearms had produced fingers with the strength of wet linguini. It was a slap too far.

Then, with a sigh, he fell off. I laughed fit to bust as I lowered him to the ground. He stood at the stance head lowered, breathing hard.

"You've just displayed all the manual dexterity of an octopus on acid," I said helpfully.

"Fuck off," he replied.

It was an inauspicious start but we eventually gathered our wits and climbed some fine routes. I felt strong and fit and enjoyed the expansive moves on the steep limestone wall. Ray seemed strangely subdued and struggled up the pitches, clearly unhappy with his form.

As we strolled down towards the car I asked him if he was okay but he waved me away saying it was nothing to worry about and that he was just a bit rusty. I knew how busy he had been with his climbing shop in Utrecht and that he had been under great pressure leading up to the holiday as plans to open a second shop came to fruition. Perhaps he hadn't managed to get enough climbing done. It was certainly very unlike him to be climbing so poorly.

I took Ray's binoculars and peered glumly at the Eiger.

"It'll never clear in time. Look at the Ramp, for God's sake. It's completely white," I said. "We've got less than two weeks left."

"I don't know," Ray said. "When I was here before I was amazed at how much sun the face got in the afternoon. It's really a northeast face, you know. This stuff might burn off faster than you think."

"Do you think so?" I asked hopefully.

"We'll see, won't we?" Ray swung his rucksack into the boot of the car. "Let's go get a beer."

I looked back at the Eiger standing proud at the head of the valley. It was a lonely and unrivalled peak, mesmerizing just to gaze on. I felt subdued in its presence. The vast blinding whiteness of mountains forces itself into your mind. I stared at the distant walls of glistening gray rock rising to spectacular heights where ribbons of water and snow fell silently from overhangs and outcrops.

The ice fields flashed white light back from the concave immensity of the north face, beautiful and ominous. It emanated a serene menace: there was about it the beckoning silence of great height.

We drove down the switchback road until level with the old

farm that I had spotted from the crag. An elderly couple sat outside the front door at a rough-hewn trestle table. The man's face was deeply lined, weathered by a hard life as a farmer on the high alpine pastures. He held a bottle of beer and waved it at us, indicating with his other hand that we should join them.

"Is that a bar?" I said.

"I don't think so," Ray said. "Looks like an old farm to me."

"Well, he seems to want us to join him."

"Might as well then," Ray said with admirable decisiveness and pulled the car into the verge.

The old farmer greeted us with an expansive open-armed gesture, a bottle of beer in one hand and a dangerous-looking bottle of clear spirit in the other. He waved us to the bench seat and swiftly opened two bottles of beer. His wife smiled and raised a small schnapps glass in welcome. Soon the farmer was pouring the peach schnapps, filling our glasses to the brim. "Chus," he said and drained his glass with a flourish. "Cheers," Ray said and took a tentative swig and immediately started coughing. "Up yours," I said, drained the glass and then sat there stunned as tears welled in my eyes and my throat burned caustically.

What followed was an increasingly animated discussion in Swiss-German that Ray replied to in Dutch while I failed to understand a word. I noticed the triconi nails hammered into the soles of the farmer's heavy boots. They were exactly the same as those used by climbers before the invention of crampons.

"He says that he used to work on the Eiger railway. He was based at the gallery windows." Ray paused, listening to the old man. "Good God!" he said when the man stopped talking.

"What is it?"

"He just told me that he stopped working there after he saw two roped parties fall past the window."

"Bloody hell!" I looked at the man who nodded gravely to me. I couldn't understand his language but his expression told me everything. "I wonder who they were? You don't think he is the man who saw the Kurz and Hinterstoisser party from the window in 1936?"

"No," Ray said. "It was later than that; in the 1950s I think. Many people died, he said. He didn't like to see them fall. It is a bad place. Now he is a farmer. It is safer," Ray translated.

"Not drinking this bloody stuff, it isn't," I said with feeling. I watched the old man as Ray pointed at the Eigerwand and then at me and spoke slowly. The man seemed suddenly very serious. His wife raised her hand to her mouth and shook her head.

"He says we mustn't go," Ray said. "It is a bad face, he says, very dangerous."

"Encouraging, isn't he?" I said. Ray laughed and reassured the couple that we would be fine. They looked as if they had heard this many times before. The old man refilled my glass before I could stop him but this time he raised his glass slowly with a grave expression in his eyes. "God be with you," he said and snapped the glass back.

We returned to the Hintisberg over the following days of fine, sunny weather, keeping an eye on the face and watching with astonishment at the speed with which the fresh snow melted away. Unfortunately Ray's run of bad form on the rock was showing no real signs of improvement. Privately I was beginning to get worried. I was climbing strongly and decided that if conditions were good and the weather remained fair I would be happy to do all the leading. Yet in the back of my mind was the nagging worry that we both had to be climbing at full strength. If we ended up in a major Eiger storm we would have to rely on our combined skills to get us through.

As we sat in the late afternoon sunshine at the foot of the crag, sorting out our climbing equipment and stashing it in our rucksacks I broached the subject with Ray. It was an awkward moment for both of us but I felt that we had to be honest with each other. We had been friends and climbing companions for so long that we could afford to be frank.

"I'm a bit worried about you, kid," I said. "You're climbing like a spanner. What's the problem, mate?"

"I've never liked this sort of climbing," Ray said defensively. "Steep and overhanging never was my cup of tea."

"Yeah, I know, but you've climbed much better in the past. Something's wrong . . . "

"It's a scary crag," Ray interrupted. "It's very exposed, especially with that steep hillside below it and the drop into the valley . . . "

"It'll be a lot worse on the Traverse of the Gods," I stated baldly.

"Well, that doesn't help, I must admit . . . "

I guessed what he was thinking. The psychological baggage of the Eiger had begun to eat into his confidence. I wondered whether he had thought it all through properly. By the time I had left England I had thought long and hard about the climb, read as much as I could, and made my decision before leaving. I suspected that in the hectic months of business leading up to our departure Ray had not had the time to consider properly what we had proposed to do. Now, faced with the menacing sight of the Eiger at every turn, he had begun to have second thoughts; doubts and corrosive fears had insidiously begun to unnerve him. He had a wife and two young daughters to think of, a business with many people dependent upon him. He had a lot to lose, far more than I had.

"We can do this, you know," I said and he looked at me searchingly. "We know what we can climb. We've seen what the face has to offer on your video. That was what made us come here. Nothing's changed. If we don't like it we back off; no recriminations, no worries."

"Yeah, I know. You're right," Ray sighed. "I'll bet once we're on that face I'll feel fine. I want to do it, I really do, it's just . . . well, I keep getting the jitters . . . "

"So? We just deal with it. *We* choose the risk—not the mountain."

"Yeah, you're right."

"Look, I reckon we should go up tomorrow and take a look at it. We can put the tent up at the foot of the face and then climb as high as the Hinterstoisser or even the Swallow's Nest and then come down again. It will give us a feel for the mountain, give us an idea of the scale and conditions. What do you think?"

"Tomorrow?" He looked a little startled.

"We've got to do it some time," I said.

"Tomorrow, well yes, why not? Yeah, it's a good idea. I reckon it'll put all these worries about the risks I'm taking into some sort of perspective."

"Exactly," I agreed. "If either of us don't like it then that's it. We go and do something else. I've got no problem with that."

"You'd be sick if we didn't do it."

"No, I said right from the start that it was our choice, both of us. Sure I might be upset but if that's what happens at least I'll know we tried. That will be good enough for me. So let's go up tomorrow."

"Right, you're on," Ray said, his expression brightening as he looked at the Eiger.

"It's funny how we deal with it, isn't it?" I said. "I mean, the risks; the way we cope with them."

"And it seems to change every time, doesn't it?"

"I never used to worry like this when I was younger. It's daft. We know so much more now, we're better climbers with superior gear and we were so inexperienced back then. Yet I'm more scared with every passing year."

"Ah," Ray said, holding up a finger. "That's because experience is something you don't get until just after you need it—that's the problem."

"The problem is suddenly realizing you're not immortal any more," I said. "I got that kicked out of me on Siula Grande. Never could think the same after that. It stays with you back deep in your mind. It's hard to deal with . . . "

"And I haven't even hurt myself," Ray agreed. "Sometimes this really does seem a stupid thing to do."

"It's just probability. Some days you're the bug, some days you're the windshield."

"Like playing the lottery," Ray laughed.

"Well, yes. And you know, if you buy a lottery ticket on Monday you have a greater probability of being dead by the time the numbers are drawn on Saturday than you ever have of winning the damn thing."

"You're kidding?"

"Not at all. It puts it into some sort of perspective, doesn't it? Winning the lottery is the equivalent of approaching a complete stranger on the street and telling him his phone number."

"Luckily I don't bother buying tickets," Ray said.

"This Eiger fear is really no more than a phobia, like being scared of flying or scared of heights."

"I *am* scared of bloody heights," Ray said sharply.

"Aren't we all? It's essential. Climbing is irrational, just like phobias. If there is an easy way why choose the hardest? If it scares you why force yourself to do it?"

"I'm still scared," Ray said stubbornly.

"It's just a phobia . . . "

"Oh, shut up will you!"

" . . . that's why we have to confront our nightmares, our phobias, your Eiger block, otherwise they'll rob us of control."

"Oh, bloody great, that is," Ray muttered and stood up, shouldering his rucksack.

"They use aversion therapy to get people over phobias. So, if you're scared of flying they make you fly and sort of force you out of the phobia. If you're scared of heights they put you in front of big drops."

"Does it work?"

"I don't know but I'm hoping I can get my fear of sleeping with supermodels treated."

"Idiot!" Ray said and began walking down the path.

"So, shall we make a recce on the lower face, just as far as the Hinterstoisser?" I said, hurrying after him.

"What? Now that you've laid my fears to rest, you mean?"

"Yes, sort of," I said as I drew level with him. "Seriously though, I think it will make all the difference."

"Do you reckon?"

"Certain," I said. "Tomorrow, okay?"

"If you say so," Ray said in a resigned voice.

TOUCHING HISTORY

THE FACE WAS SILENT, GRIPPED BY THE ICY SHADOWS of early morning. I stepped slowly across a band of shattered rocks a few feet wide. I held the ropes in my left hand, trailing them behind me as Ray followed. I was aware of the undercut rock wall that lurked on my left side. Glancing up every now and then I searched for the inverted rock triangle that the guidebook had mentioned. On its left side I would see the entry chimney, a short corner with a brutish hand-jamming crack at its back. The huge expanse of the Röte Fluh dominated the view. I knew some French climbers were up there somewhere but I had quickly lost them in the vastness of the lower wall. I had heard their voices chattering excitedly as they strode rapidly past our tent a few hours earlier.

As I had tended the glowing blue ring of the gas stove and prepared a brew of tea I had watched as the two yellow pinpricks of their head torches had dipped and bobbed on the dark wall. They had moved well left of the entry chimney and at first light I had watched through binoculars as they rapidly solo-climbed up the right side of the First Pillar. I knew it was possible to choose countless variations on routes up the complicated structure of ledges, rock walls, and snowfields that made up the lower 2500 feet of the wall. I had been tempted to follow the Frenchmen and then dismissed the idea. It would simply put us in the line of any rocks they inadvertently knocked down. I noticed as the light strengthened that the central line we were going to take was a strange brownish color, unlike the milk-white rock of the First Pillar. I thought no more about it.

At a point where a triangle of dirty névé poked down towards the band of scree that I was following I spotted the entry chimney. Immediately I began to kick steps up the névé, steadying myself with my axe. The snow gave way to a tumbled river of scattered rocks. There on the edge of the snow lay a tattered red shape. It looked like a jacket, red canvas of some sort, crumpled into the shape of a torso. I stopped, feeling momentarily shaken. I looked back and saw Ray carefully picking his way up the névé slope.

I reached forward and tentatively poked at the object with my axe. I saw a strap and then a buckle and I sighed with relief as the shape suddenly became familiar. It was a rucksack, torn and battered, partially extruded from the ice. I grabbed a strap and tugged it free. It jerked stiffly as I pulled it clear. The lid was almost torn from the body of the rucksack and one strap had been snapped. There was a jagged hole in the back section. I prized open the flattened canvas tube and peered inside, wondering what I might find. It was empty. I had thought there might be some personal items inside and was relieved to find it bare. I didn't want a connection to this object's past. I suspected it would be a melancholy one.

"I wonder whether it was dropped?" I murmured.

"I hope so," Ray said as he climbed up to my side, coiling the ropes as he moved.

There was a pedestal block behind which we could wedge ourselves and sort out the rack of hardware and slings. I kept glancing down at the red splash of color lying on the rocks, a forlorn reminder of some other person's misfortune.

"I know you said you wanted some memorabilia for the shop but that wasn't quite what you had in mind, was it?"

"No, not really," Ray said as he clipped some pegs to my bandolier. "I was thinking of a collection of old ring pitons, wooden wedges, maybe some tattered old rope, that sort of thing. It would look good hanging on a wall around a photo of the Eiger."

I examined the chimney with a jaundiced eye. There was a wet gleam of ice in the back of the crack and the walls ran with water. Although only short it would be a strenuous start to the climb. My eye was caught by a white plaque bolted high up on the left side of the corner. I read the words of memorial to two climbers who had died years before. There was no indication of what had happened to them. I glanced down at the rucksack.

"Hey, look at this," Ray called. He was looking over the side of the pedestal at the foot of the chimney. I climbed down and round the block of rock and saw another black-bordered brass plaque lying at an angle against the rock. I picked it up, noticing the empty holes that had held the bolts in place before the expansion and contraction of constant frosts had finally burst them free from wherever the plaque had been fixed. There were two names, the dates of birth and death, and some words in German.

"Poor buggers," I said, propping it against the rock wall and going back to join Ray. We had been warned about the depressing detritus of shattered and torn equipment littering the lower face but seeing it at firsthand was a sobering experience. He looked at me with a set expression.

"Well, that's a cheerful start," I said. "Come on. Let's get out of here. Have you got the ropes?"

"Yeah, I'm ready."

"It looks nasty, so I'll take my time. No point falling off the bottom 10 feet, eh?"

"Will you belay at the top?"

"I'll see but it would probably be best. We should be able to move together after that. Those French guys were soloing." I moved carefully up onto the top of the block and reached over towards the crack. I placed a Friend, an expanding camming device, in the crack and clipped it to the blue rope. I was reaching across the empty space of the chimney. The plaque leaned against the wall 30 feet below me. I felt tense, all too aware of where we had chosen to be.

"Be safe, kid," Ray said as I stepped across the gap and forced my left hand into the crack. As I clenched it into a fist jam I felt it slide then grip against the ice-lined rock.

"Watch me! It's slippery as hell," I said as I took a deep breath and swung my body into the corner. I was immediately forced off balance, dragged backwards by the weight of my rucksack, which also prevented me twisting into a more favorable position. My big mountain boots felt clumsy after the neat balletlike footwork of my rock slippers on the Hintisberg crag. It was a brief and unpleasant struggle executed with brawn rather than style before I arrived panting at the top of the corner. I moved along a narrow ledge until I came to a rusty piton hammered into a downward-facing crack. I fixed a small wire in the crack near the piton and clipped both to my ropes. Soon Ray had joined me and we stood examining the way ahead.

For a moment I felt exultation. *We're on the Eiger. On the north face at last.* We had climbed all of 40 feet but it was a momentous occasion for me. I knew that even if we had turned back immediately I could say I had been on the face. I looked at Ray and saw that he was smiling. We had left the dank corner behind with its sobering plaques and sad debris and the wall lay in front of us.

"Feeling good?" I asked.

"Yeah, very," Ray said and I knew he felt the same way as I did. Just being there was important to us. I felt a whole weight of worries dropping away from my mind as I looked up the confusing series of walls and ledges to where the Difficult Crack led up towards the Hinterstoisser Traverse. All those names in the book were suddenly real. Excitement coursed through me. It seemed so familiar—the movements, the racking of gear, the sound of the face, a silence broken by the rat-a-tat of an occasional falling stone. I realized how much I had missed the Alps.

Four hours later we had reached a point just below the top of the Shattered Pillar. Although a third of the way up the wall, I had been disappointed at our painfully slow progress. The brownish streaks I had noticed from the tent proved to be a frustrating flow of verglas right down the line of our climb. I kept glancing enviously over to the left where the French climbers had astutely chosen a dry line. We were constantly being balked by the gleam of verglas. What would have been a few easy moves became a nerve-racking, teetering balancing act. Protection points were few and far between. We moved together clipping the odd battered peg or placing a wire in the cracked, blocky terrain. Progress was further slowed by the complicated routefinding that kept leading us into dead ends that we then had painstakingly to reverse.

However, as the hours had passed I had begun to feel increasingly comfortable. The higher we climbed the easier it was to get the scale of the face into some perspective, even though we were still hemmed in by the vast wall of the Röte Fluh. At one point I glanced up to see a flurry of powder snow drifting down from the edge of a water-blackened rock wall. A tiny figure emerged on a fringe of snow at the top of the wall and began traversing slowly to the left. It was the French climbers approaching the Hinterstoisser Traverse. A stone whirled out into space with a humming, whistling sound and thudded into the top of the Shattered Pillar. I ducked instinctively. Glancing down I saw that Ray was standing on a small ledge protected by an overhanging wall. I waved and began to descend carefully towards him.

"Shall we call it a day?" I asked when I dropped my rucksack from my shoulders and placed it on the ledge.

"I thought you wanted to reach the Hinterstoisser?"

"I did but we're moving far too slowly. It's this bloody verglas."

"I know," Ray said with feeling. "Scary, isn't it?"

"I nearly fell off up there," I said. "I was doing a mantelshelf move on downward-sloping verglassed holds and trying to get my foot up onto a pile of rubble. It was stupid. There was no gear between you and me."

"Did you see the French guys?" Ray asked.

"Yeah, briefly. It made the whole face suddenly drop into

perspective. I could work out where everything was. I saw the Difficult Crack and I think I saw the door of the Stollenloch, the tunnel window on the right."

"I'm bloody glad we did this," Ray said, offering me a piece of chocolate. "All that angst I was going through has gone. It's just baggage, isn't it? I mean, you don't think about it when you're climbing, do you?"

"No, but you might do when you get down. It could all come back in a rush. Just remember how you feel now, keep it in your head."

"I reckon we've done about 2000 feet."

"Yeah, but it doesn't mean much. We're still below all the major difficulties."

"Well I'm happy just to have got this far. It was a good idea. It's special, isn't it?" Ray replied. I looked at the unsightly jumble of loose rock and scree stretching beneath us.

"It's more like a slag heap if you ask me," I said. "Come on, let's head down."

We roped down the face, careful to avoid pulling rocks down onto us as we retrieved our rappel ropes. At the foot of a short wall on the side of the First Pillar I spotted some clothing and climbed across to where it lay half-buried in scree and ice. It looked like a pair of twisted legs. The shredded black waterproof overtrousers creaked as I ripped them free and examined them. I looked around to see if there was any other impact debris. Ray came over and gazed at the overtrousers.

"No one in them?" he asked cheerily and I was pleased to see how much happier he was. I handed them over to him.

"Might have been," I said, "judging by the way they've been ripped apart. As you said, this wouldn't happen if they had been in a sack or falling on their own." I had heard enough stories of how long high-impact falls can literally strip the climber of his possessions.

"I'd rather not think about it," Ray said and stopped smiling.

"Any blood?" I asked. Ray hastily dropped the trousers with a fastidious gesture. I laughed.

"You shouldn't joke about it," he said, shaking his head.

"It's the only thing we can do," I said seriously. I threw the coiled rappel ropes into space and watched them knot themselves into a tangled mass on the first ledge they hit. I cursed silently under my breath.

As I tried to untangle the ropes my eye caught sight of a chillingly familiar shape and color half-buried in the rubble. I swung forward and reached towards the ivory-white bone, feeling squeamish. Then I was laughing loudly; too loudly.

"What is it?" Ray called and I held the bone up towards him. His expression changed immediately.

"A chicken drumstick," I said. "I thought . . . "

"I can guess," Ray said.

As we packed the tent in the meadow nestling at the foot of the Eiger we monitored the progress of the French climbers. They were moving with incredible speed. They climbed the entire route in twelve hours, reaching the summit at seven o'clock in the evening. We were flabbergasted and felt a little aggrieved at our own snail-like progress on the verglas-covered rubble of the lower face—the easiest part of the route. Apparently the climbers reported that one of the trickiest sections was a heavily iced section near the Hinterstoisser Traverse. It was encouraging to learn that the rest of the climb seemed to have dried out far better than we could have hoped for. There was no mention of heavy icing in the Exit Cracks, which we took as a good sign. The weather now seemed to be settled and warm. Luck seemed to be on our side.

"They must be good to climb that fast," I said to Ray as we climbed up the grassy slopes leading to the railway station at Kleine Scheidegg.

"There are a lot of them about."

"Makes me feel a bit silly, thinking this is such a big deal."

"It is a big deal—for us. And that's all that matters. Hell, I'm not even sure I would want to climb it in a day, even if I could."

"No, me neither," I agreed. "It would be a waste of the whole experience, wouldn't it?"

"Exactly," Ray said. "I want to enjoy it all. I'm looking forward to bivouacking at the Death Bivi or on the Traverse of the Gods. I don't want to just charge past it."

"Yeah, I know. It reminds me of the time I was in the Louvre looking at the Mona Lisa," I said. Ray looked confused. "There were few people around and I kept staring at it, trying to like it," I continued.

"Did you?"

"Not much, no. I didn't get the enigmatic smile at all. She just seemed slightly disapproving, even bored. I wondered how long she had sat there while Leonardo did his stuff. I knew she had a name. She was real. Mona Lisa Gherardini, wife of a Florentine nobleman . . ."

"Gherardini?" Ray said. "Same as the climber?"

"Well, yes, I suppose so, but I doubt they were related," I said. "Apparently her husband didn't like it and refused to pay for it."

"So he had taste then, did he?"

"Yeah, maybe. Anyway as I stood there gawping at it I imagined Leonardo having tantrums and starting all over and throwing his paints around and minions in his studio scurrying about keeping their heads down, and her worrying about whether her bum was too big . . ."

"You're a philistine," Ray chuckled.

"Not at all, I was just staring at it, thinking of its significance today and how she would never have known she would be immortalized in such a way for so many centuries. She was probably bored out of her brains and dying for a pee, hence the lopsided smile." Ray raised his eyebrows as we approached the station.

"Anyway," I continued, "while I was having these deep thoughts, about a hundred Japanese tourists rushed up to the Mona Lisa brandishing their cameras and camcorders paparazzi-style. Hundreds of flash lights went off and three minutes later they wheeled away and zoomed off like a flock of sheep to photograph something else. I was stunned. I mean, I might have not been getting much out of it, but at least I was trying."

"And that's why you don't want to do the Eiger in a day, is it?"

"Sort of," I said. "I want time to absorb it all. I want to remember the stories, and the people, and what they went through. I want to touch history—if only for a moment."

"Yeah, but there's a fine line between doing that and spending so damn long on it that it absorbs us," Ray said as we were suddenly surrounded by a horde of Japanese tourists chattering busily as they streamed off the train from Grindelwald, snapping photographs as they were marshaled by their tour guide straight into a restaurant for lunch. I don't think they noticed the Eiger.

As we stepped from the train in early afternoon sunshine I saw a figure on the platform.

"Simon?" I said cautiously and the man turned round.

"Joe! How are you? Good to see you. I heard you were here," Simon Wells said in his familiarly enthusiastic way.

"What are you doing here?"

"Oh, we're making a film about climbing the Eiger."

"Who's we?"

"It's for Channel 4. Chameleon Films are doing it for them."

"What's your role then?"

"I'm the producer. You two look as if you've been climbing."

"Yes, we just had a look at the lower face. It's coming into condition nicely. We're going to check the meteo at the guides office now and see if we'll have a weather window."

"Oh well, good luck, and here—take my mobile number and stay in touch. We must have a beer some time. Look us up at Kleine Scheidegg."

"So when are you boys thinking of going up?"

"Oh, we'll talk to Hanspeter first. He's one of three guides we've employed. He climbed the Eiger when they made that Eiger live video last year. He's done it several times so he'll know what conditions are like and we'll go on his say-so."

"Right, well we'll stay in touch then. We could do with some inside knowledge."

"That's a bit of luck," I said to Ray as we wandered up to the guides office and I explained that I had known Simon for nearly fifteen years. He lived near me in Sheffield, working as a researcher and film producer for Chameleon Films in Leeds. I'd always had a soft spot for Simon. He was a genuine, sensitive, caring person, which seemed oddly out of fashion nowadays. He also had an inquiring and creative mind and was wonderfully argumentative.

"But they might get in the way; five people, and helicopter resupply, and all the shenanigans that go with filming a climb."

"Well, we'll just liaise with them and slot in before or after they set off. But the info we'll get from the guides will be invaluable. They'll know where belay stations are, which is the best line, and they'll have intimate knowledge of the face. Brilliant."

There was also good news posted in the window of the guides office—a stable weather forecast. The synoptic charts showed steadily improving weather, offering the prospect of five clear sunny days. I felt enthusiastic about attempting the face as soon as possible. We no longer felt alone.

The following morning we returned to the Hintisberg and, to my delight, I noticed that Ray's climbing had improved immeasurably. The recce had obviously cleared out a lot of skeletons from his cupboard. We sat in the warm sunshine at the foot of the crag gazing at the Eiger through our binoculars.

"You know, kid, I think we should go for it."

"What?" Ray said, looking startled. "I thought we were going to do the Mittellegi Ridge first?"

"The guides said it was out of condition. There's too much powder up there. We can't just spend this good weather rock climbing."

"I don't know," Ray said hesitantly.

"If we go up on the first train tomorrow we'll have all day to reach the Swallow's Nest bivi. We can stop there for the night and keep an eye on the weather. If it's good and we're happy about it we'll head up the next day. We've got to do it some day. Anyway I'm sick of staring at the bloody thing all the time like some Sword of Damocles hanging there waiting to fall."

"I suppose you're right, although I don't like the simile," Ray agreed. "How much further was it from your high point to the Swallow's Nest?"

"A couple of hours, three at the most, depending on the verglas."

"Remember there's no fixed rope on the Difficult Crack," Ray pointed out. "In wet, cold conditions it can sometimes be the hardest bit of climbing on the face, especially first thing in the morning."

"We'll just take it one day at a time, eh? We can back off whenever we like."

"Yeah, you're right," Ray smiled at me. "It's a bit sudden, that was all. You caught me off guard."

"You do want to do it?" I asked and stared hard at him.

"Yeah, I do. Come on, let's go down, buy some food, and sort our kit out."

"Hang on," I said. "I just want to ring Pat and tell her our plans. I told her that I would keep in touch."

"Won't it worry her unnecessarily?" Ray asked.

"No, she's pretty understanding about this sort of thing," I said. Pat was encouraging when I told her our plans but I could hear the well-disguised concern in her voice. "Don't worry. We'll look after each other. I'll ring when we get down."

When we returned to the chalet laden down with hill food supplies Frau Alice Steuri was waiting for us in the hallway. She was a kindly lady who had looked disturbed when we had unloaded the mass of climbing gear from the car on our arrival ten days earlier. Ray had booked the room through the Internet knowing nothing about Frau Steuri, although I had mentioned to him that it was a famous name in Grindelwald mentioned frequently in *The White Spider.*

There was a Fritz Steuri Sr., an outstanding Grindelwald guide and ski racer, who, in the company of two other guides, Samuel Brawand and Fritz Amatter, had guided a young Japanese climber, Yuko Maki, on the first ascent of the Mittellegi Ridge in 1921. Years later in 1936 when Max Sedlmayr and Karl Mehringer had been swallowed by the prolonged storm that was to trap and eventually kill them during the first attempt on the Eigerwand, Fritz Steuri had accompanied Ernst Udet, one of Germany's ace pilots of the First World War, on an aerial search of the face.

In a strange twist of fate Udet had first been introduced to mountain flying in 1928 by Dr. Arnold Fanck during the filming of *The White Hell of Piz Palu*. In the film script Udet had to fly close to an icy mountain face to try to locate a stranded party of climbers and so effect a successful rescue.

Seven years later Udet and Steuri were doing it for real but there was no question of a rescue. They were simply looking for bodies. Max Sedlmayr and Karl Mehringer had last been seen on Sunday, August 25, 1935, during a break in the weather on the fifth day of their climb. They had been seen moving slowly up the immense shield of the Second Ice Field towards the distinctive arête called the Flat Iron.

The gale had returned with a vengeance. The men disappeared from sight. The guides watching their movements knew why the two men were continuing up, despite four bitterly cold bivouacs exposed to avalanches, rockfall, and the full fury of the wind. The ground below the pitifully weakened men had been turned into a terrible trap, constantly swept by avalanches and stonefall. The rock bands were either cascading waterfalls or plastered in snow and ice. Their only hope was to try and fight their way to the top or climb until they died.

A rescue attempt organized by Sedlmayr's brother was abandoned two days later at the foot of the wall. Nothing could be heard of the climbers—no calls for help echoed down from the wall. They saw nothing from the summit and the ramparts of the west ridge. Heinrich Harrer wrote:

> *A gale whipping against the rocks, the thunder of ava-*
> *lanches, the splash of waterfalls, in which the staccato*
> *rattle of falling stones mingled shrilly—these were the*
> *melody of the Eiger's Face, the funeral organ-voluntary*
> *for Max Sedlmayr and Karl Mehringer—no human sound*
> *interrupted the grim voice of the mountain.*

Three weeks later on September 19, 1935, Udet flew his plane to within 60 feet of the face in a bold display of flying skill. Acting as the spotter, Fritz Steuri saw one of the men still standing upright in the snow, frozen to death, near the top of the Flat Iron at a point ever since known as Death Bivouac.

It was always thought that the Death Bivouac was the highest point that the two men reached, but in 1952 the Viennese climber Karl Reiss and his companion, Siegfried Jungmeir, tried to force a direct line up to the Spider from Death Bivouac. It was thought that no one had tried this line before so they were baffled to find some ancient pitons on the extremely steep rock of the central pillar. They could only have been left by Max Sedlmayr and Karl Mehringer. The traverse across the Third Ice Field to the Ramp would have been suicidal. To climb directly up towards the bottom lip of the Spider was hardly a better choice. They would have been virtually blinded, in constant danger of being swept away, and contending with some of the hardest technical climbing attempted on the Eiger during the following thirty years.

It is remarkable to think how expert these first suitors of the wall were, considering the unendurable conditions they must have experienced during their attempt to escape, trapped directly beneath the Spider, which at the time would have been swept by a constant stream of avalanches and rocks. The pitons testify to the incredible strength and tenacity of Max Sedlmayr and Karl

Mehringer. This direct line was only eventually climbed by the famous joint British and German team completing the winter ascent of the Harlin Direct Route in 1966.

Max Sedlmayr's body, swept from the face by avalanches, was found the following year during the search for the remains of the Hinterstoisser party. Karl Mehringer's was not found until 1962 when his desiccated body emerged from the Second Ice Field twenty-seven years after his death. Fourteen years later, on June 21, 1976, a Czech team came across a cigarette tin. Inside was a last message from these incredibly brave climbers, probably written by Mehringer, since he had misspelled his companion's name.

> *Bivouac place on 21/8/35. Max Sedelmajr, Karl Mehringer.*
> *Munich H.T.G. (High Tour Group)*

This weathered note, written in pencil on yellowed paper, must have been an eerie reminder from the past for the two young Czech climbers.

That date—August 21—was the date of Max Sedlmayr and Karl Mehringer's first bivouac on the face. The next day they were observed slowly climbing the 300-foot rock band separating them from the lower edge of the First Ice Field. By late afternoon they had reached a cramped bivouac ledge at the upper rim of the ice field, having spent the day ducking and sheltering behind their rucksacks from heavy fusillades of stonefall.

On August 23 they tackled the second rock band, a long and arduous climb, so technically difficult that it forced them to haul their rucksacks—a time-consuming process. The watchers below may not have realized it at the time, but Sedlmayr and Mehringer were putting on a virtuoso display of climbing skill, despite their slow progress. Having overcome the second band the two men headed towards the top left-hand end of the Second Ice Field. Again they were battered by stonefall and ice fragments and forced to stop frequently and take shelter, hiding behind rocks and holding their rucksacks protectively above their heads.

Three days of climbing and they were less than halfway up the wall. A curtain of cloud descended on the face. That night the storm broke about them in a chaos of thunder cracks, hailstones, rain, snow, and tremendous blasts of wind. The next day, Saturday the 24th, the storm continued unabated and there was no sight of the climbers. The night had been murderously cold down in the valley; what must it have been like enduring their fourth bivouac with such rudimentary equipment?

On Sunday the 25th they were spotted during a break in the weather, inching their way towards the Flat Iron, climbing towards a death they probably realized was inevitable.

Three years later, in the summer of 1938, just one month before the first ascent of the wall, two Italian climbers, Bartolo Sandri and Mario Menti, were swept to their deaths in a storm probably from a point close to where Mehringer had left his penciled bivouac note. Once again Fritz Steuri led a search party and found Sandri's body at the foot of the face. Menti's body was extracted from a deep crevasse a few days later.

Years later, when Claudio Corti was rescued from high on the face by a winch-cable rescue system, Harrer mentions that Hermann Steuri, another Grindelwald guide, had been instrumental in developing the steel-cable rescue technique. It was the first successful rescue by cable from the face, although in tragic circumstances. Claudio Corti and his companion, Stefano Longhi, had started up the wall in early August 1957. At some point, probably near the Hinterstoisser Traverse, they had joined forces with the German team of Gunter Northdurft and Franz Mayer. The Germans had dropped a rucksack of provisions and Northdurft was feeling sick so the strengthened party moved as a foursome until they made a fatal routefinding error high on the face.

Mistakenly climbing 300 feet higher than the Traverse of the Gods, they attempted a far more difficult traverse line across to the edge of the Spider. Stefano Longhi fell over 100 feet from the traverse to hang helplessly in space. Despite three hours' labor the two Germans and Corti were unable to haul Longhi back up to the traverse.

He was roped down to a small ledge. Corti lowered his bivouac sack and some provisions and assured his friend that he and the Germans would race for the summit and alert the rescue services. High above the Spider near where the Exit Cracks angled up towards the summit ridge Corti was hit on the head by a rock and fell 100 feet. The Germans gave Corti their only bivouac sack since he was concussed and unable to continue. They secured him to a small ledge atop a pillar of rock. They climbed to the summit despite a thunderstorm but then died of exhaustion while descending the west flank that night. They were found four years later in 1961, still linked by their ropes, lying side by side, less than thirty minutes' walk from the safety of the Eiger Gletscher station. Disorientated and tired from the stormy descent, they had sat down to wait for morning and fallen asleep forever.

Three days later Corti was hauled to safety using the cable system that Hermann Steuri had been perfecting. The ledge he had waited on has since been dubbed the Corti Bivouac. Hanging on the cable, Riccardo Cassin heard Longhi's mournful cries rising up from far down the precipice but he was too far down the face to be reached.

Longhi lasted from Thursday, July 8, until the night of Monday the 12th when another viciously cold storm overwhelmed him. As the rescuers were lowering Corti down the west flank on the Sunday evening someone shouted across the face to Longhi, reassuring him that they would return the following day and attempt to reach him. Longhi shouted back two despairing but shatteringly clear words: *"Fame! Freddo!"* "Hunger! Cold!" I remember seeing the photograph taken from a passing plane of Longhi hanging from his rope waving forlornly at the pilot.

When they returned they saw Longhi hanging dead on the

rope. His body hung there for two years, a grotesque and macabre tourist attraction for the Eiger-watchers at the telescopes in Alpiglen and Kleine Scheidegg.

Clearly the Steuri name had a lot of connections with the Eigerwand. When I told Ray about its fame he was astounded by the sheer fluke of booking an apartment through the Internet and finding it owned by the same family. We had both wondered whether this piece of luck might provide us with some useful information about conditions on the mountain.

When Alice Steuri had asked us what we intended to climb and we had pointed towards the north face of the Eiger looming behind the chalet her reaction was fervent and unexpected.

"Oh, no, not the wall. You must not try it. It is dangerous, very dangerous," Alice said earnestly.

We were quite taken aback by her reaction and did our best to assure her that we knew what we were doing. During the following days she took solicitous care of us, inquiring about our climbing plans, letting us use her warm, dry storage rooms, and proudly mentioning our intentions to her other guests. As we struggled with doubts about trying the climb she was telling all and sundry that we were soon to set out for the wall. It became a little embarrassing.

When we came back from the Hintisberg that day and found Alice Steuri waiting for us, we assumed she had a message from Simon Wells.

"My mother, Anna Jossi, would like to show you something. Do you mind?" Alice asked.

"No, not at all," I said, wondering what it might be about. "Now?"

"In a moment I shall bring her down to the garden," Frau Steuri replied.

An hour later Anna Jossi appeared in the front garden where we were sitting with cold drinks reading books and occasionally gazing reflectively at the Eiger.

"Would you like to see this?" she said, holding out a large book. "I think it may interest you."

As we gathered around the table she carefully opened the pages of the book, which proved to be a hotel register. The date at the top of the first page was 1930. I glanced at Ray.

"My father owned the Hôtel des Alpes at Alpiglen in those days," Anna Jossi explained. "And here, do you recognize these names?"

There, written in a bold italic script in the visitors' book on a page headed August 1935 were the names of Max Sedlmayr and Karl Mehringer. I was flabbergasted and reached out to touch the words with my fingers. Alongside the entry Mehringer had penned a personal comment in German, which Ray translated.

"We are deeply indebted to Frau Jossi for her hospitality. She was always there with a helping hand. From two poor climbers, with our warmest thanks." He read the words aloud and then looked up at me in amazement.

"Frau Jossi?" I asked and Anna Jossi beamed at me. "You knew Max Sedlmayr and Karl Mehringer? You actually met them?"

"Oh, yes, indeed. They were wonderful men. So charming and friendly. Good men. Strong men."

"Did they stay with you?" Ray asked.

"Yes, yes, they stayed in the hotel and then for the last few days in an old shepherd's hut near the face. They were always polite, always kind to me. They were always helping, cutting wood, doing chores. I was very young, of course, only sixteen. Here, look."

She opened a second book, a scrapbook of photos and press cuttings, and pointed to a black-and-white photograph. Young, handsome, and smiling, Max Sedlmayr and Karl Mehringer stood on either side of a young woman with their arms around her shoulders. Her hair hung down in long dark plaits and she wore a short, dark traditional jacket over a white smock and calf-length black skirt.

"That is me," Anna said proudly. "I liked them very much.

They were kind to me." Ray and I stared at her in some wonder and then back at the photograph.

"You knew Sedlmayr and Mehringer," I said in a disbelieving whisper. History had suddenly come to life. I leafed through the album of photographs and press cuttings. I glanced again at the portrait with Anna. They looked so cheerful and confident. They were only days from lingering, lonely deaths.

Another photograph showed Sedlmayr and Mehringer standing in a meadow with a small building in the background. They wore climbing boots and puttee-like gaiters wrapped around their baggy trousers. Mehringer's rucksack was stylishly covered with his rain-coat. Both men wore trilby hats at jaunty rakish angles. Peering closely, I could just make out the words "Hôtel des Alpes" printed on a white board on the building in the background.

"I can't believe this," I said to Ray. "What's the probability of us accidentally booking into this chalet?"

"I know, weird, isn't it?"

"My father did not want them to attempt the climb," Anna said, looking grave. "He told them many times that it was a dangerous place. He had heard the rockfall. He knew what happened to the face in bad weather but they would not listen."

"Did you watch them climb?"

"Oh, yes," Anna seemed torn between pride and sadness. "At first they climbed very fast, so strong, and then they went slowly, very slowly. My father had arranged with them to shine their torches at us each night. My father built a fire every night for them to see so they knew we were looking for them and then the storm came in and they did not reply to our fire. It was terrible, terrible." She shook her head, saddened at the memory.

"After two days of the storm we knew they were gone," she said and paused. "And we cried and we cried and we cried," she added simply and tried to smile. I felt a chill run through me.

Anna had brought them suddenly to life and given us a melancholy sense of how much they had lost. When she spoke of their long-drawn-out death she shook her head sadly and when she said "and we cried and we cried and we cried" I felt chastened by her pity.

I thought of all the hopes and ambitions that had driven them to this place to meet, however fleetingly, with Anna and touch her with the brilliance of their lives, and then they were gone, and Anna's life was forever colored by the memories of their kindness and humanity.

We live within such a tiny capsule of time yet it seems vast until death rudely makes it so insignificant. It humbles us. I glanced up at the Eiger bathed in warm afternoon sunshine and thought of those terrible storm-torn days sixty-five years ago and a young girl staring up at the face hoping against hope that the young men would return.

"Did you know Hinterstoisser and Toni Kurz?" Ray asked and Anna shook herself from sad memories and smiled in recognition.

"Oh, of course," she said. "In the early years we met many of the climbers coming for the wall."

"You met Toni Kurz?" I was aghast.

"Yes, yes, he was a fine boy."

"Who was the leader? Was it Hinterstoisser? He was supposed to be the master climber."

"Yes, perhaps he was, but it was Rainer who was the leader. He was so strong, like this." Anna broadened her shoulders to mimic a bodybuilder's physique. "A strong man. He was the leader."

"And Hinterstoisser?"

"Yes, he was good but not the leader. We watched them climb," Anna said. "I saw Angerer hit by the rockfall. Rainer bandaged his head."

"How?" Ray asked in amazement.

"We had a big telescope outside the hotel. I was always watching. It is upstairs if you wish to see it. We took it down from Alpiglen when we decided to sell the hotel."

"Yes, that would be good to see," Ray said.

"What was Angerer like?" I asked, feeling a little guilty at interrogating Anna so insistently but I couldn't resist the opportunity to hear about these men at first hand. I knew the story of their lives and deaths so well that I wanted this chance to know them more intimately, to have them brought vividly to life by the fond and melancholy memory of an old lady who had witnessed their passing.

"Oh, Angerer," Anna said with a fond smile. "He was so pretty. He was like a girl, so slim, and his face, very smooth just like a girl. And always he was looking at his sweetheart. He had a photograph of her hanging around his neck and always he was looking . . . "

It was a poignant detail that neither of us had ever considered. After all they were simply names on a page. It had never really occurred to us that they had loved ones. I thought of the three long bitterly cold bivouacs that Angerer had endured after being struck on the head by a rock. When they had reached the Flat Iron it became apparent that his condition was worsening. By the time they had retreated to the Swallow's Nest and Hinterstoisser was desperately attempting to reverse his Traverse, Angerer was observed to be slumped to one side, no longer taking any part in the proceedings.

"And Kurz? How was he?" Ray asked.

"He was young. They were all so young," Anna said. "His was a terrible death, very sad."

I thought of a boyish Kurz sitting in a meadow with alpine flowers at his feet, shelling a boiled egg, staring back at me from that old photograph. It was he who had brought me here. His life and his death, insignificant, I suppose, given the countless tragedies that had ensued in the intervening years, had stayed with me from the moment I had first read about him. Anna's story had suddenly made him as real as if he had sat by me only days before.

The world has a life of its own. Nothing we do affects it. It goes on and on, never looking back, unaware of a past, oblivious to the future, never hesitating in its inexorable progress through time. If life were not to have death at its end and had death not been preceded by life, neither would have any meaning. We need to die or our lives are meaningless. The poet Yasar Kemal seemed to sum it up when he wrote:

Anybody, whether a novelist or not, must have purpose in life. And that purpose is to understand human reality in the face of death. Death only exists because there is life. That is the great poetry of the world. That is its reality.

If Toni Kurz had not died on the Eiger, if Max Sedlmayr and Karl Mehringer had not passed this way then nor would I. They gave meaning to my actions.

"Did they stay in the hotel?" Ray asked.

"Oh, no, they were very poor. We let them stay in the wood shed. One franc a night," she added, chuckling. "They cut wood for us, always helping out."

We spent an hour listening to Anna's reminiscences, avidly looking through her extraordinary scrapbook of history. When at last she left we sat back and stared at each other in amazement.

"Well, that's made the holiday," I said. "Whatever happens, it won't beat that."

"No," Ray agreed and stood up. "I'm going to sort out my kit for tomorrow. What time's the first train?"

"Seven, I think," I said. "I'll set the alarm early and get a good breakfast on for us. We should be on the face by eight-thirty. Anyway, there's no rush. We'll have all day to reach the Swallow's Nest."

"Yeah, that's true." Ray turned and walked back to the room. I rang Pat Lewis, my long-suffering partner, to tell her the great news about the forthcoming climb. She seemed a little less enthusiastic than me. She started to tell me to be careful and then stopped. We had been through that scenario too many times. "Take care of Ray for me," she said. She had a soft spot for Ray and I promised I wouldn't let him out of my sight.

"I'll ring you as soon as we get down. I won't have the phone on to save the batteries. Don't worry about us. We'll be having fun."

I opened my book and tried to read, but the setting sun was painting the mountains in crimson light and distracting me from the words.

I put my book down and glanced up at the mountain as the sun angled across the ice fields illuminating the Ramp in a wash of gold. We were making an attempt on the face the following morning but the combination of sunshine, a strong gin, and a second reading of *Corelli's Mandolin* had helped drive the prospect clean from my mind. It was a wonderful, hypnotic novel of fabulous scope, swinging between joy and bleakness: lyrical, angry, and earnest. I felt calm and relaxed as I watched an isolated cumulus cloud drift in to the great amphitheater of the face. A breeze scattered it into tendrils of mist that hung around the icy rim of the Spider until the sun burned it from existence.

I read for an hour, struggling with the fading light, completely enthralled by the words, forgetting for the first time in weeks the insistent, mesmeric pull that the Eiger had been exerting on me; I had escaped its shadow. As I returned to the book it occurred to me that the only reason I was here was because of reading; it was the reason I began to climb.

There is something about reading that takes you beyond the constrictions of space and time, frees you from the limitations of social interaction, and allows you to escape. Whoever you encounter within the pages of a book, whatever lives you vicariously live with them can affect you deeply—entertain you briefly, change your view of the world, open your eyes to a wholly different concept of living and the value of life. Books can be the immortality that some seek; thoughts and words left for future generations to hear from beyond the grave and awaken a memory of another's life.

Climbing taught me how to look at the mountains, how to read their secrets and survive on their heights. More recently, particularly since I began to write, it taught me how to look at people—myself included—to see how we behave, how climbing changes us. I feel that the frontier of climbing is no longer technical or geographical but ethical. This is what climbing should be about: using the tradition, ethos, and passion of our sport to arouse greater responses within ourselves, echoes of what we would like to be.

After having climbed a great classic route I always thought that I never wanted to repeat it. It was unique, intensely personal, and I never wished to lose that perfect sense of it or the passion that had driven me to climb it.

It had always seemed to me that passion, like love, should never fade. I had read that in love you should not do things by halves, that if you love a woman you should love her entirely, give everything. You don't make love to other women, you don't take her for granted. It is something I am painfully aware that I have always failed to do. The mountains had made me selfish and I could love no one entirely because of them, or so I told myself. Then again I had once thought that I loved mountains in this way, unequivocally, selflessly: once this was true to the loss of everything else. With the eroding passage of the years I now sometimes think that even here I failed.

As I sat reading in the sunshine, sipping an iced drink, and glancing occasionally at the looming majesty of the Eigerwand rearing out of the meadows in front of my chalet, I realized that I was finding it difficult to leave the mountains. In a way I had come back to my roots, but with the passing of the years and of so many friends I suspected that my passion had been eroded.

DO NOTHING IN HASTE

I AWOKE BEFORE THE ALARM BEGAN TO BEEP and quickly deactivated it lest it woke Ray. I lay still for a moment, staring into the darkness, thinking about the day and feeling a rising swell of excitement. I ran quickly through a tick list of the items I had packed in my rucksack. Stove, gas cylinders, food, duvet jacket, hardware, rope, harness, bivi bag, camcorder, spare batteries and film, contact lens case. I tried to think of what I might have forgotten, wondering whether our tactics were right. We had decided to leave the bivi tent and our lightweight sleeping bags behind to save weight. I hoped a duvet jacket would be up to the rigors of two, maybe three, long, cold September nights. We should have at least two bivouacs on the face.

I had been told not to bring down equipment on the wall because the wet nature of the climb quickly degraded its insulation properties. Jerry Arcari, who works for Rab Carrington, had supplied us with two Rab down jackets with a special waterproof breathable outer layer, assuring us that they would be fine. I had tried one out on Bridalveil Falls, spending ten minutes standing in a veritable shower of icy water, convinced the down feathers would be turned into useless soggy lumps. To my astonishment the down had remained dry, so I had persuaded Ray on the basis of this impromptu experiment that the jackets were good enough to allow us to leave the tent and sleeping bags behind. I smiled at the thought of what he would say when we were shivering through our second night on the face.

Unable to think of any pressing reason to stay in bed I threw back the covers and pulled a thermal top over my head, shivering at the touch of the icy morning air. I switched on the stove ring to heat water for coffee and busied myself with preparing breakfast. Bacon was soon sizzling in the pan and the smell of fresh coffee filled the room. I turned to look for my thermal trousers and the rest of my clothing and noticed that Ray was sitting up in bed, back propped against the wall.

"Oh, sorry, I thought I'd wake you with all the clatter. Breakfast should be ready soon."

"I wasn't asleep," Ray said in a subdued voice. "I've been awake since two."

"You're not ill, are you?" I said anxiously as I sat down to pull on my knee-length socks. He remained silent. I began pulling myself into my fleece salopettes, struggling to find the braces hanging down my back.

"I'm not going, Joe," Ray said flatly and I stopped looking for the buckle and glanced at where he sat with his arms crossed defensively.

"I've been going over it all night," he said. "It's doing my head in. I keep seeing all the things that could go wrong. I can't take that risk. I'm not going."

"Right," I said in shocked surprise. "Okay, right, you're not going."

"I'm sorry, Joe," Ray said calmly. I said nothing.

I poured myself a coffee, opened the patio door, and stepped outside to sit at the table. I lit a cigarette and tried to think. I felt sick with disappointment. *We weren't even going to make an attempt!* I tried to think of what I could say that might make Ray change his mind and realized immediately that there was nothing. Morally I had no right to put pressure on him. It was his decision. I knew he would have been agonizing over it these last few hours. He was aware of how much this climb meant to me and he also was painfully aware that he was the cause of reawakening my dream. I knew he felt terrible.

When we had been packing our gear the previous evening I had noticed Ray looking at the photographs of his two young daughters and I had felt a pang of guilt. I was keenly aware of what they stood to lose. Then I shook the thought from my head. After all, he had made the same choice on every climb we had embarked upon in the past.

I sipped my coffee and looked at the shadow of the north face. The sky was lightening and I could make out the outline of the west flank and the Mittellegi Ridge. A bright yellow light shone out from the center of the face. It was the gallery windows where the old farmer had watched two roped parties fall past him. In the end I drank too much coffee and smoked too many cigarettes and stared glumly as the first train made its way up through the picturesque meadows towards Kleine Scheidegg. I stood up and went inside.

"I'm going to see if I can find a partner," I said, not looking at Ray. He said nothing. "I understand, Ray. It's not a problem."

"You're no good at lying," he replied bluntly.

"Maybe not," I conceded. "I just think I won't get another chance, that's all. I was wondering whether Nick Bullock is around."

Nick was a friend of Bruce French, who I had been told was climbing in Chamonix that summer and had plans to come over to try the Eiger in mid-September. I was hoping his partner might have dropped out. I almost laughed at the irony that once again I was in exactly the same position as I had been twenty years before when Dave Page had said he wouldn't climb the Eiger with me.

"Failing that, I'll ring Simon Wells. He's using some guides. He might know how much it costs to be guided on it." Even as I said it I felt mildly guilty at the thought of being guided. It was anathema to me. We had all taught ourselves to climb. All of us had been furiously independent and the very idea of paying to be led by others was the antithesis of everything we hoped to do in the mountains. Apart from the expense, and I had no doubts how costly a Swiss guide's rates on the Eigerwand would be, I would also not be allowed to lead anything on the route. In fact I suspected that no guide would take a client on such a serious route without having climbed with him beforehand. I didn't have enough time for that. I hoped that the guide might have heard of me and then chuckled at the idea of the German-Swiss edition of *Touching the Void* being a recommendation to any aspiring climbing partner. *He would probably run a mile.* But there was no other choice.

In truth, I didn't want to be guided because I wanted to experience the climb with a close and trusted friend; someone who thought the same way about the importance of the climb as I did. I had no ego problems about using a guide since I knew I could climb the route and it wasn't as if I would be being dragged up something completely beyond my ability. Yet I wanted to do it with Ray so we could grow old with the memory of it, so that it would always be something special, something shared. However good the guide, it would always be an isolating experience and I knew I would miss Ray.

Deep down I knew that Ray wanted to do the route more than any other climb he had ever attempted. I knew he would regret this decision. If I went and climbed it successfully with a stranger it would only make his recriminations worse. I felt that I should explain this to him but that would be tempting him to change his mind against his better judgment. I had to respect his choice. I wanted to shout at him that he was wrong.

After an hour of fruitless ringing around I was no better off. Simon Wells knew of no British climbers in the area so it looked as if Nick Bullock had changed his mind about the Eiger. He also said that he would ask Hanspeter Feuz, his head guide, what the rates were and if there were any guides available. He was sympathetic but there was nothing he could do for me. He had his hands full with his own filming project.

I left a message for Samuel Zeller, a Swiss guide from

Interlaken introduced to me by Jerry Arcari, but learned that he was guiding in another area of the Alps. Simon Wells then called me back to say it would cost nearly £1500 to be guided and that he thought it unlikely a guide would take me on the Eiger untried. It was no more than I had expected. I wondered whether I could justify spending so much money on a guide and knew immediately that I would have paid double if the opportunity arose. Simon added that his team was starting up the face the following day, Monday, September 11. The plan was for Heinz Zak and Scott Muir to climb the face as they were filmed by Will Edwards. Will was to be looked after by two guides, Hansruedi Gertsch and Godi Egger. The forecast was stable. There was supposed to be some overcast weather on the Tuesday and then it was set fair until Thursday, possibly right through to Saturday. The French climbers who had climbed the route in twelve hours had reported that the face was in dry condition and improving with every day of sunshine. I put the phone down, sickened by a curdling mixture of envy and disappointment.

Later that day I strolled up to our favorite restaurant and ordered a beer on the terrace. The waitress asked why we were not on the wall. We had made the mistake of telling her our plans the previous evening.

"Ah well, my friend has had a change of mind," I said diplomatically.

"That is good, no?"

"Not really," I said and I gave her a vague disingenuous story about our future plans. I rang Pat to tell her what had happened. She was understanding and concerned about Ray's welfare. She also knew how disappointed I was, but I sensed the relief in her voice.

"We may come home early," I said. "See you soon." And I rang off.

I read the paper and tried not to keep glancing at the mountain. Leafing through one of the magazine supplements, my eyes were drawn to a page of astrological predictions. Out of curiosity I read what it said for Leo, my star sign.

Believe it or not, with Mars in your birth sign, it could be that certain people are thinking along the same lines as you.

"Bollocks!" I said a little too loudly, startling a group of American tourists at the adjacent table. They glared at me and I glared pleasantly back.

However, this is not easy for them to admit, so you might have to spring into action, rather than walk off and miss your chance. Having said that, you could find yourself sucked into a situation from which there is no way out. As you begin the week you are still disgruntled over sudden developments that involved the use of your resources and certain individuals who insisted on making decisions for you. These may have been both unfair and unwise, but battling to reverse them achieves little.

"Too bloody right!" I snapped angrily and watched as the Americans paying their bill threw disapproving looks in my direction. I searched the horoscope page for the Taurus prediction, Ray's star sign.

As you don't have total control over current situations you must make sure that colleagues will be there when you need them. Making the best of it demands only that you go along with sudden—and unsettling—changes.

I burst out laughing at the irony of it. It was me who was having to deal with sudden—and unsettling—changes. I ordered another beer and morosely thought of what could have been.

"How are you doing, kid?" I looked up to see Ray standing by the table.

"Okay," I said. "Didn't get much joy from Simon. Maybe Samuel will be able to help. I've left him a message. I'm prepared to pay fifteen hundred, more if I have to. It'll be worth it even if it's not quite what I wanted."

"Listen, I've been thinking this through," Ray said, drawing up a chair. "And don't get me wrong. I don't feel pressured by you in any way. In fact, I was quite surprised. I expected you to blow up."

"I did, inside," I said. "But we said from the start we would respect each other's decisions. It was your choice. There was nothing I could say."

"I want to do it."

"What?" I stared at Ray.

"I've been thinking about it," he continued. "I let it get to me. All that psychological baggage stuff. I couldn't stop thinking about it. You know, worst-case scenarios and all that."

"Yeah, I know. I did that thing months ago," I said, somewhat bitterly.

Ray shrugged. "I've sorted it out now. Got it into perspective. I thought about climbing up to the Stollenloch the other day and how much I enjoyed it. I'll kick myself if I don't at least give it a proper try. I want to do it."

"Are you sure?" I looked at him. "This is all a bit muddled."

"Yeah, I know, I'm sorry. I feel pretty stupid about it all. I just got a bad feeling and couldn't shake it off. I was scared. You know what it's like."

"Yes, we've all been there," I said. "We can't go tomorrow, even though the forecast is great."

"Why not?"

"Simon told me that Heinz and Scott are heading up tomorrow. If we try to reach Death Bivouac there will be seven of us spending the night there. And it will screw up their filming schedule if we keep getting in the frame."

"First train on Tuesday, then?" Ray suggested and I nodded agreement.

"We'll go up tomorrow and have a look at how they're getting on. We should be able to monitor them through the big camera—see what the conditions are like—and we can also check out the west flank descent route."

"Good idea."

"Hello," the waitress greeted Ray and placed a beer on the table. "So you are not climbing the wall?" she said in a loud voice. I put my head in my heads.

"We've changed our minds," I said.

"Yes, your friend is not going," she said, and Ray scowled at me.

"He is now," I said.

"I changed my mind again," Ray said with a grin. "It's my prerogative. I'm a man."

"You are crazy. This is bad decision. The wall is dangerous," she scolded him.

"Let's not go into that again," I said and watched as she stalked away.

The next morning as we disembarked from the train at Kleine Scheidegg I saw Mark Stokes fussing over the camera that was set up on a large tripod outside the hotel. It was weighed down with heavy sandbags to prevent camera shake. Simon stood talking earnestly to Hanspeter Feuz. I glanced at the wall looming in the background and wondered how the team were getting on. Simon spotted me and waved us over.

"Hi, guys. How's things?" he said.

"Oh, fine," I said. "Our usual decisive selves, you know. Are they on the wall?"

"Yes, Scott and Heinz are climbing up to the Stollenloch. They should be there within the hour. Will and the two guides will pick them up from there. They just went up on the train. Hanspeter has an arrangement with the railway to let people out of the tunnel."

"Good thinking," I said as Simon turned away. I looked at Ray. "I've got a cunning plan," I said.

"Oh, God. What?"

"Well, since we've already climbed up to the Stollenloch and it was a load of rubble why don't we ask whether we can get let out of the window on the first train tomorrow? That way we can get to Death Bivouac easily in a day."

"Wouldn't it be cheating?" Ray said dubiously.

"If we hadn't already climbed that part of the face, yes," I replied. "Do you want to do that again?"

"Not especially," Ray agreed. "It's not as if it's good climbing."

"It's a dangerous slag heap," I said.

"But would they allow us to stop the train?"

"As for the train, well, that's where my cunning plan comes in. Simon knows we would have gone up today, right?"

"Yeah."

"And he knows we held back so we were not in his way. I'll bet he'll put a good word in for us with Hanspeter. After all, we've done him a favor by holding back."

"Cunning, very cunning."

"Anyway I've always fancied stepping out of the train straight onto the face. It would be surreal."

"You have a weird idea of fun, Joe."

"Hey, Joe, Ray," Simon called, smiling mischievously. "Come over here. There's someone I think you guys would like to meet."

We wandered over to where a knot of people were gathered around a table laden with cameras, sandwiches, and beer bottles. A man stooped with age and wearing a black jacket stood with his back to us as Simon extended his arm towards us in greeting. The man turned around as Simon introduced us and Ray and I stood stock-still in shock.

"Anderl, I have some friends here who would like to meet you. Ray, Joe, this is Anderl Heckmair. I think you may have heard of him."

"Hello, good to meet you," Anderl Heckmair said, removing a vicious-looking black cigar from his mouth and extending his hand. I shook it and mumbled something inane about honor and privilege. Ray shook his hand wordlessly. "This is my wife, Traudl," Heckmair held his hand out to a petite lady who smiled broadly and shook our hands.

"Simon tells me you are going for the Eigerwand tomorrow," Traudl said.

"Er, yes, that's right," I said. "We wanted to go today but didn't want to get in Simon's way."

"You be careful, boys," Traudl said and waved us towards the table. A waitress brought fresh beers and I watched in admiration as Anderl drank freely and kept relighting his cigars during the hour we spent chatting with him. At ninety-one years of age he seemed pretty sprightly. At one point a tourist approached proffering a camera.

"Herr Maestro Eiger," the tourist greeted Heckmair, the first man to climb the Eigerwand. A group of his friends stood respectfully in the background. Clearly Heckmair's fame in Switzerland was widespread. I took a photograph of the tourist standing beside his hero and Heckmair smiled and then grimaced as the man departed.

"I don't understand why these people think of me like this. They are not climbers. They do not know," he said sorrowfully.

"Is it very irritating?" I asked.

"No," he shrugged. "I just don't understand it. I prefer the company of climbers. I know they understand."

"I think this climb you made," Ray said, "was the greatest mountaineering feat of its time. It still is. That is why we want to climb it."

"It was a climb. One of many," Heckmair replied modestly. "I didn't think it would still be with me so many years later."

"When I read *The White Spider* at fourteen years of age I vowed never to be a mountaineer," I said. "I was so scared of the Eiger and now here I am twenty-five years later and I meet you. Amazing."

"Have you climbed many mountains?" Traudl asked.

"Well, yes, I suppose so. Not as many as Anderl of course, but yes, we have climbed in Nepal, Africa, India, and South America."

"South America? In Peru? Did you ever read that story about the English climber who broke his leg and was crawling many days alone? What a story!"

"Er, yes," I said warily and saw that Ray was smirking.

"This is the man," Ray said to Traudl and she stared at me in surprise then clapped her hands together in delight and reached out her arms to give me a hug. She spoke rapidly to Heckmair and I felt my ears begin to redden. He simply looked at me and nodded his head slowly with his lips pursed in a knowing smile.

"It was so hard for you, no?" Traudl asked.

"Yes, it was hard but it was our mistake. These things happen in the mountains. We were lucky."

"But so strong. Alone, all those days."

"Accidents happen in these places," I said, feeling embarrassed. Heckmair nodded in agreement. "When you were on the wall it was a very close thing, wasn't it?" I said to him.

"Yes, it could have been different," he said reflectively and I thought of him falling on the Exit Cracks and Vorg holding up his hand and having his palm pierced by Heckmair's crampons. They had been so very close. They could just as easily have been one of the Mehringers or Hinterstoissers of the Eiger's history and I could see he knew that all too well. Perhaps that was why he felt so uncomfortable with the hero-worship of nonclimbers. As he said, they didn't understand.

We, of course, immediately became hero-struck schoolboys posing proudly as Simon took our photographs with the great man and his wife. As we set off to scramble up the west flank Simon waved us over to the camera.

"You can just see them now," he said. "I think they're starting up the Difficult Crack."

I peered through the viewfinder, momentarily lost as the scale of the wall swam in and out of focus.

"Just right of dead center," Mark suggested helpfully and suddenly I spotted the two tiny figures dwarfed by the immense surge of the Röte Fluh looming over them. I drew a sharp intake of breath and then stood up and stared at the face. I could see nothing with the naked eye. Ray rose slowly from the eyepiece and glanced at me.

"It certainly puts it into perspective, doesn't it?"

"It's bloody huge."

Simon introduced us to Hanspeter Feuz and I put forward my plan about leaving from the Stollenloch the following morning. Hanspeter seemed happy to help out and we agreed to meet on the first train up in the morning. He would swing it with the stationmaster, no problem, he said.

At the top of a spectacular rock pillar protruding from the west ridge Ray and I sat eating sandwiches and discussing our plans for the morning. Behind us lay a 1000-foot drop down into a vertiginous gully falling towards the meadows at the foot of the north face. The face was obscured from our view by the bulk of the Röte Fluh looming into the air on the opposite flank of the gully.

"Listen, if we get a good head start from the Stollenloch we could consider going beyond Death Bivi tomorrow," I said.

"Well, maybe," Ray said reluctantly. "You mean, try and reach the Traverse of the Gods and bivi there?"

"It would be a long day, I admit," I replied. "But I suppose it depends what time we reach Death Bivi. I wouldn't want to cross the Third Ice Field to the Ramp in the afternoon. Too much risk of stonefall."

"There is a bivi site in the Ramp," Ray pointed out. "The Spanish bivouac, it's called."

"I thought that was up in the Spider where Rabada and Navarra died?" I said, referring to the two Spanish climbers who had been pinned down near the top of the Spider in August 1963.

"Who were they?" Ray asked and I described what had happened to the two Spaniards.

After obstinately fighting their way up the face in almost continuously bad weather Albert Rabada and Ernesto Navarra had succumbed to exhaustion and hypothermia after six days' desperate climbing. It seemed strange that at no point on the climb, despite the ferocious weather, did the two men once consider retreating. It was a decision that would slowly kill them over the ensuing days of storms. Harrer, writing in *The White Spider,* had been struck by the Spaniards' courageous and stoical persistence but equally baffled by it.

> *The tragic part was that they were both endowed with too much noble courage and spirit; alas, they matched it with too little and poor equipment, totally inadequate protection from the cold, and too little experience. In the reality of mountains it is fatal to lose one's sense of realities.*

The men were last seen on August 16. One man, Navarra, had reached a stance on the rocks at the top of the Spider while his companion, Rabada, lay slumped on the icy slopes of the Spider 100 feet lower. In December of the following winter three Swiss climbers, Paul Etter, Ueli Gantbein, and Sepp Henkel, rappelled from the summit and reached the top of the Spider where they found Navarra encased in ice standing on a small rock stance. He was securely tied to a rock piton holding the wire-tight rope leading down to his friend. He still wore his crampons from which the front points were missing and his ice hammer was hanging from his wrist. One hundred feet below Rabada lay as if asleep, almost encased within the ice of the Spider. He was wearing a blue fleece jacket and held his ice axe across his chest in calm repose. He had removed his crampons, also without front points, and laid them on the ice above him. The taut rope ran through two well-set ice screws up to where Navarra still stood in death hauling hard on the frozen rope.

The Swiss spent three hours hacking Navarra out of glacial armor before they could lower his body down to the point where Rabada now lay entombed within the stomach of the Spider. The men bivouacked at this macabre campsite and spent six hours the following morning trying to extricate Rabada, who, by all accounts, was a huge man. Lashing the two corpses together the three men then rappelled and lowered their gruesome burden directly down to a bivi at Death Bivouac, thus avoiding the complicated traverse into the Ramp and back across the Third Ice Field. When they awoke, the two bodies were gone. The pitons had ripped free, perhaps shattered in the icy winter temperatures or more likely swept from the face by rockfall or a falling cornice in the night. Over the following two days the three men descended the rest of the face, so making the first-ever descent. Their main intention, however, had always been to relieve the rescue services from a commitment that few wanted to undertake.

"So, that bivi they made with the bodies in the Spider was what you thought was the Spanish bivi?" Ray asked.

"I've never heard of a bivi in the Ramp. What if it stormed in the night? I've heard the Ramp can turn into a continuous waterfall."

"Yeah, I heard that, too," Ray agreed. "And it's somewhere below the Waterfall chimney pitch. It's also pretty small and cramped."

"No, I don't fancy that," I said. "But if we can't reach the Traverse of the Gods in a day I've read that there is a good bivi site to the left of the Ramp ice field: good enough for six people apparently. The French party with Rebuffat used it in 1952 during that epic ascent when they joined up with Hermann Buhl."

"Well, that's certainly a better option," Ray commented. "At least there we will be out of the main drainage line of the Ramp. Having said that, it would be a shame not to stay at Death Bivouac. It's just one of those places you have to stay at, isn't it?"

"Like a night in the Ritz?" I said. "I know what you mean, though. It's so redolent of all that history it would be a shame just to rush past it."

"Well, we've got all those options, haven't we? Let's just see how things pan out and adapt ourselves to whatever seems to be the best plan, eh?"

When we returned from our sortie on the west flank we spent an hour watching as Heinz Zak and Scott Muir climbed the Second Ice Field. The two tiny figures were joined by three others, Will Edwards filming them as they climbed, belayed by his two guides.

In an instant the face came into perspective. When previously we had searched the wall with our binoculars, vainly trying to recognize distinctive features such as the Hinterstoisser Traverse or Death Bivouac, we had been confused by the sheer immensity of the mountain. Now that we could watch tiny figures creeping up the Second Ice Field the scale of everything suddenly became apparent. It was good to be able to watch them on the Difficult Crack and know at last exactly where it was instead of the vague idea we had been used to. But on the other hand, it was quite sobering to see how utterly insignificant the climbers appeared in the center of that massive amphitheater. Peering through the huge camera lens of the Channel 4 crew was an extraordinary experience. The climbers, although small, were no longer simply dots barely distinguishable from rocks on the ice field. I watched, fascinated, as the arms and legs of the climbers made distinct and familiar movements, swinging axes, clipping gear, taking in the ropes. The moment I pulled back from the eyepiece and stared at the face they disappeared as if they had never existed.

Hanspeter Feuz arrived by the camera and asked us about our plans for the morning. We explained the options we had run through and he seemed to favor a stop at Death Bivi. In the course of our conversation we took turns at the camera watching the climbers' progress and gleaning invaluable advice from Hanspeter. He had been part of the team that had been filmed live climbing the face the previous year and I promptly blamed him for awakening the dream I had cherished after Ray had sent me a video recording of the climb.

Hanspeter was trim, athletic, and obviously incredibly fit, which made us very conscious of our own lack of preparation in that department. His immaculate English and open, charming friendliness soon put us at our ease and banished my suspicions about arrogant and aloof Swiss guides. The insights he gave us on key sections of the face were both priceless and confidence boosting. As we watched Heinz and Scott start up the Second Ice Field he pointed out the best place to exit the Ice Hose and where to break left across the ice towards a distinctive inverted triangle of rock breaching the top of the ice field.

"Have you been involved in any rescues?" Ray asked, a little too hopefully.

"Oh, yes," Hanspeter replied. "Too many."

"On the face?"

"Yes, I work with the mountain rescue service as well as guiding."

"I imagine that there are regular accidents each year on the face," I said. "But I've heard that the guides now use long-line techniques and can reach victims on virtually any part of the wall."

"Yes, that's true but it is still very dependent on the weather," Hanspeter replied. "We use 180-meter wire cables and suspend a guide from these and fly them into the face. This way the helicopter can remain high and far enough away from the face to avoid rocks hitting the rotors."

"One hundred and eighty meters?" I said in astonishment. "That's 600 feet, for God's sake." Hanspeter laughed at my expression. I had once been suspended 60 feet below a helicopter in a dramatic rescue on the Drus above Chamonix, and watching that silk-thin wire twisting and clicking as I wheeled through the sky thousands of feet above the Nant Blanc glacier had been a deeply unsettling experience. The idea of a 600-foot wire was nightmarish.

"Yes, it is exciting but it works," Hanspeter said. "There have been no fatalities on the wall for ten years now."

"Ten years?" Ray and I echoed incredulously.

"I'd have thought there would have been at least a death every year," I added.

"Well, that was true before we developed the long-line system," Hanspeter agreed, "because in those days it took a long time to get onto the wall safely and we could only reach a limited number of places. I think because of this there were fatalities either because injured climbers had to wait too long for rescue and died of their wounds or they tried to descend, or even climb out in bad conditions and this killed them."

"Well, that's worth knowing," Ray said. "You don't happen to have a mobile phone number for us?" he added in jest.

Within minutes I was keying in Hanspeter's number, the number of the Grindelwald guides office, and the Mountain Rescue center number.

"Let's just not have an accident, eh?" I suggested.

"Yeah, the phone bill would be enormous."

"We might film you guys on the ice field tomorrow, if you don't mind," Simon said. "It will be a long-distance shot but it's the only way we can film two climbers without the cameraman and guides in the frame."

"No problem," Ray replied.

"I've got to go now, guys," Hanspeter said, picking up his rucksack and radio. "I'll see you on the first train in the morning." We waved goodbye as he hurried away, talking urgently into his radio.

"Are the team stopping at Death Bivouac tonight?" I asked Simon.

"Yes," Simon said. "In fact, Hanspeter has just left to arrange the helicopter drop. He's talking to the pilot now."

"Helicopter drop?"

"Yeah, we're dropping them thermoses of hot water, prepared hot meals, and beer. Heinz insisted on beer."

"Beer? What about dancing girls?"

"Not enough room. Beer was more important, apparently."

"Now that's the way to climb," Ray said approvingly as we headed for the train.

"How do you feel about it now?" I asked.

"Good," he said as the train pulled in. "And bumping into all these people from history."

"He's a real hero of yours, isn't he?"

"Heckmair? Definitely. All those Munich climbers were amazing, Hermann Buhl as well."

"I suppose you're right," I said. "It was guys like Cassin and Bonatti who really inspired me. I suppose I admired Heckmair for the Eiger but I've never really known that much more about him. Still, I'm glad I've met him. That's Cassin, Bonatti, and Heckmair ticked off."

"Where did you meet Bonatti?"

"At the Banff Film Festival. I could barely speak. I felt like a snotty schoolboy. We shook hands and he rattled on in Italian, very passionate and expressive and I didn't understand a word of it. His wife translated and said how much he had enjoyed my book. I nearly choked. I picked up a menu and asked him to sign it, feeling like a fool."

"I felt like that with Heckmair," Ray nodded. "We've got to climb it now," he said fervently as the train pulled out of the station and we both craned our necks to look at the face sliding past the windows.

"You know," Ray added thoughtfully. "It's not every day you meet someone who has had a personal audience with Hitler."

I stared at him open-mouthed. It suddenly put the history of the man into sharp perspective.

The wildest dream: George and Ruth Mallory (courtesy Millikan family)

Moon rises over the Walker Spur, Grandes Jorasses, Chamonix
(Photo by Bradford Washburn)

RIGHT: *Chris Bonington cutting steps into the Spider on the first British ascent, 1962* (Photo by Ian Clough; Chris Bonington collection)

Don Whillans
climbing the First
Ice Field using
an ice dagger
(Chris Bonington
collection)

LEFT: *Brian Nally retreating across*
the Second Ice Field after the death
of his partner, Barry Brewster
(Chris Bonington collection)

RIGHT: *Tom Carruthers and Anton*
Moderegger on the Second Ice Field
before they fell to their deaths.
(Photo by Ian Clough;
Chris Bonington collection)

Entry in the visitor's book of the Hôtel des Alpes, Alpiglen: "We are deeply indebted to Frau Jossi for her hospitality. She was always there with a helping hand. From two poor climbers, with our warmest thanks." (Rudolf Rubi collection, reproduced in *Eiger: The Vertical Arena,* ed. Daniel Anker)

Karl Mehringer and Max Sedlmayr waiting for good weather at the Hôtel des Alpes, Alpiglen, August 1935 (Rudolf Rubi collection, reproduced in *Eiger: The Vertical Arena,* ed. Daniel Anker)

"Bivouac on 21/8/35. Max Sedelmajr, Karl Mehringer, Munich. Munich H.T.G. Section Oberland." In June 1976 a Czech rope team found a cigarette tin with this yellowed note on the Second Ice Field, forty-one years after it was written. It was probably Mehringer who wrote the note, since he misspelled the name of his climbing companion. (Rudolf Rubi collection, reproduced in *Eiger: The Vertical Arena,* ed. Daniel Anker)

A young Toni Kurz smiles back at us from the past. Alpiglen, 1936
(Taken from *Um die Eiger-Nordwand*, Munich, 1938, reproduced in *Eiger: The Vertical Arena*, ed. Daniel Anker)

"If only the weather holds," said Andreas Hinterstoisser to the photographer, Hans Jegerlehner. Unluckily for Hinterstoisser and Kurz, the weather did not hold. But that was only one reason for the disaster. (Taken from *Um die Eiger-Nordwand*, Munich, 1938, reproduced in *Eiger: The Vertical Arena*, ed. Daniel Anker)

Austrians Heinrich Harrer and Fritz Kasparek and Germans Anderl Heckmair and Ludwig Vörg (left to right) on July 24, 1938, after the first ascent of the north face of the Eiger. (Rudolf Rubi collection, reproduced in *Eiger: The Vertical Arena*, ed. Daniel Anker)

Stefano Longhi, trapped above the Traverse of the Gods, waves to a passing plane. "Fame! Freddo!" were his desperate last words. (Ludwig Gramminger/Archives Hans Steinbichler, reproduced in *Eiger: The Vertical Arena*, ed. Daniel Anker)

Using a 370-meter steel cable, Claudio Corti is recovered from the face. This was the first time a climber was rescued from the Eigerwand. (Ludwig Gramminger/Archives Hans Steinbichler, reproduced in *Eiger: The Vertical Arena*, ed. Daniel Anker)

LOOK WELL TO EACH STEP

THE TRAIN RATTLED SLOWLY THROUGH THE LUSH MEADOWS past the hamlet of Alpiglen, curving beneath the foot of the Eiger's shadowed north wall as it headed towards the cluster of hotels at Kleine Scheidegg. Both Ray and I craned our necks to look up at the face. It was gray, menacing, and inhospitable. We were silent, each quietly contemplating the coming climb. I looked at Hanspeter Feuz, tanned, handsome, and smiling. I wondered what I looked like. *I've probably got pupils like saucers.* I smiled and glanced back at Ray, who hadn't taken his eyes from the face.

Looking over his shoulder I could see where ice dribbled from the lower reaches of the Spider, hanging in the weightless chill of frigid air above the colossal roof of the Second Ice Field. The dark gash of the Ramp cut leftwards from the top of the prominent aréte of the Flat Iron. For some reason the Third Ice Field was obscured by the angle we were looking at the mountain. I thought of being up there alone. I thought of Adi Mayr and wished I hadn't.

Of all the dramas of success and tragedy that have been enacted on the Eiger's vast north face it was Toni Kurz's fate that affected me most powerfully. Brave, resourceful, obdurate, he died alone, despite Herculean efforts to save himself. Few could fail to be moved by the pathos of his lonely and torturously drawn-out death. It has stayed with me throughout my climbing life and after Siula Grande it became an even more poignant, haunting memory.

Adolf Mayr's fate, or Adi, as the young Austrian climber was known to his friends, also struck me with resounding force. When I learned that some climbers actually chose to climb alone—solo climbing as it is known—I was quite dumbfounded. The concept seemed so overwhelmingly dangerous I couldn't for the life of me work out why anyone would even consider undertaking such a rash and perilous ascent.

On a few occasions I have tried my hand at solo climbing and I confess that I am not a great fan of the pastime. Sometimes it has made sense to unrope and solo up ice fields, when moving roped together would otherwise entail the risk of both climbers being pulled to their deaths if one slipped or was knocked off. I have climbed a few alpine peaks alone and gained a certain degree of satisfaction afterwards, but it was mainly to do with being glad to be alive.

Although physically and technically quite capable of solo climbing, I feel that mentally I am poorly equipped for the task. Soloing on mountains I feel alone and miss the shared companionship of a partner to enjoy the adventure. On rock I am simply intimidated. What I can never get out of my mind is that however well I might be climbing there are two elements that make what I am doing an unacceptable gamble.

First, I am keenly aware that we are all fallible, even the very best. We don't plan to do it; it just happens. Climbers die because they make mistakes. Death is the price you pay if you are too human at the wrong time.

The second thought that I find hardest to shake off is that even if I climb immaculately there is no guarantee that the medium I am climbing—be it snow, ice, or rock—will behave in the same accommodating manner. The tiny edge of rock that I am pulling on may snap with such startling speed that I would be falling before I have a chance to grab another handhold. However much I might believe in myself, I still have to play Russian roulette with the chance of a hold breaking off.

Sadly, a couple of friends have been caught out by this very problem and some brilliant lives came to an abrupt end. It was what they chose to do and willingly, in the full knowledge of the possible consequences, so I never felt that they had wasted their lives; rather that we were the ones who had lost something brilliant and precious. It was after all what had defined them, made their lives distinct and rich.

Having said that, I have always admired those who can do such feats. It seems to me to be the ultimate challenge of climbing, the most aesthetic expression of climbing that can be made—one person's skill, nerve, and self-control against the rock or ice or mountain. It strips the climber of any connection with the world and he moves into a dimension that few of us would dare enter. It demands respect, even if one privately feels it is an act of madness. I have always made a point of carefully standing to one side when watching a solo climber at work.

On August 28, 1961, Adi Mayr made the first attempt to climb the north face of the Eiger alone. At first he climbed smoothly, confidently, and without hesitation. The watchers gathered around the telescopes on the hotel balconies began to feel reassured that here was an expert climber truly in his element. When he reached the Ice Hose he chose to avoid it altogether by climbing a variant line up the brittle and awkwardly stratified rock on its left side. Like many climbers from the eastern Alps, Adi felt more comfortable on rock than ice and when he reached the Second Ice Field his speed dropped and he was forced to cut steps in places where the ice was steep and hard. Nevertheless, he had reached Death Bivouac by two-thirty in the afternoon where he chose to rest until the following day.

Although a sensible and logical decision, it may have been his undoing. He no doubt reasoned that with the sun on the upper part of the face the traverse of the Third Ice Field to reach the Ramp would be too dangerous, bordering on suicidal. Rocks melted free by the heat of the sun were funnelled into the Spider and then spewed directly down the Third Ice Field.

Adi was providing good business for the telescope owners as the queues of paying spectators waited patiently for their turn to gawp at him. I wonder how many half-hoped to see him fall. The weather was fine and the proximity of the sheltered rocks of the Ramp a couple of rope lengths away must have been a great temptation to Adi. With at least six hours of daylight remaining and the Ramp in sunshine he could reasonably have hoped to reach the Traverse of the Gods—even the Exit Cracks—before nightfall. With luck the rock in the Ramp would have been dried by the sun, except where spray from the melting ice in the Waterfall Chimney pitch had leeched down, dampening the adjacent rock walls.

Climbing wet rock would not have been a problem for a man of Adi's skill. The Waterfall Chimney pitch, sometimes sodden with water and sometimes glazed with ice, is frequently the hardest section of climbing in the Ramp. In winter it can be completely jammed with a plug of ice near its top where the walls rear outwards and arm-thick icicles can block progress as effectively as a portcullis. He chose instead the fifteen-hour bivouac at Death Bivouac's sheltered cave, a long time to sit alone and think of what you have committed to. The freedom of intense concentration and precise climbing technique were no longer there to keep his fears at bay.

In the morning Adi was observed traversing the Third Ice Field slowly and with great care, cutting steps as he went. It was icy cold and his choice to bivouac and avoid the rockfall seemed a wise one until he reached the first few rock pitches of the Ramp. Here the rock is sound and by no means technically difficult, yet Adi was observed to be climbing in a cramped, hesitant manner. Had the long anxious night eroded his spirit, eaten away at his confidence and élan?

As they watched him climb into the shadowed, icy maw of the Ramp they noticed that he had still not chosen to get out his rope and use a self-belaying system. If the difficulty had been troubling him then this is the first thing that he would have done: perhaps he was moving slowly because he wasn't fully warmed up after the long bivouac and the previously wet rock was now heavily iced with a treacherous patina of verglas.

As he approached the Waterfall Chimney pitch his progress slowed dramatically. He had to make a delicate traverse just beneath the chimney. It is at this point that a feature called the Silver Trench becomes apparent when the sun strikes deeply into the Ramp in the late afternoon.

Like many names on the mountain the Silver Trench is a pleasant name for an otherwise intimidating section of climbing. I had often wondered how these evocative and sometimes lyrical names had come into being. Perhaps the Traverse of the Gods was so-called not because of its magnificent and exposed position on the edge of a 5000-foot chasm but because climbers edging across it had the unnerving feeling that they would be joining the gods rather more quickly than they had planned.

The Silver Trench, however, was coined not by climbers but by the spectators at Kleine Scheidegg and Alpiglen because only they could see the sun flashing brilliantly back at them, reflected from the gleaming plate of ice covering the traverse at the foot of the Waterfall Chimney. Early that morning as Adi cautiously attempted a bridging step across the traverse the face lay in shadows and the watchers could not see the deceptive glitter of the Silver Trench.

They watched as Adi stretched a foot far out to his left. His boot slipped suddenly and he withdrew his leg to regain his balance. Poised above such an immense fall, it is hard to understand why he did not reverse his movements to a point where he could get out his rope and use a self-belay. Perhaps he did not want to waste time? Maybe because it was just one small step he knew he only had to raise his courage and then all would be well. The defiant way to regain confidence would be to force yourself to confront the impasse that has stymied you. Perhaps Adi, already unnerved by the treacherous conditions, had reached just such an impasse.

Backing off and resorting to the rope would be an admission of failure. It might open the floodgates of fears that could quickly wash away whatever self-belief remained to him. He was being watched by an attentive, expectant audience. Perhaps he felt he couldn't back down; just one long stride and he might regain his poise. It was a time to be brave: it was what he lived for.

He stretched his boot out once again, a jerky, tense movement, and again returned warily to his stance. Then he worked on the foothold with his ice axe. His movements reflected the actions of a tired and nervous man.

They saw him make another agonizing attempt. Nothing was different from his previous strides but perhaps this time he managed to raise sufficient courage to transfer his weight to the glassy foothold. At twelve minutes past eight in the morning Adi risked the step. Heart pounding and adrenalin coursing through his body, he weighted the hold momentarily and then fell silently from the Silver Trench. His body flew from the Ramp and hardly struck the face during its fall of 4000 feet.

I too have paused many times at a particularly tricky move, hesitated as I tried to bolster my courage, and then stepped up or reached a tiny handhold at full stretch and breathed a sigh of relief. It is the essence of climbing. For an endless moment everything is concentrated on the outcome of one shift in body weight, one calculated decision to move, upon which the outcome of the entire climb—if not your life—is dependent. For an instant you are intensely alive. Good memories of climbs are as much about these brilliantly intense experiences, milliseconds of movement, confrontations with infinity, breath held until you have won through. I glanced up at the face thinking of Adi's fateful step. Sometimes we lose.

The train rattled to a halt at the Kleine Scheidegg station and the air compressors hissed as the doors swung open. Most of Tokyo seemed to disembark onto the platform and rushed after a chattering tour guide holding aloft a pink umbrella as a marker point.

"Where do they all come from?" Ray said as he watched the Japanese tourists perform a pincer movement around a St. Bernard dog and fire off fusillades of well-aimed camera shots. The dog looked bored, lay down, and began to lick his genitals. The tour guide raised her pink umbrella, barked a sharp Japanese order, and her entourage dutifully streamed off behind her in the direction of the hotel. I saw Simon and the camera crew take up defensive positions around the camera tripod.

"God knows," I sighed and then turned to Hanspeter.

"Do we go straight up to the Eiger Gletscher station now?" Ray asked, like a condemned man hoping the scaffold had collapsed.

"First I must clear it with the stationmaster and then talk to Simon about the helicopter, but don't worry, we shall still catch the first train up."

"Great, wonderful." He heaved his rucksack onto his shoulder.

We wandered up towards the group huddled around the camera. Everyone seemed to be in high spirits. Simon Wells grinned broadly and gave us the news that the team was already on the move heading up the Ramp. Hanspeter had a hurried conversation with Simon and then it was time to go. We shook hands all round and waved farewell as they shouted encouragement and we followed Hanspeter back towards the platform. I would rather have gone straight up onto the face without meeting anyone. I hate farewells.

As the train climbed up past the Eiger Gletscher station with a full complement of Japanese tourists aboard, the lights in the two carriages flickered on as we drove into the guts of the mountain. I watched the morning light fade to a pinprick dot and then disappear as the tunnel entrance receded behind the train.

I glanced at Ray, who was looking serious. I felt edgy and suppressed the urge to laugh. I aimed my video camcorder at the carriage full of faces who all began smiling back at me. Obviously I was learning their language. I panned across and filmed Ray as the train hissed to a stop and the side door opened.

"Come on," Hanspeter called as he jumped down onto the tracks. "Come round the front of the train. You'll see the Stollenloch door on the left."

I switched the camcorder off and hefted my rucksack out of the door, following clumsily into the darkness of the tunnel. Walking around the front of the train I waved my thanks to the driver who smiled and held up a thumb in encouragement. A short corridor had been carved into the side of the tunnel and we clambered up a slight rocky incline towards where a weathered wooden doorway blocked further progress. On the left of the corridor I was astounded to see a fluorescent green neon advertising display that I had no time to read.

In moments we were alone and suddenly a blast of wind began hurtling up the tunnel. Hanspeter had pushed open the small trap-door set within the main wooden door. The wind was strong enough to suck me off balance. I saw Ray say something but couldn't hear the words in the rush of the wind. A gray light glimmered into the tunnel, silhouetting him against the morning sky.

"This is bloody ridiculous!" I heard Ray exclaim as I poked my head out of the door. He looked nervous. Hanspeter smiled.

"What a way to start the day!" I exclaimed, turning to Hanspeter and Ray. "This is weird." I dumped my sack on the broad ledge outside the door and looked straight down 2500 feet to the meadows below us. "Hell, it's not every day we get a chance to do something like this, is it?"

"Thank God," he said and began to step into his harness. I quickly sorted out the rack and tightened the harness around my waist.

"I'm glad we've done this, you know," I said as I uncoiled the green 60-meter (197-foot) rope. "I thought I would feel guilty about missing out the bottom bit, but we've already climbed it once and this is the scene of so much history. Just imagine all the people who have come this way."

"Yeah, usually trying to save their lives," Ray said sharply and handed me the end of the blue rope.

"You have company," Hanspeter said, pointing towards a triangular rubble-topped pillar about a hundred meters (328 feet) away. Two men sat side by side on the rubble. One was smoking a cigarette and his companion chewed on a sandwich. Thirty-one-year-old Matthew Hayes, from Hampshire, and Phillip O'Sullivan, twenty-six, a New Zealander living in Britain, had started up the face early that morning. We never talked to them on the climb but heard enough shouted commands to know that they were Brits.

"Damn," I swore despondently. The last thing we wanted were people in front of us.

"They must have started at first light," Ray said as he clipped a sling through a shiny new bolt set into the rocky mouth of the tunnel.

"Ah well, we'll have to see how they're going," I said. "There will still be room for us at Death Bivouac if that's where they're headed."

I glanced at the sky, making a quick weather check. There was a line of grayish white on the western horizon. The forecast for the day was for some overcast cloud cover in the afternoon that would clear during the night to be followed by three, possibly four, days of fine weather. I checked my Casio barometric altimeter, which gave altitude readings and more importantly, air pressure changes every hour.

As I stepped around Hanspeter and onto the face proper he clapped me on the shoulder and wished us well. At the last moment I asked if I could take a quick look at the Difficult Crack through his binoculars.

The black rock sprang into focus and I twirled the dial to adjust it to my eyesight. The first thing I noticed was the sheen of water dripping down the buttress of rock that the Difficult Crack cut through.

"It's streaming with water."

Suddenly a figure appeared, clinging to the rock.

"Damn, there's another climber," I said and looked more closely. "He doesn't seem to have a partner," I added as I examined the first and final stances of the Difficult Crack.

"God! He's soloing," I added, feeling despondent. I didn't want to be anywhere near a soloist on the Eiger. "And what's more he's not using a back rope and he's wearing bloody rock shoes."

"Bugger!" Ray said pointedly.

"I just hope he's good," I said fervently, thinking of Adi Mayr. "And lucky."

"Okay, guys, I had better get going," Hanspeter said. "I have to run up to the Gallery station before the next train comes. Good luck."

When I turned to run a rope-length out horizontally across from the Stollenloch to the rubble-topped pillar I saw that the two resting climbers had hurriedly started climbing. Clearly they wanted to stay ahead of us. I imagined that they were pretty annoyed to see two climbers pop out of a window in the face and almost get ahead of them. Still, I wasn't about to start racing them. We wanted to do the climb in our own time, in control, and not get ensnared with another party. I was happy to let them go first.

The terrain was easy but deceptively dangerous and I was very aware of the sucking gulf on my left side. Above the pillar I found a large sling clipped to an old peg and a shiny new bolt. A hurriedly discarded half-eaten sandwich and the butt of a cigarette lay nearby. I watched Ray as he moved nervously across the ledge and began climbing the pillar. He moved with an exaggerated caution that betrayed his tension.

"How are you feeling, kid?" I asked when he hauled himself up beside me.

"A bit freaked-out to tell the truth," he said. "I'll need a while to get comfortable with this place."

"I might as well just keep leading until you settle down. What do you think?"

"Fine by me," Ray said, and grinned. "Bloody hell, this thing's big," he added as he peered up at the immense wall of the Röte Fluh that blocked any view of the rest of the face. A flurry of powder snow rustled out into space hundreds of feet above us and over to our left.

"That must be the solo climber," I said, pointing at the snow drifting away on the breeze. "God, I hate being on this with him above us."

"Forget him. It's his choice," Ray said emphatically.

I glanced up, searching for the two climbers ahead of us. I saw a red rucksack and white helmet moving leftwards beneath a yellow band of rock.

"That must be the Wet Cave bivouac," I said and Ray nodded. I could look down from where I stood to the top of the Shattered Pillar and several thousand feet below the distinctive rounded tumuli of the First Pillar marked where we had started up the face four days earlier. We climbed up a faintly defined rib, moving together, carefully keeping several pieces of protection clipped on the rope between us. Most of the gear was of dubious quality, old rusted pitons hammered into downward-sloping cracks and bent over against the rock. We moved slowly, trying to get a feel for the terrain. The hand- and footholds were disconcertingly smooth, downward-sloped, and verglas and wet snow made otherwise easy scrambling an alarming experience. I would find myself unexpectedly tiptoeing around smears of ice desperately looking for some protection with a 100-foot fall lurking beneath me.

Ray took over the lead and climbed a series of slabby white limestone rock walls, then stopped for a long time. I began to feel impatient at our slow progress. A few irritated shouts elicited a pregnant silence. A stone clattered by, making me duck for cover as the ropes began to move through my hands.

When I reached the point that had slowed Ray I felt bad about my impatience. He had been perched a long way above a frail piton runner faced with delicate balance moves made desperately hard by large weeps of verglas. I thought about putting my crampons on and then decided that it would waste too much time. As the Vibram rubber sole of my left boot was skittering across the glazed slab I regretted my impetuosity. Hooking an axe pick against an icy nubbin of rock saved me from falling in a long sweeping swing across the wall. I arrived beside Ray breathing heavily and a little shaken. I moved up to a rectangular low-roofed cave burrowed into a rock buttress.

"Hey, Ray, this is the Wet Cave bivouac!" I yelled down excitedly. "And I can see the Difficult Crack now, directly above us. Those lads are at the belay. I'll see if I can catch them up."

Finding these sites that I had only ever seen in books had filled me with elation. It was a confirmation that we were on the route we had dreamed about for so long. I felt a childish, irrepressible joy just at being there. I wanted to shout down to Ray that we really were on the 1938 route but I decided he had probably already worked that one out.

As I traversed left towards a short vertical chimney I looked up and saw ropes snaking up over a jutting roof. It was Matthew Hayes and Phillip O'Sullivan climbing the Difficult Crack. Slings clipped to protection pitons slapped against the rock as the rope came tight. A voice shouted a familiar English climbing instruction. The second climber appeared by the overhang and began to reach his hands into a soaking wet crack cutting through the roof.

"Climbing, Matt," he yelled in response and then glanced down at his feet. I waved to him and held my thumb up.

"All right, mate?" I shouted. He said something in reply that I couldn't understand. I had hoped that I might have reached his stance before he began climbing. The thought that he might take one of our ropes up with him and fix it for us had been playing on my mind but that possibility was gone. In a way I was secretly quite pleased. I wanted a go at leading the Difficult Crack and felt uncomfortable about relying on another climber's help, even if it would have saved us a lot of time.

I edged across the traverse, my rucksack bumping against the roof and forcing me out over the drop to my right. I began crawling across the ledge, hampered by the friction of the ropes dragging heavily behind me. At its furthest end I found an old ring peg and clipped myself securely in place. I shrugged my rucksack from my back and pushed it to the back of the cave.

There was something familiar about the cave. And then I remembered a photograph in Chris Bonington's book, *I Chose to Climb*, of Ian Clough stirring a pot of stew at a bivouac. The roofed cave was the one they had used during their first British ascent of the Eigerwand in 1962.

Although most of my climbing heroes came from the generation of the 1930s, Chris Bonington's career and his many books had been a major influence on my climbing development. It was his first autobiography, *I Chose to Climb*, that really inspired me to go and climb routes like the Eiger and the Walker.

I had always admired Bonington's tenacity and determination to climb the Eiger. In 1961 he had arrived in the Alps directly from a 7000-mile road trip from Kathmandu after a successful attempt on the south face of Nuptse. He and Don Whillans had planned a protracted summer of Eiger-watching, determined to be the first British climbers to scale the north face.

On their first attempt they reached the Difficult Crack before retreating from the threat of bad weather. This was the highest point yet reached by British climbers. After a period of bad weather Bonington and Whillans headed off for Chamonix and, teaming up with Ian Clough and the Polish climber Jan Djuglosz, they made the first ascent of the Central Pillar of Freney. It was a significant coup made all the more impressive by the fact that the terrible tragedy on the Pillar experienced by Walter Bonatti had occurred only two months before.

The Italian party of Bonatti, Roberto Gallieni, and Andrea Oggioni had joined forces with a strong four-man French team led

led by Pierre Mazeaud, with Robert Guillaume, Antoine Vieille, and Pierre Kohlman. In early July they reached the foot of the Chandelle, a distinctive 400-foot-high rock obelisk that stands atop a 2000-foot plinth of broken granite. Bad weather moved in and the party was pinned down on a cramped ledge for three days and nights. Pierre Kohlman was struck by lightning on the first day of the storm and severely weakened. With ineffective plastic sheets and no bivi tent the group huddled together for warmth.

On the fifth day of their climb they attempted to retreat down the Pillar, across the Col du Peuterey, and down the Freney glacier. Hoping to reach the safety of the Gamba hut, they soon found themselves wading through chest-deep snow. After sheltering for a night in a crevasse they continued down. Antoine Vieille collapsed and died of exhaustion. Hours later Guillaume also succumbed. Bonatti's great friend Oggioni was the next to collapse at the foot of a couloir leading up to the Col de l'Innominata, still 2000 feet above the Gamba hut. Pierre Mazeaud bravely chose to stay with his companion while Bonatti forged ahead.

Shortly thereafter Kohlman, deranged by the insidious effects of hypothermia, displayed signs of delirium and tried to attack Bonatti and Gallieni. They were forced to untie from their ropes and flee down to the hut. Of the seven who had set out only Mazeaud, Gallieni, and Bonatti survived and the story became one of the most renowned and harrowing accounts of survival and tragedy in alpine mountaineering.

Undeterred by its serious reputation Bonington, Whillans, Djuglosz, and Clough raced a competing French team of René Desmaison and Pierre Julien to the summit of the Central Pillar of Freney.

The Freney, the Walker, and the Eiger had always inspired me. I had climbed the Freney early in my alpine career and stopped at the ledge where Bonatti's party had been stormbound. I then kept a sharp and wary eye on the weather. I remembered Whillans's hand-jamming his way over the roof at the top of the Chandelle as

I hung in that same upside-down, exposed position with 4000 feet of clear air sucking at my struggling body.

Whillans and Bonington then returned to Grindelwald for yet another attempt on the Eiger, this time accompanied to the foot of the face by a photographer from the *Daily Mail,* which had agreed to finance their attempt. They retreated from the Swallow's Nest and Bonington decided to call it a day and return to England. As he packed his gear in Alpiglen, intending to get the next flight back to England, they heard that a climber had been seen falling down the north face. They set out for the foot of the face to confirm their worst fears. A pompous German tourist was standing guard over the corpse, proudly pointing out the terrible head injuries suffered by the victim. Chris and Don covered the climber with a blanket and tried not to hit the tourist.

The following summer Chris was back on the Eiger with Whillans again, fighting for their lives as they went to rescue Brian Nally after Brewster's death on the Second Ice Field. Having then gone on to climb the north face of the Badile with Whillans, Bonington went to Chamonix and joined Ian Clough on the first British ascent of the Walker Spur. Less than forty-eight hours later the pair were in Alpiglen. On the rubble-strewn lower rocks Bonington was disturbed to notice blood trails and a piece of flesh attached to some bone. He chose not to tell his partner. Later Ian told Chris that he hadn't mentioned it for the same unspoken reason.

As they settled down in the cave to camp at the foot of the Difficult Crack where I was now belaying Ray they were surprised by the appearance of two climbers—Tom Carruthers, a well-known Glaswegian climber, and Anton Moderegger, an Austrian climber. Bonington and Clough were baffled to learn that not only were they complete strangers but neither could speak a word of each other's language. While Bonington and Clough went on to climb the face with one more bivouac on the Traverse of the Gods, Anton Moderegger and Tom Carruthers were last seen moving very slowly halfway up the Second Ice Field.

I saw the grainy photograph of the pair that Ian Clough had snapped from the top of the Flat Iron. The tiny figures had been crudely circled to mark them out on the immense expanse of gray rock-pitted ice. They were moving so slowly that there was no chance that they would reach the Flat Iron, one of the most dangerous places on the face, before the heat of the afternoon released the daily barrage of rocks. The rock slabs of the Flat Iron are scarred and pitted by the incessant impacts of falling stones that turn the place into a death trap in the afternoon. As Bonington and Clough anxiously watched their snail-like progress they could sense the uncertainty in their movements, two tiny spots becoming overwhelmed with fear.

Confident, rational decision-making would have been impossible given that they didn't speak each other's language—only mixed messages. In the center of the ice field they were sitting ducks, vulnerable to the random bombardment of stonefall. Clough and Bonington tried to shout a warning but they were too far away to hear.

The photograph, despite its poor quality, had a powerful effect on me. It seemed to sum up everything that was bleak and lonely about the north face of the Eiger. It was a last glimpse of short lives caught by chance on film that filled me with a sense of pity and pathos. I wondered what might have gone so terribly wrong. Were they swept from the face by rockfall? Did one fall and pull his companion to his death? We would never know. They simply disappeared unseen from an eerie world of dirty rock-pitted ice and plunging rock.

I glanced around the cave as Ray came into view at the end of the traverse. For a moment I had begun to feel uneasy about what we were doing. Perhaps I had read too many books and knew too many horror stories.

"Hey, this is good," Ray said with an infectious grin.

"Well, you've cheered up," I said, noting Ray's surge of confidence.

"Oh, yes, I've got over that," he said dismissively. "Just morning sickness. Hey, I recognize this place," he added, looking around the cave.

"It's a good bivi site. Better than the Swallow's Nest, apparently."

"Did you meet those guys?" Ray asked as I sorted out my gear in preparation for leading the Difficult Crack. "I thought they might have fixed a rope for us."

"No, I just wished them luck. Anyway I quite fancy leading this," I said and started to move to the right where a crack cut through a bulge of rock dripping with icy water. I clipped the ropes through an old twisted piton.

"Rather you than me," Ray said as he fed the ropes out.

"Look, I'm leaving my sack here," I said as I clipped it to the piton. "When I get up I'll tie the blue rope off and you can use it as a fixed rope while I belay you on the green."

"What about your sack?"

"I'll pull the green rope through the runners, drop it down to you, and I'll haul the sack up."

"Yeah, okay, sounds good."

At the first touch of the crack, which was streaming with water, I marveled at the nerve of the solo climber who only hours earlier had tackled the pitch without the security of a back rope. The water trickled down my sleeves and along my arms, sending icy rivulets into my armpits. I shivered and tried to get a better grip of the rock. I pulled up to the overhang and stretched to clip a tattered loop of rope protruding from the crack. I had no idea how strong it was or even what it was threaded through. Above it I could see another contorted, rusted piton. My fingers were quickly numbed. I knew I couldn't waste time. Reaching as high as possible I managed to get a tenuous finger-jam in the slimy crack and, pressing my boots as high up under the roof as I could manage, I pulled nervously upwards, praying that my hand wouldn't suddenly shoot out of the crack. I struggled to clip a carabiner through the bent peg and breathed a sigh of relief when the green rope was then safely clipped in. I noticed with some apprehension as I pulled through the roof that the tattered rope loop I had clipped to was only loosely jammed in the crack.

Above the roof the climbing eased and I began to enjoy myself as I followed the crack rightwards to a stance at the top of a short corner. To my surprise I could find no pitons or places for wires. Looking up I saw the way lead back left, traversing into a rocky corner directly above where Ray was standing. As I moved across to it I was dismayed to note a series of blocky roofs jutting from the corner beneath me. It would make hauling my rucksack a time-consuming task. After 100 feet of climbing I came to a secure stance at the top of the corner with two good pitons and a bolt to belay on.

"Okay, Joe," Ray yelled and I began to haul on the green rope that I had dropped down to him. I watched as the rucksack swung into sight from beneath the first roof and hauled hard to get it clear of the obstruction. It flipped upside down as it bounced over the lip of the roof and I watched my crampons swing from the attachment points on the top of the rucksack. After 30 feet the rucksack jammed hard under another roof. I couldn't free it. I shouted to Ray to tell him to start climbing the blue rope using a sharp-toothed camming device to grip the rope. I couldn't belay him until he freed the rucksack and I could throw down the green rope.

Ray had found the prototype lightweight camming jumar in his shop and had thrown it into his sack as an afterthought. Now he was using it for the very first time and finding it almost useless. The grip relied too heavily on the sharp teeth in the metal cam. I could see an alarming amount of white core appearing on his rope. It was shredding the sheath. Ray was grunting and swearing as he pulled over the roof, fighting with the recalcitrant device that was steadily eating its way through his lifeline with alarming efficiency.

When he could reach across to free my rucksack I hauled hard, with the result that it promptly jammed 15 feet higher under yet another roof. I started swearing angrily. On Ray's third attempt to free the rucksack I noticed that the straps holding my crampons in place had almost worked loose. A solitary strap remained in a loose loop and the only thing preventing the crampons from disappearing into space was that one of the points had punctured the nylon tape. I yelled a warning and Ray managed to grab the crampons before they became Eiger junk.

When Ray arrived at the stance he was breathing heavily and swearing about the useless lightweight jumaring device.

"Bugger, that," he said, throwing the piece of aluminum into the depths. "It nearly killed me."

"Look, sorry I got angry with you, mate," I said. "I thought you were making a pig's ear of it."

"I was."

"Yeah, but it was my fault for not thinking about the haul line."

"No worries," Ray said and clapped me on the shoulder. "Oh, and well led. It looked hard."

"More like wet and cold," I said. "Anyway, let's have a drink and sort these ropes out. They're a mess."

As we chewed on some tough Swiss sausage and dried fruit I noticed the clouds had built up in the west. There was no longer a thin gray line on the horizon but a whole series of cumulonimbus clouds piling steadily into the sky. I glanced at my watch. One-thirty in the afternoon.

"Hell, we've wasted an hour and a half at least," I said angrily. "Have you seen those clouds?" I nodded to the west.

"They said it was going to be overcast in the afternoon."

I didn't reply. There was something I didn't like about the way the clouds were forming. I checked my watch again. The pressure was plummeting.

THE FATAL STORM

WE HURRIED UP A ROCKY GULLY LEADING TOWARDS the base of the Röte Fluh. We moved together in an ascending 500-foot traverse over easy ground that led us leftwards over a series of snow-covered walls to a shield of rock. As I approached the wall I recognized the distinctive shape of the Hinterstoisser Traverse and felt a gathering excitement that we were about to pass another historic landmark. I found a tattered fixed rope clipped to some ancient but strong-looking pitons and quickly brought Ray up to the stance. Looking directly above the belay I saw an overhanging rock wall about 150 feet high. A thin trickle of water fell into space from its edge and I felt the spray cool my face.

"That's where Don Whillans rappelled when they rescued Nally," I said to Ray.

"Must be," he said.

I didn't answer because I had looked at the sky again and was now deeply troubled at what I saw.

"Bloody hell, kid," I said and Ray turned to see what I was looking at. The western sky was now filled with dark thunderheads. The boiling white summits were building massively and even as we watched, great plumes of coiling clouds were climbing thousands of feet into the air with every minute that passed.

"We're in deep shit. That lot is going to go off any moment. It's big. This is no overcast afternoon," I said curtly.

"That happened quickly."

"They can build very fast. I noticed the wind rising earlier. It's the gust front pushed ahead by those cumulonimbus clouds. They're all joining together. Come on, let's get the hell out of here. It might be short-lived but it's really going to dump on us."

I reached up and grabbed the fixed rope that was draped across the traverse. In three or four places the sheath on the fixed rope had been torn away and thin strands of white core was all that was left. I was filled with a nervous urgency, made worse by the oppressive and electric atmosphere of the onrushing storm front. There was no time for delicacy so I simply heaved myself across on the fragile rope, hoping it wouldn't snap, clipping my own ropes through every battered piton I came to.

I glanced back and was astounded to see how dark it had become. Ray seemed to be standing on a cloud and behind him the ramparts of the Röte Fluh had disappeared. There was an ominous rumble of thunder from the surrounding clouds and water began to splash down across the slabby rocks of the traverse. The overhanging wall protected me from the worst of the deluge as I hurried across the rock, grabbing and clipping and hauling as fast as I could. I winced as another heavy explosion of thunder rumbled behind me. Glancing up to my left I saw a mass of fist-sized rocks spinning out into space from the top of the wall. I watched, transfixed, as they whistled past and spat down with sharp staccato reports into the rocky terrain several hundred feet beneath my feet.

An insistent rushing, sluicing sound began to increase in volume. I looked directly above me and was alarmed to see a curtain of water, hail, and stones spewing over the wall at the top of the Hinterstoisser Traverse. Fortunately, the heavier debris sprayed far out into space, although the water and hail began to flow in torrents across the slabs I was traversing. I glanced back at Ray who was hunched at his belay stance, his hood over his helmet, in the direct line of a now-heavy waterfall. Since I was preoccupied with climbing the traverse safely I simply registered these facts but didn't feel unduly troubled. If anything I felt a mounting anticipation at the turn of events. The storm was dramatic and spectacular and, in a peculiar sort of way, enjoyable. For the moment we were safe and the security of the Swallow's Nest beckoned.

After 130 feet of traversing I came to a vertical crack running straight up, bounded on its right side by a jutting roof. I knew that I should stop and bring Ray across, but with ropes nearly 200 feet long I gambled that I might just reach the shelter of the Swallow's Nest. I climbed the crack as fast as possible, tugging hard on the fixed rope as the sky around me began to explode with heavy cracks of thunder. Lightning flickered within the clouds and water and hail began to rush down onto me. As I emerged at the top of the crack I saw a small snow ledge at the base of an angled rock wall. A flat roof projected protectively out over the ledge. There were bolts and an old fixed rope on the wall that I hurriedly clipped myself to and shouted down to Ray to come up. There was no response. I doubted that he had heard me above the tumult of the storm. I pulled on the ropes until they came taut and then gave three sharp tugs, which was our signal to climb if we were out of earshot.

I clipped the ropes through my belay plate, dropped my ruck-sack onto the ledge, clipped it to a sling, then lay back against the sloping rock wall, which was completely dry. A fine curtain of water was spraying over the lip of the roof. I lit a cigarette, keeping the ropes taut in case Ray started moving, and stared across the First Ice Field. It was at that point that I fully appreciated how powerful the thunderstorm had been. The ice field was a continuously moving sheet of hail and water. Individual rocks bounced down the ice and sprang into space from the lower edge of the ice field. I leaned forwards and craned my neck to look up at the rest of the wall, which had now opened up as I had escaped the confines of the Röte Fluh. I gasped in shock at what I saw.

Far out to my left, in line with the Spider, a great waterspout was spewing from the lower edge of the Second Ice Field and cascading in a free-falling torrent hundreds of feet high. Higher up the wall there was a ceiling of gray cloud level with the Traverse of the Gods, but I could make out the Ramp ice field and the dark diagonal gash of the Ramp. Another waterfall was spraying out from the top of the Ramp ice field in a triple-headed torrent. The main mass of the water was falling the entire length of the Ramp in a 300-foot arc, pounding into the rocks at the start of the Third Ice Field. A continuous barrage of rocks was flying off the Second Ice Field, some impacting the First Ice Field in front of me with sharp, cracking sounds and whirring out to fall 3000 feet to the meadows below.

I stopped feeling elated and felt alarmed instead. I had never seen such a transformation on a mountain face in my life. The entire wall was a confusion of falling rocks, hail, small avalanches, and waterfalls. I thought of Heinz and Scott, and Will Edwards and his guides, and wondered where they were. I hoped they weren't in the Ramp because I doubted anyone would survive such a battering if they were trapped in that deluge. If they were not swept straight out of the fissure they would surely be drowned.

Then I thought of the solo climber and something clenched tight and cold inside. *Could he have reached the Ramp this quickly?* I thought and then dismissed the idea. *No, but he could well be on the Second Ice Field.* I stared at the debris discharging from the lower rim of the ice field and knew that anyone caught out on that vast expanse of ice would be having a torrid time with little chance of survival. *If he was moving without any back rope he wouldn't stand a chance. If he tried using a back rope system he would be so slow he would certainly be hit. Some choice! He's probably already dead.* I thought of Adi Mayr's long, silent fall. *What about the Brits? They can't be very far ahead of us. With luck they should be able to get back to the shelter of the Swallow's Nest.*

I looked around the bivouac site. Normally it is a narrow 18-inch-wide rock ledge suitable for no more than two people. With the bad weather of the past week there was enough snow banking out the ledge for us to stamp out a reasonable platform that two of us could lie down on and still be sheltered by the roof. *It would be damned cramped for four of us,* I thought and felt the ropes give and slacken. Ray was crossing the Hinterstoisser. I spat the cigarette out and watched it tumble down onto the ice field and slide away into space. *We'll have to change our game plan.*

When the storm first broke, Scott Muir, Heinz Zak, Will Edwards, and their two guides, Hansruedi Gertsch and Godi Egger, were just about to move across the Traverse of the Gods towards the ice of the Spider. A few hours earlier, as Hansruedi had been safe-guarding Will Edwards he happened to glance down and saw a lone climber moving fast at the bottom of the Second Ice Field. No partner appeared behind him. Glancing back a short time later he saw that the man had disappeared. He noted the weather and assumed that the soloist had taken the prudent option of retreat-ing to the Swallow's Nest. Distracted by the seriousness of their own position he gave no more thought to the matter. They were now high on the mountain, committed to climbing out of the wall with thunderclouds massing rapidly in the west, and he knew that the hail and water would be rapidly funneled down the cone of the Spider.

That morning they had left Death Bivouac in fine weather and enjoyed good, dry rock climbing in the Ramp. Despite the slow-ness that a filming schedule imposed and the congestion of five climbers in the narrow confines of the Ramp they had climbed efficiently up onto the Ramp ice field, crossed the Brittle Ledges, and climbed the loose and steep rope length up the Brittle Crack to reach the relative safety of the Traverse of the Gods. There was a good bivouac site at the left end of the traverse, but despite the gathering storm clouds they felt confident that they could reach the Exit Cracks at the top of the Spider and climb out of the face that day. The storm caught them at a highly vulnerable point.

The Traverse of the Gods is aptly named, given its lofty and exposed position and the fragile, loose nature of the climbing.

From the top of the Brittle Crack there is a reasonable belay at the left edge of the traverse, but from there on for 400 feet towards the Spider the points of protection—weak, damaged pitons, battered into shattered downward-sloping cracks—are marginal, to say the least. Most climbers would prefer not even to weight such pitons statically, let alone fall onto them. For the most part the climbing was not technically difficult but the rock is suspect and the drop beneath the climbers' feet is 5000 feet of clear air. The wall beneath the traverse is especially steep and undercut, hugely increasing the sense of vulnerability. The hardest climbing comes right at the end of the traverse around a protruding prow of rock close to the edge of the Spider. There was a good belay to be found at the far end but nothing reliable in between.

It is no place to fall. In fine weather and dry conditions it is a traverse that would alarm all but the most dishonest climber, however easily they might have climbed it. With snow covering foot- and handholds it becomes a seriously unpleasant enterprise. As the guides saw the oncoming storm they made an immediate change to their climbing order. They roped together as one party of five climbers and the guides set off from the security of the left-hand belay with the firm instructions that the last climber was not to unclip from the pitons until he knew the good belay at the far end had been reached by the leading guide.

At the most inconvenient moment the storm broke. Scott Muir was attempting to climb around the prow of rock at the end of the pitch and could see Heinz Zak belaying him from the edge of the Spider. Already unnerved by the exposure, his composure was broken when a wave of hail and water rushed down the rocks as thunder cracked and lightning flashed around the summit ridge far above him. The storm front had collided with the mighty ramparts of the Eiger and the Scheidegg Wetterhorn and in a very short time had unleashed its massive load of water. The entire mountain appeared to be flowing downwards in an unstoppable flood of hail, water, and rocks. Scott slipped and cried out in alarm.

Down at Kleine Scheidegg, Simon Wells and his crew had been monitoring the progress of Matthew Hayes and Phillip O'Sullivan, the two climbers above us. Hanspeter was scanning the face with his binoculars as Mark Stokes tended to the camera. A curious crowd of onlookers hovered around the tripod. Having spotted the two men near the Ice Hose, Simon had assumed that they were Ray and I, unaware that there was a party ahead of us. The previous day he had been unable to get a long-distance shot of Heinz Zak and Scott Muir alone on the Second Ice Field because Will Edwards and the two guides were always in the frame. It was an ideal opportunity to get the shot they wanted and they knew we would appreciate a minor role in their documentary. They set the big camera to run unattended, filming the pair as they struggled very slowly up to the Ice Hose.

As the storm swept in, the summit area quickly disappeared into clouds and an ominous blue-black light filled the amphitheater. When it broke Hayes and O'Sullivan were at the foot of the Ice Hose, sheltering from the mass of debris washing over the rock band, extending 300 feet above their heads. It must have been a terrifying experience. While the storm lasted the First Ice Field was being raked with stonefall and avalanches and it would have been suicidal to attempt the two rappels down to the shelter of the Swallow's Nest. They had no choice but to sit the thunderstorm out leaning against the security of the rock.

Ahead of them lay the Ice Hose, streaming with water. This 300-foot-high gully connects the First and Second Ice Fields and provides the easiest line through the rock band. Sometimes it can be completely iced up, presenting a steep vertical ice climb, but more frequently the ice is thin and loosely bonded. In hot years it can be no more than a damp flow running through the rock band that must be climbed on awkwardly sloping smooth holds, sometimes smeared with a thin film of verglas.

Perched on the Traverse of the Gods 2000 feet above where Hayes and O'Sullivan had taken shelter by the Ice Hose, Scott

Muir was convinced that he was falling. Suddenly engulfed in a wave of hailstones so heavy that it obscured the rock he was traversing across in a bewildering moving white mass, he was unable to find the crucial foot- and handholds that would lead him around the prow. With his hands and feet disappearing into the gathering tide of hail, Scott had the unnerving sensation that everything was moving down: the hail, the rock he was holding onto, and himself. He seemed to be standing on a moving white carpet. Then he slipped, a heart-stopping lunge towards the abyss that elicited a yelp of fear almost as soon as the slip was halted by crampon points biting securely onto a hidden hold. Heinz Zak, who was calmly belaying Scott from an exposed position on the edge of the Spider, could see that his partner was on the edge of panic. He urged Scott to steady himself. A fall could be disastrous to them all. As thunder exploded above him Heinz reassured Scott that he wasn't falling and belayed him across to the ice of the Spider.

Fearing that their position had become critical with astonishing speed, they knew that they would have to climb fast to reach the shelter of the rocks 350 feet above them at the top of the Spider. As the storm clouds deposited masses of hail, snow, and water it would flood down the summit ice fields and into the maw of the Spider. With every moment that passed the risks of heavier and heavier avalanches increased.

By the time the party began to climb the Spider the storm had passed with amazing rapidity. The hail and watery slush quickly dissipated and the sky lightened. They had been reprieved.

Despite its ferocity and thunderous noise the storm was short-lived, probably lasting no more than forty-five minutes, and had dumped most of its precipitation in the first twenty. By the time Ray had reached the Swallow's Nest the sky was already clearing. In the distance protesting thunder reverberated as the storm clouds swept eastwards across the towering pillar of the Scheidegg Wetterhorn, ripping themselves to pieces as they crashed against the ramparts of the Lauterbrunnen Wall.

"Well, that's our first Eiger storm," I said as I set the stove and balanced a pan of snow on the hissing blue flames.

"And our last, I hope," Ray said, looking damp and bedraggled from his impromptu soaking in the waterfall. The torrent had been so powerful that he had been forced to endure a twenty-minute dousing, waiting for the pressure to ease off, despite my shouted curses and impatient triple yanks at his harness.

"Tea or cappuccino?" I said, holding up a tea bag and a foil packet of instant coffee.

"Cappuccino," Ray said. "It's not bad here is it?" he added, admiring our sheltered eyrie.

"Yeah, I've been thinking about that," I said. "If we stamp out a ledge and build it up on the outside we should be able to make a lie-down bivi here."

"What, and not carry on?"

"I don't fancy it," I answered and watched as a flurry of stones swept the First Ice Field. I raised my eyebrows at Ray, who had been watching the stones.

"No, maybe not," he agreed.

"Let's have a brew and see how the weather develops. My feeling is that the storm has done its worst, cleared the air now, and we should get a sunny afternoon."

"With luck."

"It's three o'clock now, okay," I said, handing Ray a mug of frothy coffee. "We might have six hours of daylight to reach Death Bivouac, maybe less. But we have no idea how hard the Ice Hose will be after this storm and it might well slow us down."

"Yeah, and I'm not sure I fancy sticking my head out onto the Second Ice Field. Look!" Ray said, pointing upwards. A volley of stones was winging out into space from the wall above the Hinterstoisser, thrumming as they spun down through the air. "They might not be that big but I don't fancy one in the face. It would ruin my modeling career."

"Yeah, I was thinking that," I agreed. "And we'll end up climbing the Flat Iron in the late afternoon. I think the effect of this down-pour will still be kicking rocks down for a long time yet." As I spoke there was a heavy thud from the First Ice Field and we turned to watch a football-sized stone bound in great leaps down the ice.

"That settles it," Ray said emphatically. "We've got plenty of food, a good bivi site, and a settled forecast for three, maybe four days. Let's sort this place into a really comfy bivi."

THE HAPPINESS OF A LIFETIME

WE BEGAN TO ARRANGE A CAT'S CRADLE OF ROPES linking the bolts that had been fixed to the back wall of the bivi ledge. Soon we had fixed a washing line of rope hanging with hardware, slings, axes and crampons, cameras, and rucksacks tidily out of our way as we methodically stamped the ledge wider, banking the outside edge to stop us slipping off in our sleep. We paused every now and then to watch the flurries of stonefall. The bombardment didn't seem to have eased up very much. After an hour's work we felt satisfied that our sleeping arrangements were as good as we could make them and we made a thin mattress on the snow by coiling our ropes in wide S-bends and placing our empty rucksacks on top of them. Once we had put our insulated sleeping mats on top of them it began to feel quite palatial.

We were in high spirits, delighted to have found such a fine bivi spot and feeling that everything was in control. We were happy to change our game plan and not force a way on towards Death Bivouac. Why take unnecessary risks?

I was sitting at the far edge of the ledge overlooking the Hinterstoisser Traverse and the sweep of the First Ice Field, which ended abruptly in a lurching abyss some 80 feet below me.

"Good God! This is where Hinterstoisser and Kurz tried to rappel," I said, pointing at where the ice field plunged over the huge overhanging rock band. Stones rattled down the ice and I thought of the desperate position they must have been in. They were in a full-blown storm, not some vicious passing thunderstorm, and the avalanches spewing down the ice field must have been frightening.

"Remember Anna Jossi saying she saw Angerer, the guy with the head injury, slumped here, not moving?" Ray said.

"God, it must have been awful," I said fervently.

I stared at the ice field, imagining their crouched, battered figures hacking a stance from the ice, trying to find good placements for the pitons. I thought of Hinterstoisser moving out to one side searching for a crack in the rock while Angerer crouched passively on the ice, a bloody bandage wrapped around his head. I imagined the sudden heavy rush of that final avalanche or the thunder of the rocks that swept Hinterstoisser cartwheeling helplessly out into the void. I thought of the brutal impact of Kurz's and Anger's falling bodies wrenching Rainer hard against his belay piton and strangling the life from him. I shuddered at the thought of Kurz's last moments.

"What time is it?" Ray asked, breaking the spell.

"Nearly five. Why?"

"I sort of expected to see those Brits appear by now."

"Yeah, that's a point," I said. "I was worrying about the solo climber. Do you think he survived?"

Ray gave an eloquent shrug of his shoulders. His grimace confirmed what I already feared.

"Shit!" I muttered and got to my feet. I tied myself into the end of the green rope and pulled some slack free from beneath the sleeping mats. "Here, watch me on this," I said to Ray, handing him the rope. "I'm just going to go up and have a look around the corner. They might be coming down."

"Watch it, kid," Ray warned. "There's a lot of crap coming down." I nodded and stepped past him, grabbing a tattered length of fixed rope that was tied to a rocky outcrop 20 feet above me. I used it to swing myself out to the left onto the slushy névé of the ice field and then pulled myself hand over hand up the rope. Clipping a sling to the piton that the weatherworn rope was tied to I leaned around the corner and peered up the First Ice Field.

"Any sign?" Ray asked.

Above me the ice field angled up for 300 feet until it ended at a rock band. I saw the distinctive white line of the Ice Hose cutting left to right through the rock band. It appeared thin and unstable. A flurry of snow drifted down. There was no sign of the climbers. Large chunks of ice peeled off the edge of the Second Ice Field.

There was an unusual slumping sound and a cluster of ice chunks rained down as if something large was coming. I swung quickly behind the rock and ducked my helmeted head down low. It was a strange noise that I couldn't explain. It was neither a heavy impact nor a slithering sound. I cautiously raised my head and examined the Ice Hose with a critical eye. I had been worrying about it all day, curious to see how hard an obstacle it might be. The ice appeared honeycombed and rotten. I swung hurriedly back down to the ledge as another volley of rocks sprayed down the ice field.

"What does it look like?" Ray said with excited impatience.

"It's no distance away at all," I said, grinning. "If this stonefall eases up we could run the ropes up to the Ice Hose this evening and then climb them quickly in the morning. We'd be there in less than an hour."

"Really? That's brilliant. What about the Ice Hose?"

"Not good," I shrugged. "Hey, I'm getting excited about this, youth. I've got a gut feeling about this one. I think it will go."

"But what about those other guys?"

"I don't know," I said gravely. "They must be climbing. I kept seeing chunks of ice tumbling down, the sort of stuff that comes down when you're digging out stances, clearing ice to place screws, that sort of thing."

"Going up?" Ray said incredulously.

"I know, that's what I was thinking," I said, settling into a sitting position on the mats. "It doesn't make sense."

Ray shook his head and stared at the rocks bounding down the First Ice Field.

"What I don't understand is that they're climbing themselves into a trap," I said. "Think about it. If they're on the Second Ice Field now the chances of being hit are horrendous."

"You know, our cock-up with the sack-hauling might have been a blessing in disguise," Ray pointed out.

"How do you mean?"

"If we hadn't wasted all that time we might be up there with them by now."

"No bloody way. We're too cowardly for that," I said. "It's only a couple of rappels back down to here. We would have been running for shelter the minute we saw that thing overdeveloping."

"Yeah, you're right."

"Even if they get to the top of the ice field in one piece what are they planning on doing?" I asked and Ray shook his head. "They'll get some shelter from the rock wall at the upper rim but then they'll have to traverse right across towards the Flat Iron and up that to Death Bivouac."

"The crap coming down the Spider would be lethal," Ray added.

"Jesus, I hope they're not hurt," I said and stared into Ray's eyes. "We're nearest to them. We'd have to go and help them . . . " I left the question unspoken, feeling a little scared.

"Would you go up?" Ray asked quietly. I stared at the First Ice Field as more stones zipped past, then I looked back at Ray. He seemed troubled. I thought of Simon and Mal, who had put so much on the line to save my life on Siula Grande and Pachermo.

"We'd have no choice," I said somberly. "We'd have to make an attempt at least. I'd have to go."

Ray looked away. "I'd go with you, kid," he said and we were silent. The sudden excitement of seeing the way ahead and knowing we were in a good position to climb the wall had dissipated.

"Shit!" I swore again and looked at Ray. Already I was mulling over the practicalities of a possible rescue that in my heart of hearts I was crying out not to have to attempt.

"I've got my emergency first-aid kit," I said. "It's not much."

"We've got to reach them first."

"If they need help it will depend on where they are," I said, trying to work out a plan."

"What are you thinking?"

"Well, first we'll have to climb the Ice Hose—if we can. Then we'll see what it's like. No point killing ourselves."

"Agreed."

"We'd have to lower whoever is injured down the Ice Hose, then we could double our ropes and do a single lower to here."

"What if they're both injured? What if . . . "

"I dunno," I muttered and shook my head irritably. "We'll have to decide when we get there but we'll have to get them off the ice field. They'll be too exposed otherwise. It might be better to fix lines from where they are and get them up to the shelter of the rim, wait for a rescue helicopter there. Dig a big stance in the ice. I . . . " I trailed off as I caught Ray's expression.

"We'll go if we have to," Ray said quietly.

"How will we know?"

"We could phone Simon," he suggested and I stared at him in astonishment.

"Phone Simon? What the hell are you talking about?"

"You've got your mobile with you," Ray pointed out and laughed at my expression.

"Good God, I'd forgotten about that," I said and felt the tiny phone in my chest pocket.

"Good things, modern gadgets, eh?"

I stood up and moved to the far left edge of the ledge, peering down the line of the Hinterstoisser. A familiar sound came whirring up from the valley. Helicopter! I glanced at Ray in surprise and he got to his feet and moved over to my side.

"Where is it?" he said as we scanned the sky. The whop-whop-

whop sound of the rotors was creating confusing echoes that bounced off the surrounding walls. The din rapidly grew in volume, thudding back off the walls in disconcerting reverberations.

"Down there!" I shouted, pointing straight below us. "Coming up the Shattered Pillar. It's heading towards us."

We watched as a red helicopter with a white cross on its door rose in a steady series of climbing circles. We could look straight down into the spinning disc of the rotors flashing with a strobe-light effect. A man was hanging far out from the doors, searching the face.

"It looks like Hanspeter," I said.

With a great roaring noise the helicopter rose up until it was hovering directly opposite us, only a hundred feet away. Ray and I held up our thumbs to indicate that we were safe and Hanspeter waved back in acknowledgment. The helicopter suddenly peeled away in a great spiraling arc out over the meadows, losing height rapidly.

"Well, that was nice of them," I said. "They must have been worried about us and just came over to check us out."

"I'm not sure about that," Ray said as he tracked the path of the helicopter. "Look, it's coming back. Why would it do that if it knows we're safe?"

I watched as the aircraft hovered down near the screes at the foot of the face, making steady beats sideways across the face, gradually gaining height.

"What are they doing?" Ray asked.

"Searching," I replied. "They're looking for something—or someone," I added.

"The soloist?"

"Yeah, that's what I was thinking." The helicopter had flown level with the top of the First Pillar, some 2000 feet below us.

"Hang on," I said. "It's landing. They've seen something."

"Landing? On what?"

"The First Pillar," I said, staring through the viewfinder. "They've put down a skid on the top. Two guys have just jumped out."

The helicopter immediately rose up and curved away to hover above the safety of the meadows. I watched as two figures wearing red guides' jackets ran from the top of the pillar in towards the face. They appeared to be crouching as they moved rapidly to the left of the pillar and then slowed down. One man knelt down, gently examining something lying on the rubble-strewn ledge. I watched as he spoke into a radio. Then both men rose and ran back to the top of the Pillar. The helicopter immediately swung in towards the face in a smooth curve to place one skid delicately on the rocks and the two men jumped aboard. It rose quickly, climbing steadily in the sky above the meadows before turning and flying directly towards Kleine Scheidegg. I felt a cold cramping sensation in my stomach.

"Someone must have fallen," I said. "They've found a body down there."

"Are you sure?" Ray asked. "Why didn't they put it in the helicopter then?"

"Too dangerous," I replied and watched rocks roll down the ice field and launch into space to fall directly in line with the First Pillar. "I think they took a big risk just doing what they did."

"Are you sure it's a body?" Ray persisted. "It might just have been a rucksack, some debris. There's plenty around."

"They knew exactly where to look. They'd seen something fall. I'll bet it was the solo climber." I glanced up at the top of the First Ice Field and caught Ray's questioning expression.

"I know," I said. "Just what I was thinking. How could anyone have fallen without us noticing? Maybe you're right and I'm just being paranoid."

"Ring Simon Wells," Ray urged. "If that was Hanspeter then he'll have been talking to Simon."

I fiddled with my mobile. My fingers felt shaky. I heard the number being dialed and then there was a click.

"Hello?"

"Simon?" I said, recognizing his voice with relief. "It's Joe."

"Joe! God, Joe, you're alive! Thank God for that. You're alive," he said, in a rushed, relieved tone.

"Well, yes," I said, realizing with dread that it meant someone else wasn't. "We're fine. We're safe."

"I kept ringing your mobile and getting this stupid recorded message. I was sure it meant you were dead."

"I'd just turned it off to save the batteries," I said. "What's happened, Simon? What did the helicopter find?"

"Hang on, Joe." There was silence and then I heard Simon talking into a radio. "Are you there, Joe?"

"Yeah, still here," I said. "What's going on?"

"They've found the others."

"Others? More than one?"

"Yes. Look, you know those two lads who were climbing above you?"

My stomach tightened. I glanced at Ray, who was watching my conversation intently. "What of them?"

"They're dead, Joe." Simon paused. "Hanspeter was looking through his binoculars and he saw the lead climber fall from the top rim of the ice field. We thought it was you. We'd been monitoring you all day."

"What do you mean, he fell?" I said, somewhat exasperated. "Maybe it was a rucksack?" I added hopefully.

"No," Simon said insistently. "It was them. We had the camera running. We rewound the film. They both fell. The leader hadn't put any gear in on the ice field. They were moving together. The second was pulled off. They're gone."

"Have they found them?"

"Yes. Down by the First Pillar. There's too much rockfall to get them off . . . "

"Hang on, Simon," I interrupted him and moved to the edge of the ledge. I looked down at where the bodies had been found and back up the ice field above me. "We never saw anything. Never heard a thing." I thought of that strange, heavy, slumping sound.

"They went straight over the top of you," Simon said bluntly. "We saw the fall."

"Oh, God, no. Look, I'll ring you back," I said and closed the phone. I turned to Ray, who was looking quizzically at me. "Those lads are dead." He swore and turned away, rubbing his face with his hands. I explained what Simon had seen and for a long moment we stood silently on the ledge staring at the huge drop beneath us. Ray moved to one side and crouched down, resting his head in his hands. I stared out at the storm destroying itself on the rock buttresses of the Wetterhorn. It was strangely beautiful. I felt dazed and wondered whether I was simply trying to see what was good and ignore what I had learned from Simon. I felt detached and thought of the lads falling and what it must have been like. I thought selfishly of myself and felt ashamed. We wouldn't have to attempt a rescue now. I watched as the light and colors danced in the dying storm clouds. For a long silent moment I was lost, trying desperately to understand what had happened. I lowered myself to the mat and put my head in my hands. I wanted to cry for them but I didn't know how.

Stones clacked by, shaking me from my thoughts and I looked wordlessly at Ray. I could see in his eyes what he was thinking. *It could have been us.*

"I didn't see anything," he said helplessly. "Didn't hear anything." He looked up at the boundary wall above the Hinterstoisser and we did not need to answer his question. They had cleared the First Ice Field in one sickening free fall out into the chasm 3000 feet below.

I felt weak at the thought.

"What do we do now?" I said and Ray swore in frustration. "Do we carry on?"

"I don't know," Ray said. "What do you think?"

"Nothing's changed," I said callously. "I mean, the weather forecast, our plans. If it's fine tomorrow we can carry on."

"I suppose you're right," Ray said hesitantly and I shared the feeling that we might be doing something wrong. The joy had been instantly extinguished from the climb. My phone rang shrilly in my pocket.

"Hi, Joe. It's Simon. Look, I don't know what your plans are but I should tell you that Hanspeter has said that the forecast has changed. There's bad weather moving in tomorrow—I don't know how bad. Then it should improve over the following two days. I just thought you might need to know."

"Yes. Thanks." I glanced at my watch. It read a quarter to six. Dark in three hours, maybe less. "By the way Simon, when did the lads fall?"

"Oh, about forty-five minutes ago. About five o'clock."

"Right," I said, thinking of the strange sound when I had looked up at the Ice Hose. "I see."

"What are you going to do?"

"Ray?" I called. "Bad weather tomorrow. Do we sit it out and go up or go down now to the Stollenloch?" Ray held my gaze for a moment and then nodded his head downwards. I smiled in agreement.

"Simon," I spoke into the phone. "We're coming down. We'll head for the Stollenloch but we have to get ourselves sorted out first. There's a lot of rockfall so we'll be slow."

"Okay, I'll get Hanspeter to ask the railway people to leave the doors open at the entrance to the tunnel. We'll be in the hotel. We'll wait up for you. Be careful."

"Will do and thanks." I closed the phone. "Let's get the hell out of here," I said, even as I watched Ray rolling up his sleeping mat.

At half past six I grasped the fixed rope leading down the vertical crack towards the Hinterstoisser Traverse and swung myself off the ledge.

"Be careful, kid," Ray said. "And clip everything you can."

I lowered myself swiftly hand over hand down the weathered rope, glad of the chance to be doing something instead of brooding on what had happened. When I reached the edge of the traverse I saw that it was streaming with water. A few rocks hissed by and flew harmlessly into space off the ice field above, rattling down the wall below. Reversing the traverse was awkward. I clipped my ropes behind me through the line of old pegs to safeguard Ray and skittered across the slippery, wet rock.

When I reached the belay at the far end I had to raise the hood of my jacket. Water was flooding off the top of the wall, coursing down my sleeves, and soaking my arms as I held the fixed ropes. I yelled up at Ray to come down and felt the ropes moving.

The sun was low on the horizon, bathing the face in warm light. I glanced down at the First Pillar, now swathed in frigid shadows, and tried not to dwell on what lay there. Ray and I had a job to do as safely and as efficiently as possible. That was all there was to consider.

I watched as Ray swung across the wall with water spattering across his shoulders and rucksack. The sunshine glittered on the silver streams. I glanced at the horizon and knew that we would not get to the Stollenloch before darkness fell. I dropped my ruck-sack to the ground and found my head torch. As I was fastening it to my helmet Ray swung down to the stance. I looked at the ground we had to cover to reach the top of the Difficult Crack. I remembered that protection was sparse on the way up and we had clipped only a couple of pitons on each rope length. Down-climbing the traverse was our fastest descent option but it would be awkward and if either of us slipped the consequences were all too obvious.

"What do you reckon? Downclimb or rappel?" I said.

"Rappel," Ray replied confidently.

"It's all sideways. It might be a bitch getting the ropes down."

"It will but we're in no rush. Let's be super slow, super safe, eh?"

"Fair enough."

We threaded the ropes through the belay, coiled them, and threw them out and sideways. They hit the first snow ledge and rolled into a bundle of tangled loops. I slid down the ropes and painstakingly freed the knotted coils and threw the ropes down separately. There was a high-pitched sound and I ducked as a handful of rocks peppered the slope to my right. Glancing up, I saw that we were moving out from the protection of the rock wall.

The light was fading fast by the time we gathered at the top of the gully leading down to the Difficult Crack. Ray pulled the ropes through as I threaded the next rappel point. Stones had been falling almost continuously since we had left the Hinterstoisser. I felt oddly detached. It didn't concern me that I might be hit. There was nothing I could do about it so I simply ignored the impact sounds around me. As I stood watching Ray making his way cautiously down towards me, ducking as rocks hit close by, it occurred to me that we were doing exactly what we had read about in so many books. It was a strangely surreal thought.

As I began to rappel down the gully I switched on my head torch and looked up at Ray. He was grinning broadly and I realized with a start that he was enjoying himself. I realized that I, too, was grinning. We were in control. All was well. It was a matter of some pride. Even though our plans had been wrecked I was pleased that we could retreat calmly and in good order. Making the right decisions and acting competently in a stressful situation was almost as satisfying as a successful ascent.

I reached the top of the Difficult Crack and tried to see whether the rappel would reach the belay ledge beneath the roof. The beam of my head torch picked out the ropes as I flicked them out into space and tried to guess whether they were long enough. I decided that they would just reach on the stretch of the ropes and lowered myself down into the airy space of the corner. My boots touched the ledge just as the knot in the end of the ropes came hard against my hand. Clipping myself to a bolt, I carefully released the ropes from the belay plate and kept a tight hold on the knot.

"Okay." I heard Ray's faint cry of acknowledgment that the

ropes ran free and I let the knotted rope ends bounce away up into the darkness above me. A few moments later there was a scrabbling sound and rocks dislodged by Ray tumbled down the corner as he stepped down the gully. I ducked under the protection of the roof.

"It won't budge," Ray muttered as he heaved down on the green rope holding the knot joining the two ropes.

"Here, let me help." I reached over and added my weight to the rope. It stretched, slipped a few inches, then held fast.

"Bugger." Ray eased the pressure on the rope. "That's the last thing we need."

"I've put this cam on the rope," I said, indicating the small brass camming device gripping the rope tightly. "If I stand in this sling I can jump off the ledge and put my entire weight onto it."

"Is that wise?"

"I'll tie into the other bloody rope. I'm not a complete idiot." I tied off a length of the blue rope to the piton and clipped it to my waist. "The sudden impact might rip it free. I reckon it's jammed in that thin crack at the top of the gully."

"You'll go flying," Ray pointed out helpfully.

"Thanks. I know," I said, glancing down into the darkness below. I checked that the blue rope was secure. "Okay. Let's pull as much stretch down as we can."

When we could gain no more rope I took a deep breath and jumped off the ledge with the sling wrapped around my boot, tensing for the sudden jerk and the fall. I bounced in the air a foot lower than the ledge, feeling rather stupid—and Ray burst out laughing.

"Ah, well, bugger that for a game of soldiers. I'll climb up the green. You belay me on the blue."

"It might pull free."

"I'll clip the pegs in the crack as I go."

"It's not worth it," Ray said firmly. "It's just a rope."

"It's brand-new," I complained.

"It's still not worth your life," Ray said. "Leave it, youth." He let go of the green rope and it sprang up into the darkness out of reach. He untied the knot, releasing the blue rope.

"If we go straight down we should be able to reach the stance where we made that long traverse to the left," Ray pointed out. "After that we won't need a double rope."

"Well, we haven't got one now, have we?" I said sharply. "Is it more than 30 meters (100 feet)?" I added, peering down into the darkness.

"You'll find out," Ray said confidently as he threaded the single blue rope through the belay, knotted the ends, and dropped the doubled coils down the wall below. They disappeared into the darkness. I peered anxiously into the depths, whipping the rope out with my hands, trying to spot the knot. I could see nothing.

Forty feet from the end of the ropes I caught sight of a snow-covered ledge. The knot swung disconcertingly high above the snow. As my feet touched it the rope was at full stretch and I struggled to release it from the belay plate. I glanced along the ledge that ran to the left. It was about 18 inches wide and covered with wet snow lying on top of loose scree. Gripping one end of the rope I searched for a piton or a crack into which I could place a wire. I was sure that there was a belay somewhere near me but in the darkness and the flickering light of my head torch I could find nothing. The rock was compact and featureless. Reluctantly, I let the rope go and it whipped out of reach. I shouted up for Ray to come down and then stood still, keenly aware of the gulf behind me. I knew that there was reasonably easy ground from where I stood leading to the door of the Stollenloch tunnel 300 or 400 feet horizontally to my right. We were nearly there. I began to relax.

With heart-stopping abruptness a rock the size of a football thudded into the snow ledge 6 feet to my right. It hurtled off into the night. I listened as it cracked down the wall, dislodging a flurry of smaller rocks. Fright galvanized me into action and I frantically searched the rock wall again, spotted a hairline crack, and pounded a knife-blade piton into it until the eye was hard against the rock. It was impressive how fear could make previously invisible things suddenly apparent. I clipped myself securely to it just as a shower of stones rushed down from the wall above, striking me painfully on the arm.

Ray came swiftly down the ropes and landed beside me on the stretch.

"That's a piece of luck," he said as he released the rope and pulled one end down to him. "I didn't think it would reach."

"Thanks for telling me," I said and he laughed.

"Did you hear that rockfall?" Ray said. "I was hit on the shoulder."

"Are you okay?" I asked.

"I'm fine, just bruised." He shrugged nonchalantly. "Let's keep going."

At ten o'clock I traversed across the broken, snowy ledge towards the yellow rock wall at the base of the Röte Fluh. My head-torch beam picked out the dark shadow of the Stollenloch door set into the rock. Clipping the bolts by the door I dropped my rucksack to the floor and shouted for Ray to come across. As he stepped up onto the ledge outside the door I reached an arm around him and gave him an uncharacteristic hug, feeling slightly self-conscious. I thought of Tat and knew he would have squeezed the life out of me in the same circumstances. Ray was grinning broadly and clapping me on the back.

"Well done, kid. Well done," he said.

"And you. I'll ring Simon, let him know we're safe."

I had to extend two 8-foot slings from the bolt and hang far out over the face before I received any reception. Even then I kept getting cut off just as I heard Simon answer the phone. After five attempts I pulled myself back into the doorway.

"Come on, kid, forget it. Let's go," Ray said.

"I can't," I replied. "Simon heard me trying to get through. If we don't tell him that we're safe he might think we're in trouble and call out a rescue."

"Damn."

"Hi, Simon? Is that you?" I said as the phone rang.

"Joe? Are you guys okay?" His voice sounded strained and concerned. He had endured a long, bad day.

"Simon, we're fine. We're in the Stollenloch. We're safe."

"That's great news. We were getting worried. It's been four hours . . ."

"It wasn't easy, mate. Rockfall, lost ropes, darkness. You know the score. Listen, we're heading down the tunnel now. Should be with you by eleven, I reckon."

"Good. Hanspeter says the door has been left open for you. We've got food here for you. We'll be waiting."

"Hey, get some beers in for us before the bar closes, will you?"

"We got the lot, don't worry."

"What about Heinz and Scott and the boys? Did they get off the wall?"

"Yeah, they're safe, bivouacking on the Mittellegi Ridge right now."

"That's grand news. See you soon." I closed the phone and smiled at Ray. "Let's go, Ray. It's over."

We hurriedly stuffed our harnesses and hardware into our sacks, coiled the rope, and clipped our axes and crampons onto their holders. As Ray heaved at the wooden door, releasing a latch, it suddenly burst open with the force of the updraft, almost pushing him off balance. I chuckled as he stumbled and grabbed at the walls for support. Squeezing through the trapdoor, we emerged into a strange greenish light faintly illuminating the tunnel. We pulled the door shut and dropped the latch and the wind instantly stopped. It was silent, calm, and warm. I stared at an incongruous green neon sign advertising beer, chocolate, or something inane and then stared at the wooden door. One moment we were exposed to rockfall on the north face of the Eiger, next minute we were reading adverts.

"Bizarre," I muttered. "It's almost as if today never happened."

"I know," Ray said as he turned to walk down the narrow boardwalk running alongside the rack railway. "It would be funny but for those lads."

The tunnel seemed to go on forever as we tramped down at a toe-bashing angle, leaving the green neon glow behind. At one point Ray slipped on some grease stain on the wooden boardwalk and crashed onto the rails. His torch flickered out. He cursed and struggled to his feet. It was pitch black. It would have been a nightmare without our torches. Half an hour later we trudged out of the tunnel entrance and walked through the deserted Eiger Gletscher station. The lights of the hotels at Kleine Scheidegg sparkled half an hour's walk below us. Suddenly I felt weary. It hadn't been a hard day, but knowing during our descent that two men lay broken and lifeless on the rocks beneath us had gotten to me. I let Ray stride ahead and followed slowly, thinking about the mountain. I wondered whether it was worth the risks. I knew in my heart that I still wanted to climb the face but some of my romantic idealism about the route had been destroyed.

They had known the risks, I told myself. *We all do. Nothing's changed—not for us anyway.* When we came around the curved ridge leading down to Kleine Scheidegg I looked back at the vast black amphitheater silhouetted against a starlit night sky. In its center the gallery windows' light glowed gold from the black depths of the wall. I wished we were still up there, regretting our decision to retreat. It had been there for the taking. We might not get another chance. I wondered whether Ray still wanted to try again. *Maybe not this year.*

As we pushed open the glass doors of the hotel I saw Simon Wells standing in the foyer, smiling at us. He came forward and put his arm around my shoulders.

"It's good to see you, Joe, I thought I had just watched you die." He looked subdued. "Worst day of my life." He looked shattered and it suddenly dawned on me what he had gone through. It must have been an awful experience to have witnessed the death of a friend whom you had known for fifteen years and have to wait helplessly as the guides went to recover his body. We were in the middle of it. All we had to do was deal with our situation. It was what we knew. For Simon it must have been agonizing.

Simon's immediate reaction had been one of denial when Hanspeter had put down his binoculars and said, "Scheiss! They've gone. They've fallen."

They had all stood in shocked silence for a moment. What had been a game had suddenly become a harsh reality. Everyone knew it was a dangerous climb but it is only climbers who fully understand the risk. Mark then remembered that the camera had been running and focused on the two climbers. They rewound the film and played it back and there it was—the shattering sight of two men falling to their deaths from the Second Ice Field.

I had never witnessed a man fall to his death as some of my friends have and I felt it might corrode whatever flimsy rationale I had erected to convince myself that taking risks was an acceptable thing to do.

"Come on in," Simon said. "We've got food for you . . . "

"Beer?"

"Yes, plenty of beer." Simon led us through to a room with a table laden with sandwiches and cold meats. He opened two bottles of lager and Ray and I chinked bottles and drank deeply. I had no appetite for the food, even though we had eaten only a few snacks since the morning. Simon passed round a bottle of vodka and I drank hungrily and passed it on to Mark Stokes, the cameraman.

"Thanks," he said. "And welcome back."

"Hey, did any of you lot see what happened to the solo climber?" I asked and was met by blank faces.

"What solo climber?" Simon asked and I explained the man that we had seen on the Difficult Crack.

"No, we never saw him."

"Well, he was on the face in the middle of all of that. In fact when we saw the helicopter we were both sure that it was he who had fallen. To hear that a two-man roped party had fallen was a real shock. We couldn't understand how that could have happened."

"Actually, it's strange," Mark Stokes said. "When Hanspeter said he had seen you fall there was a whole group of us standing around the camera and obviously it caused quite a stir. I remember this tourist standing near me. He was British. He just said something like, "Wow! That's the second guy I've seen falling today.""

"You're kidding?" I stared at Mark.

"No. I remember thinking what an odd thing to say and then we had so much on our minds with checking the film, knowing that you had fallen, and sorting out the helicopter I sort of forgot about it. I just put it down to some dumb tourist who didn't know what he was talking about—but maybe he did see something."

"We'd better talk to Hanspeter in the morning," Ray said. "If he didn't fall he might be hurt or in some sort of trouble. It's odd that no one saw him on the Second Ice Field, though."

"Yeah, and the only way he could retreat was to come past us and we saw no one," I added. "Here, pass me that vodka. I need another drink. This is a bad day."

We talked long into the night, drank too much, and then tottered off to bed. Ray and I had planned to bivouac on the patio outside the hotel but Simon insisted on putting us up in the Edwardian luxury of the Scheidegg Hotel. I fell into bed unwashed and unsettled.

HALF SILENCES

I AWOKE IN THE MIDDLE OF THE NIGHT feeling disorientated. *What was I doing in a comfortable bed under a down duvet?* Thinking I was bivouacked at the Swallow's Nest, I thought I must be in some strange dream and I had to wake up. I saw moonlight through the windows and the humped shape of Ray snoring in the adjacent bed and remembered the storm and the two lads falling. I got up and drank water from the tap, drenched my face in the basin, and went over to the window to stare at the Eiger. It was going to be with me forever.

The following morning after breakfast Simon mentioned that a guide and a policeman were coming to the hotel to debrief everyone and take a statement about what had happened. I walked into the foyer and saw Mark fiddling with the camera.

"What's up?" I said.

"Oh, we're making a digital copy of the fall for the authorities. The police and guides requested a copy to take with them after the debrief. It's here now. I've just rewound it."

"Listen, Mark," I said. "I'd like to see it if I could. I know it sounds odd, but I'm not being morbid. I've been thinking about it all morning. I need to know what those lads did wrong. People don't usually fall like that; not roped together anyway. It's bugging the hell out of me. What on earth happened to them?"

"That's no problem, Joe," Mark replied. "Here—you can view it through the eyepiece. It's color film but you'll only see it in black and white in this mode. I've seen it a number of times and it doesn't make sense to me, but then I'm not a climber. Maybe you can work it out, see something I missed."

I stepped up to the eyepiece of the camera feeling unsure about whether I wanted to see the fall. I glanced at Ray, who looked troubled. Then I took a deep breath and bent over the eyepiece as Mark ran the film. I knew that I had to see what had happened, not out of any macabre curiosity but because I needed to know, for my peace of mind. I had to find out why. If I didn't see the fall I would always be plagued with doubt about exactly what had occurred above us that day.

The ice field flickered into view and I spotted a tiny figure crouched against the ice. Following the ropes above him led my eye to the leader, who was traversing the edge of the upper ice field, walking sideways to his left, stepping one foot over the other on the rim between the rock and the ice. I glanced at where his partner perched on a blackened crest of ice protruding from the ice field 150 feet below him. The dark rocks bounding the top of the ice field were spattered with patches of wet snow.

As the leader traversed leftwards, stepping carefully on the swath of soft wet snow that had accumulated on the upper rim, I saw his ropes draped down the ice field, swinging to the left as he moved away from the climbing line of his partner. Suddenly the soft snow slipped away beneath him.

The fall was slow, almost lazy. He stepped across his left foot with his right and planted his feet parallel to the ice field. Then he fell. He wasn't hit by falling rocks and there was no indication of a hard impact, no sudden, violent loss of balance. His feet simply slithered away beneath him and he went down onto his right hip and then onto his flank.

It seemed to be the fall of a tired man—a typical slip that every climber has experienced at some point in his climbing career.

The figure twisted round swiftly onto his stomach, raised his ice axe, and aimed a hard blow at the ice field, to little effect. The band of soft snow absorbed the ice pick but gave no purchase.

Immediately he swung with his other axe but it cut through just as easily as the first. He tried again with the axe. Nothing happened. He still seemed to be sliding down with deceptive, almost languid slowness. It seemed as if he could stop this whole irritating affair at any moment with ease. As he made a final swing with his axe—more hurried as if with the first hint of desperation—his body moved onto the snow-free hard ice and he accelerated away with brutal abruptness. There were no more blows from the axe. He hurtled down with frightening acceleration in a long, smooth slide. There was no tumbling, no indication that his crampons had caught and flipped him over; he simply fell away.

His partner appeared to be looking at him. He did nothing, since there was nothing to be done. The now loose ropes connecting the climbers whipped downwards. I waited to see the rope come tight against an ice screw. There were no sudden jerks, no angular tension in the line of the rope to indicate that a screw had temporarily halted the fall. The leader fell away to the second's left side straight down the 750-foot ice field—a dark shape whipping past his colleague in a blur. Then, in a fluid motion, the second was ripped away and followed him down. I winced. There was no resistance. There had been no belay. They had been moving together without the protection of ice screws.

They fell directly in line with the Swallow's Nest, positioned on the edge of the First Ice Field, which was separated from the Second Ice Field by a rock band some 200 feet high. I knew that we were in the picture somewhere and shuddered. The pair flew off the ice and into the air and began the long fall down to the broken rocks at the foot of the face; a fall of nearly 3000 feet.

I stood up abruptly, feeling shaky. "No belay, no gear," I said incredulously.

"I know," Mark nodded.

"They just fell," I said in confusion. "Nothing hit them, nothing."

Ray stepped up to the eyepiece as Mark replayed the short

segment of film, then pulled away sharply the moment he saw the leader begin to fall, not wishing to see any more.

"I expected them to be hit by rocks, but they just slipped," he said, staring at me. "It looked so commonplace, something we've all done."

"I know, but not there, with that stonefall, not there," I said and turned away. We walked out into the sunshine and I lit a cigarette and inhaled deeply.

"I wish I hadn't seen that now," I said, feeling subdued.

"I don't," Ray said firmly. "I know what they did wrong now. I know we won't make the same mistakes."

"But they made so many mistakes," I persisted. "It doesn't make sense. Why move together in that rockfall? Why no ice screws at least? Why didn't they back off? If they hadn't fallen off they were climbing into a nightmare on the Flat Iron."

"We all make mistakes, Joe," Ray said, "for all sorts of reasons. Maybe they were scared—stressed out—not thinking straight. That ice field must have been terrifying. Remember what Simon said about watching them ducking and trying to take shelter all the way up?"

"All the more reason to put gear in. Stones are no respecters of climbing ability."

"Well, they took a gamble and it didn't pay off," Ray said. "Perhaps they thought the climbing on the ice field was easy, so moving together was the fastest option. Their decision-making was bad, but we all get it wrong sometimes. With luck they might have gotten away with it and we'd be none the wiser."

"Maybe," I shrugged. "It doesn't matter now, I suppose. It just makes me angry."

"Look, they were simply doing what we wanted to do, climbing the Eiger, living a dream. It was their choice and their risk. We can't blame them for that."

"No, I know. You're right," I agreed. "Hell, I've screwed up enough times in the past, so who am I to talk?"

"I suspect you wouldn't have done that, though," Ray said.

"Too cowardly?"

"Too experienced, I'd say."

Hanspeter and a policeman arrived and we went inside to give our statements. When I asked about the solo climber neither the policeman nor Hanspeter seemed overly concerned, which puzzled me. I had thought that a search of the face with a helicopter was the least that should be done, but the official policy seemed to be that if no relatives requested a search then nothing would be done. It seemed a strange policy to me. I pointed out that the three of us had seen the climber and he had never been seen again but it was to no avail. If the man had turned up in Grindelwald, having told no one about his plans for the Eiger, how would any relatives begin to know where to initiate a search?

The mystery deepened a few hours later when Heinz Zak and Scott Muir arrived at the hotel, having descended from the summit that morning. They were stunned to hear of the fatalities and even more appalled to learn that the party had been moving together without protection. Heinz Zak pointed out that the ice had been perfect and that good screws could have been set quickly.

"I don't understand it," I agreed. "Perhaps they were distracted. That rockfall would have been very stressful."

I asked whether anyone had seen the solo climber. Everyone presumed he had retreated in the face of the obviously deteriorating weather. Yet no one had come past us. Perhaps he had come to grief trying to rappel down the Ice Hose? We would never know.

I mentioned to Hanspeter that an English tourist had spoken of seeing two falls that day but the feeling was that either the solo climber would turn up or some day his remains might be found at the foot of the face. I let the matter rest, although it disturbed me. I glanced up at the wall and hoped he was climbing safely out of the Exit Cracks as we chatted in the sunshine. In truth, I felt certain that he was dead. I remembered the huge waterfalls and the curtains of hail and the endless noise of the rockfall.

Early that afternoon Ray and I boarded the train and rode down to Grindelwald. I didn't look at the face as the train rattled past its base. We walked slowly, feeling subdued and introspective, up to the front door of the chalet and were surprised when it flew open and there were Alice Steuri and Anna Jossi staring at us as if we were ghosts. Anna threw up her arms.

"You are alive! You are alive!" she cried and held her face in the palms of her hands, looking as if she were about to cry. "Those poor boys. So bad, so bad."

"We heard about the accident," Alice said. "We heard it was two Englishmen so we knew it was you. It was so terrible."

"I have come from the church," Anna said. "I was saying a prayer for you boys. So many times they do not come back and now, again, it had happened. I was very sad. But you are alive. It is a miracle." She opened her arms and hugged us both affectionately.

We were quite taken aback. We had been so caught up in events that we had completely forgotten that Alice and Anna might have been concerned for our welfare. We apologized profusely but they kept smiling and thanking God.

That evening we drank gin on the lawn and watched the sun setting on the Eiger.

"We've got a week left," Ray said. "Shall we have another go?"

I stared at the face, remembering the film.

"I'm not sure I want to," I said.

"Good," Ray said. "That's what I was thinking. We could go somewhere else, I suppose. Maybe have a look at the Piz Badile?"

"No, I've had my fill of climbing," I said, glancing at Ray. "Let's go home."

"Tomorrow?"

"Might as well. I've had enough of looking at that thing," I said, nodding at the Eiger.

"I'd still like to climb it," Ray replied, looking expectant. "I really enjoyed being up there. I want to go back. How about it? Next winter? Next summer?"

"Yeah, maybe," I said uncertainly. "I'm not sure what I think right now. I don't want to die on that bastard," I said vehemently. "I said that on Chaupi Orco after the avalanche. I said it after Alea Jacta Est with Tat. I said it after Siula Grande and Pachermo. I've said it a lot. And one day it will happen. Perhaps I should listen to myself. I'm tired of all this . . . this death thing . . . " I waved my hand helplessly at the mountains.

"I know," Ray agreed. "But I don't want to leave it on this note. It's been everything to us. We can't end like this. It could have been so good, meeting Anna Jossi and Heckmair, and all that. It still can be."

"Do you think so?" I looked at Ray, who shrugged. "I'll sleep on it," I added.

The next morning as we packed the gear into the car Anna Jossi came down and invited us into the chalet. Lying on her dining-room table was the Alpiglen hotel register, open at the page where Mehringer and Sedlmayr had signed their names. She asked if we, too, would put our names in the book. We were flattered but protested that we hadn't climbed the wall and didn't deserve to put our names in such a revered book. Anna insisted that we did so.

"You came back," she said solemnly. "That is important. You came back."

We signed our names on a fresh page and took photographs of Anna and the register, and Alice Steuri presented us with gifts of Swiss chocolates in a box incongruously shaped like the north face of the Eiger. As we turned to leave Ray smiled at Anna and said, "We'll see you next year."

"Oh, no," Anna said. "You are not going on the wall again?" She looked searchingly at the pair of us.

"Maybe," Ray said. "We're thinking about it." I said nothing.

As we drove out of Grindelwald I thought of our plan to drive away, having successfully climbed the face, and throwing our climbing gear out of the car windows. It would have been good.

"Hang on," Ray pulled the car into the curb.

"What?"

"We haven't told the girls."

"What girls?"

"The waitresses at the restaurant. They probably think we're dead."

He swung the car around and we drove back into the town and parked in front of the restaurant. We wandered onto the balcony and took our favorite seat in the sunshine.

"You're alive!" a startled voice said behind me and I glanced at Ray.

"This is getting repetitive," I muttered as she rushed off to fetch her friend. They, too, had heard the news of the accident and knew we had been killed.

"I told you it is dangerous," they chorused.

"It's as dangerous as you make it," I qualified their comment and listened as we were told off yet again. When Ray mentioned we might return next year I thought we were going to get our beers poured over our heads. We waved farewell as we drove off on the ten-hour slog back to Holland. Ray took the first three-hour stint at the wheel and I sat brooding on what had happened. I hadn't appreciated how distressing the experience had been. Ray seemed to have dealt with it with pragmatic and sanguine confidence. As far as he was concerned our safe retreat and sensible decisions made him feel all the more sure that we could climb the face safely. It was ironic that the accident seemed to have erased any worries that he had previously held and yet it had hit me harder than I had expected.

For two weeks I wished that I had not chosen to view the film of the fall. The stark black-and-white images kept replaying through my mind. I would wake in the middle of the night with a start, having seen it in my dreams. Sometimes I was watching from a distance and occasionally I awoke in a cold sweat, having somehow become one of the falling figures. There was something chillingly familiar about the film sequence that seemed to be affecting me profoundly. I knew it wasn't the shock of watching the two young men die. We had tried to be rational about it, coldly analyzing what had happened. It evoked a sense of pity for their fate, anger at why it had happened, and a somber realization that it might very well have been us.

I think Simon Wells's obvious distress had probably influenced me most of all. I was suddenly confronted with a friend who believed he had witnessed my death. It made it very personal indeed.

When I returned home I mulled over the idea of returning to the Eiger but because I was unable to get the images of the fall out of my mind I felt uncertain about committing myself to going back. There soon followed a number of reports on the accident in the national papers, some of which were appallingly inaccurate. The habit of taking stories from wire services and believing the facts to be true without making any attempts to check them seemed remarkably irresponsible. Perhaps more importantly than simply being sloppy journalism, it was confusing and upsetting for the relatives and friends of the two men to read such conflicting and inaccurate reports.

Consequently I was telephoned by a representative of the British Mountaineering Council and asked whether I could call Matthew Hayes's brother and describe what had really happened. I was willing to make the call but uneasy. I was angry that people already suffering traumatic grief should be put in this position by shoddy journalism.

When the phone was answered I was taken aback to find that I was talking to Matthew Hayes's mother. At first I didn't know what to say. "Sorry" seemed so inadequate. She was calmly philosophical and remarkably controlled. I tried to describe the storm and the events that had followed but I shied away from offering any criticisms or personal details. She told me that Matthew had been a great fan of my writing and said that he would have loved to have met me. I didn't know how to respond.

The mountains were the love of Matthew's life. He had told his mother that he always felt that if he had a choice in the matter he would prefer, when the time came, to die in the mountains. I understood the sentiment, but as always it made me feel guilty to have survived so many accidents and be a helpless witness to someone else's fate.

Later Matthew's brother rang me. He had introduced Matthew to climbing. This time I was a little more detailed in my account of what had happened and although I had to say that the pair had made mistakes I did not intend to be critical. I knew that his brother, as a fellow climber, would want to know all the details. We both knew that climbers, all climbers, make mistakes. Every friend of mine who has died has at some point made a mistake that has led to their deaths.

When Simon and I did not take enough gas on Siula Grande it was later to force us into a series of actions that led inevitably to the cutting of the rope. It was our fault. When Mal Duff and I moved together in high winds on the north ridge of Pachermo without placing protection I was dragged off when his crampons failed and he fell. I could try and argue that the crampon failure was out of our control but that would be avoiding the issue. A couple of well-placed screws would have saved me from the injuries the fall was to inflict. When I was avalanched on Les Courtes in 1981 I was guilty of being lazy and inexperienced and reckless. I don't suppose anyone could have guessed that the huge rock pedestal that Ian Whittaker and I bivvied on while climbing the Bonatti Pillar on Les Drus would detach and fall into space forty-five minutes later. Our error lay in looking for a bivi ledge after night had fallen. In daylight we might have been able to see that there was something unstable about the pedestal. We were responsible for the subsequent accident and subsequent rescue simply by having made that choice.

Before I had set off for the Eiger I had signed a publishing contract to write a book about what the mountain meant to me. It had always fascinated and repelled me in equal measure. *The White Spider* had an enormous influence on me as a youngster and the images and stories had left an indelible mark upon my mind. Ray and I had wanted to climb the north wall mainly to pay homage to those heroes of ours who had been that way so many years before. If we had succeeded it would have been the crowning achievement of both our climbing lives. As climbers of a generation brought up on a diet of alpine mountaineering literature, the Eiger had dominated our thoughts from the time of our very first alpine seasons. We knew that if we quit climbing without at least having one attempt on the wall we would always regret it.

I had decided to attempt the face long before I thought of writing the book. The book was never meant to be about our climb and it was certainly not dependent on our success. What interested me were the psychological barriers that we would have to confront, the fears and personal weaknesses that might be exposed. In the end the experience exposed rather more than I wished and reawakened bad memories that I had thought had been well buried.

Both Ray and I had reached a crossroads in our mountaineering lives and we had made a choice to make the Eiger our last route. Whether it was age or cynicism, fear or weakness, somehow we both sensed that mountaineering was no longer the passion it had once been for us. I had felt guilty thinking such thoughts, as if it was somehow a betrayal. I had always thought I would just go on and on, returning to the mountains at will until fate took its course.

As it turned out, I fell back in love with the Alps. The time spent in Grindelwald, the people we met, and the climbing we experienced made the trip a very special time for both of us. The fact that it ended so tragically didn't present any reasons for not returning and attempting the face again. If anything, it strengthened our desire to climb the route. It was everything that we had hoped it would be and we didn't want to walk away with that fatal storm as our last climbing memory. We had confronted our own deep-set fears about the climb and come out stronger for the experience. We had a clearer sense of the scale and geography of the route and had been given a graphic reminder of how unexpectedly dangerous the mountain could become, however easy or hard the technical climbing. Above all, and to our enduring delight, we had felt comfortable to be climbing on this famous route and our confidence had been boosted by the experience. We loved every moment of it, even the storm and the stonefall. Feeling confident in such conditions and effecting a safe and efficient retreat was a satisfying confirmation that we knew what we were doing. We had completed a long apprenticeship in the mountains and had a greater depth of experience to draw upon than we had hitherto realized.

At first I could not understand why the sight of two men falling had had such a deep effect on me when Ray had been able to get over the experience so swiftly. I took it as a sign of weakness and felt irritated with myself. Of course such a sight would be upsetting to anyone but it went deeper than simply distress. There was, I realized, something alarmingly familiar about the fall. It was Pachermo all over again. It was almost as if I was seeing myself falling in that same helpless state and it brought back a rush of memories and fears that I hoped I had seen the last of.

As I had viewed the film footage I felt that I knew what these two men were desperately hoping for. I surfaced from the brutal impact of my fall in a concussed and bloodied state. I had been lucky. I saw in those fleeting black-and-white images how it should have been for me and felt shaken. I took it as a warning. It was, I suppose, a purely selfish response that I couldn't help.

When I thought of the fall it took me back to the time I had stood at the Swallow's Nest after hearing the news of the deaths from Simon on the phone. I had looked away at the distant storm clouds broken on the buttresses of the Wetterhorn. The late afternoon sun had lit their bellies with a sheen of gold. Some, still darkened with the last of the storm's fury, roiled in the chill, clear air—vainly putting up a fight, their detonations noiseless now, the flames of lightning muted and compressed as the storm drifted away across the mountain. The light seemed shot through with layered colors as the clouds drifted on the wind and the heat of the sun ate through their disintegrating forms. The cool swirling colors of the fading storm made for a dreamlike air and I felt as if I was floating in the summer shallows of a river pool looking up at the passing clouds. I knew I was trying to see the beauty before my eyes, trying to block out the ugliness of what had just happened.

As the clouds dissipated into smaller separate white layers I recalled being told that clouds are rafts for souls as they drift towards paradise, breaking their bonds with earth. As the departing soul rises the colors become lighter, more refined, blue through gold to the sharpest silver until there is no more than a luminous white, too bright to comprehend. Eternity in its flawless balance can be nothing other than the most brilliant white. I turned and stared into the sun until the intense light seared my retinas in a sharp white flash and for a moment my vision was black. I heard Ray swearing softly beside me.

I thought of their endless frictionless fall, numbed in their last moments of consciousness by the full enormity of what was happening. I knew exactly what it must have been like—the long gathering slide with such fearful acceleration that one's mind cannot keep up and the violent speed of the fall becomes distant and the mind falls silent, resigned, save for that one unanswered plea. *Will it hurt?* Once I, too, had been there in that longing, headlong fall.

Almost as a blessing to salve the terror, there is no time for fear. Life was rushing by me so fast that I had no time to grasp it, only mutely register what was happening and be calmed by my helplessness. I had felt a faint anger trying to rise, a mild resentment at the unfairness of it all, and then instantly I was gone into blackness, pounded into painless unconsciousness by the impact. Only when I awoke, struggling to rise through a foggy, concussed consciousness, did I begin to feel the pain.

With the resignation had come a sense of calm, a tranquility held like a bubble, sheltered from the whirling, spinning violence of the fall. I had given in to that relaxing calm with ease, accepting without question that there was nothing I could do. It was over. The peace had been marred only by a dim, aching dread. And that was it, no terror, no frantic screaming all the way down; just numb acceptance.

No pain. That at least is a blessing, I thought, and stared down at the First Pillar, thinking of them lying there tangled in their ropes, side by side, quieted now into perpetual stillness, all hopes and dreams gone. We didn't hear them go. They didn't scream.

The dead make their anonymous presence felt, pervading everything with their torn-off senses, drawing on the tomorrow that they had expected and deserved. I was keenly aware of their presence lying far below us who now stood safe, untouched, alive, and bemused on a small ledge on a mountain wall.

I was struck by the sudden silence and wondered whether it was real or the creation of a damaged mind. I scanned the mountain walls, sensing the eerie quiet and feeling much as if I was in a cathedral. There was the same stillness, the familiar sense of up-wardness in the structures of the mountain buttresses and the same chilled awe in my soul. I had never known such calm, never felt the world suspended between breathing in and breathing out.

I looked down at where they lay and for a moment I held a clearness and an understanding going so sharp and deep, down into unimaginable depths, that it pulled on my soul. There was something secret and private inside being dragged out into the open where it had no wish to be. I felt overcome with a mixture of pity and shame and self-reproach.

I felt guilty at the feeling of relief that had hovered in the back-ground of my mind when I had heard the news of their deaths. *We wouldn't have to go up there. There was no need for a rescue.* I felt ashamed at my selfishness and surprised to realize how nervous I had been at the thought of trying to go up onto the ice fields.

They would have done it for me. I knew they would. They were climbers. They were our own and I felt base and tried to push the thoughts away.

We didn't know their names until we read the newspapers. We hadn't seen their faces. I had spoken to one of them and received no answer. They were strangers and yet we were brothers bound together by the same dreams, following the same paths. We are such stuff as dreams are made of. The rest is silence. Our meeting of their lives, like their passing, had been so swift, so silent, it was as if they were sublimated away from us, that moment when a solid becomes a gas without melting, like snow in the sunshine, like mist in the wind, disappearing before your eyes as you watch.

The sound of stonefall shook me from my thoughts and I looked wordlessly at Ray. I saw in his eyes what he was thinking. *It could have been us.* Each of us saw our own expression on the other's face, sadness touched with our fear of death so close we could feel it in the air. We were scared. I always would be.

The silence and lucidity had been broken by the stark impacts of the rocks, gone forever. I had felt sickened and weak and sat down slowly on the mats and put my head in my hands. I didn't have the understanding to cry for them.

Perhaps other climbers are better equipped than I to deal with some of the experiences I have had in the mountains. I have found that over the years it has become harder and harder to drive away the memories. Maybe I am not pragmatic enough, not sufficiently detached to cope. Sometimes I feel completely unnerved, wary of the cupboard crammed with skeletons that sometimes seem to constitute the sum total of my climbing memories.

As the weeks passed I recalled the film less and less. The fears ebbed. I looked through *The White Spider* and felt myself smiling at the memories that the photographs evoked. I remembered the days sitting in sunshine under the towering crags of the Hintisberg, peering at the Eigerwand through the binoculars, watching thin veils of cloud dissipate in the sun as I scanned the mile-high ramparts of rock and ice. I was subdued in the presence of such an immense mountain. It emanated power, a lonely and unrivalled peak, silent, distant, and unapproachable. It made me feel like a lovesick suitor hoping to be chosen and believing I would be rejected. It made me edgy. I thought of the ominous, incessant noise of falling rocks and the white sound of ice and water falling and flowing and knew I wanted to be there.

I watched as a warm wind rustled through the valley below, swaying through stands of pines and meadows patchworked in a dappled coat of greens. I wanted to be up on those walls of glistening ice-streaked rock watching snow fall from overhangs and outcrops beneath my feet. I wanted to be lost within the heart of a mountain, choosing our destiny, playing games with eternity.

The essence of beauty can only be properly appreciated in contrasts. The sound of a striking clock exists only because of the silence that came before. Music is wrought half from silence, half from sound. Mountains have always been my half silences. The peace and beauty of the valley meant nothing to me without the somber, foreboding presence of the mountain wall above.

Mallory wholeheartedly believed there was no dream that must not be dared; his life stretched to the very end. Perhaps, like him, we have no choice but to go back and dare our dreams. We had looked up at the vastness of the Eiger filled with a mixture of exultation and apprehension about what we were about to do in the morning. To me that is everything mountain climbing is about—the outcome uncertain, the spirit subdued, the challenge open—a free choice to take up or walk away from. More than anything it is about taking part—not success or failure, simply being there and making the choice.

There is about the mountain the beckoning silence of great height; a siren call that lures me back against my will. I knew then that Ray was right and that the images of the film would fade with time but not the memory of those two lads. We would return in the summer and try again and all the time be thinking of them. If we succeeded then we would walk away from the mountains at last—or we just might drive up to the Bregalia and have a look at the north face of the Piz Badile. Just a look, mind, nothing more.

ACKNOWLEDGMENTS

THIS IS ALL RAY DELANEY'S FAULT. Thanks for being there, Ray.

It has been said that writers are all made up of patches and quotations of other forms, other stories, thoughts of generations gone before us. In this I am especially culpable. I cannot acknowledge all those authors from whom I have gleaned phrases, been offered inspired thoughts, and taken their philosophies and bent them to my ends, because I am, at the end, unaware of which book they have come from. To all those who might recognize their words in mine I offer my thanks and hope you will forgive my innocent plagiarism.

It has also been said that when a philosopher dies there is one less star in Heaven. Philosophers guard the spy-holes in the firmament. They are supposed to tell us of the Great Beyond. Well, clearly then, I am not a philosopher but I have tried in this book to make some sense of the life I have led and what the mountains have blessed me with. The essence of the work has been to try to come to terms with the fear and love, grief and death that mountains have induced in me and to come through it to a positive life-enhancing state of mind. I do not know whether I succeeded; that is for you to judge. It is an entirely personal analysis but I hope it evokes a sense of familiarity in those who read it.

I have listed a bibliography of those books from which I researched heavily but there are some authors I would mark out for particular notice. Heinrich Harrer's *The White Spider* was an enormously influential work that has informed my entire climbing career, and this book is as much an homage to those climbers whom he wrote so vividly about.

Chris Bonington's *I Chose to Climb* was the second mountaineering book I ever read and I put it down knowing that because of his example one day I too would climb the Eiger. Thanks for the inspiration.

Mark Helprin, author of *A Soldier of the Great War,* may not be a mountaineer but he thinks and writes as if he has spent his entire life in the hills. His ideas wonderfully mirrored my own thoughts. Thanks to Kimberly Unger who kindly gave me the book.

Peter and Leni Gillman's biography of Mallory, *The Wildest Dream,* was inspirational and conversations with Peter about his own Eiger experiences were encouraging and invaluable.

Thanks also to all those who helped with the photographs: Ray Delaney, Alison Claxton and Brian Mucci, Thomas Ulrich, Jane Tattersall, Daniel Anker, Chris Bonington, and Bradford Washburn.

I owe Val Randall an immense debt of gratitude for her unstinting and selfless help with making this book what it is. My admiration for her literary erudition, editorial eye, and her ability to see at once how to say a little thing edgily, is unbounded. Thank you, Val.

Thanks also to my brother David for the enlightening conversations, the patient task of line editing, and schoolmasterly but perceptive corrections.

Tony Whittome, who so generously became my editor at the last moment following the death of Tony Colwell on November 22, 2000, had the unenviable task of working in the shadow of a man who had taught me everything that I knew. He has been patient, encouraging, and unswervingly enthusiastic and we have forged a working relationship and a friendship that I hope will be long and fruitful.

Megan Hitchin, Caroline Michel, and Dan Franklin of Random House were all hugely supportive.

I am indebted to Vivienne Schuster who convinced me that I could still write at a time when I had decided to give it all up.

Margaret and Catherine Colwell offered support and encouragement at a time when my worries were the least of their problems. And yes, Margaret, you were right; Tony was looking over my shoulder all the time—always will.

Joe Simpson
Sheffield, July 2001

SELECTED READINGS

Anker, Daniel. *Eiger: The Vertical Arena.* Seattle: The Mountaineers Books, 2000.

Bonatti, Walter. *On the Heights.* London: R. Hart-Davis, 1964.

Bonatti, Walter. *The Great Days.* London: Victor Gollancz, 1974.

Bonington, Chris. *I Chose to Climb.* London: Victor Gollancz, 1985.

Bonington, Chris. *Mountaineer: Thirty Years of Climbing the World's Great Peaks.* San Francisco: Sierra Club Books, 1999.

Brown, Joe. *The Hard Years.* Seattle: The Mountaineers Books, 2001.

Bühl, Hermann. *Nanga Parbat Pilgrimage: The Lonely Challenge.* Seattle: The Mountaineers Books, 1999.

Cassin, Riccardo. *Fifty Years of Alpinism.* Seattle: The Mountaineers Books, 1982.

Curran, Jim. *High Achiever: The Life and Climbs of Chris Bonington.* Seattle: The Mountaineers Books, 2000.

Desmaison, René. *Total Alpinism.* London/New York: Granada, 1982.

Dickinson, Leo. *Filming the Impossible.* London: Jonathan Cape, 1982.

Diemberger, Kurt. *Summits and Secrets* in *The Kurt Diemburger Omnibus*. Seattle: The Mountaineers Books, 1999.

Fleming, Fergus. *Killing Dragons: The Conquest of the Alps*. New York: Atlantic Monthly Press, 2002.

Fowler, Mick. *Vertical Pleasure: The Secret Life of a Taxman*. Seattle: Cloudcap Press, 1995.

Gillman, Peter and Leni. *The Wildest Dream: The Biography of George Mallory*. Seattle: The Mountaineers Books, 2000.

Gillman, Peter and Dougal Haston. *Eiger Direct*. London: Collins, 1966.

Hargreaves, Alison. *A Hard Day's Summer: Six Classic North Faces Solo*. London: Hodder & Stoughton, 1995.

Harrer, Heinrich. Hugh Merrick, trans. *The White Spider: The Classic Account of the Ascent of the Eiger.* New York: Penguin USA, 1998.

Haston, Dougal. *Eiger.* London: Cassell, 1974.

Haston, Dougal. *In High Places*. Seattle: The Mountaineers Books, 1997.

Helprin, Mark. *A Soldier of the Great War.* New York: Harcourt, 1991.

Krakauer, Jon. *Eiger Dreams: Ventures Among Men and Mountains*. New York: Anchor Books, 1997.

Krakauer, Jon. *Into Thin Air.* New York: Anchor Books, 1998.

MacInnes, Hamish. *High Drama*. Seattle: The Mountaineers Books, 1981.

MacInnes, Hamish. *Look Behind the Range*s: *A Mountaineer's Selection of Adventures and Expeditions.* London: Penguin, 1981.

Messner, Reinhold. Tim Carruthers, trans. *The Big Walls: From the North Face of the Eiger to the South Face of Dhaulagiri.* Seattle: The Mountaineers Books, 2001.

Messner, Reinhold and Horst Hofler. *Hermann Bühl: Climbing without Compromise.* Seattle: The Mountaineers Books, 2000.

Patey, Tom. *One Man's Mountains: Essays and Verses.* Seattle, The Mountaineers Books, 1997.

Rebuffat, Gaston. *Starlight and Storm: The Ascent of the Great North Faces of the Alps.* Oxford: Oxford University Press, 1968.

Robertson, David. *George Mallory.* London: Faber, 1969.

Roth, Arthur. *Eiger: Wall of Death.* New York: Norton, 1982.

Tasker, Joe. *Savage Arena.* New York: St. Martin's Press, 1983.

Terray, Lionel. *Conquistadors of the Useless.* Seattle: The Mountaineers Books, 2001.

Unsworth, Walt. *North Face: The Second Conquest of the Alps.* London: Hutchinson, 1969.

Whillans, Don. *Portrait of a Mountaineer.* London: Heinemann, 1971.

THE MOUNTAINEERS, founded in 1906, is a nonprofit outdoor activity and conservation club, whose mission is "to explore, study, preserve, and enjoy the natural beauty of the outdoors. . . ." Based in Seattle, Washington, the club is now the third-largest such organization in the United States, with 15,000 members and five branches throughout Washington State.

The Mountaineers sponsors both classes and year-round outdoor activities in the Pacific Northwest, which include hiking, mountain climbing, ski-touring, snowshoeing, bicycling, camping, kayaking and canoeing, nature study, sailing, and adventure travel. The club's conservation division supports environmental causes through educational activities, sponsoring legislation, and presenting informational programs. All club activities are led by skilled, experienced volunteers, who are dedicated to promoting safe and responsible enjoyment and preservation of the outdoors.

If you would like to participate in these organized outdoor activities or the club's programs, consider a membership in The Mountaineers. For information and an application, write or call The Mountaineers, Club Headquarters, 300 Third Avenue West, Seattle, WA 98119; 206-284-6310.

The Mountaineers Books, an active, nonprofit publishing program of the club, produces guidebooks, instructional texts, historical works, natural history guides, and works on environmental conservation. All books produced by The Mountaineers Books fulfill the club's mission.

Send or call for our catalog of more than 500 outdoor titles:

 The Mountaineers Books
1001 SW Klickitat Way, Suite 201
Seattle, WA 98134
800-553-4453
mbooks@mountaineersbooks.org
www.mountaineersbooks.org

 The Mountaineers Books is proud to be a corporate sponsor of Leave No Trace, whose mission is to promote and inspire responsible outdoor recreation through education, research, and partnerships. The Leave No Trace program is focused specifically on human-powered (nonmotorized) recreation.

Leave No Trace strives to educate visitors about the nature of their recreational impacts, as well as offer techniques to prevent and minimize such impacts. Leave No Trace is best understood as an educational and ethical program, not as a set of rules and regulations.

For more information, visit *www.LNT.org*, or call 800-332-4100.

Other titles you might enjoy from The Mountaineers Books

Available at fine bookstores and outdoor stores, by phone at 800-553-4453, or on the World Wide Web at *www.mountaineersbooks.org*

Dark Shadows Falling by Joe Simpson. $18.95 paperbound. 0-89886-590-5.

Storms of Silence by Joe Simpson. $19.95 paperbound. 0-89886-512-3.

This Game of Ghosts by Joe Simpson. $14.95 paperbound. 0-89886-460-7.

The Mountaineers Anthology Series, Volume I: Glorious Failures edited by The Mountaineers Books Staff. $16.95 paperbound. 0-89886-825-4.

The Mountaineers Anthology Series, Volume II: Courage and Misfortune edited by The Mountaineers Books Staff. $16.95 paperbound. 0-89886-826-2.

The Mountaineers Anthology Series, Volume III: Over the Top: Humorous Mountaineering Tales edited by Peter Potterfield. $16.95 paperbound. 0-89886-889-0.

Ghosts of Everest: The Search for Mallory and Irvine by Jochen Hemmleb, Larry A. Johnson, and Eric R. Simonson. $24.95 paperbound. 0-89886-850-5.

Detectives on Everest: The 2001 Mallory and Irvine Research Expedition by Jochen Hemmleb and Eric R. Simonson. $19.95 paperbound. 0-89886-871-8.

The Mystery of Mallory & Irvine: Fully Revised Edition by Tom Holzel and Audrey Salkeld. $18.95 paperbound. 0-89886-726-6.

A Life on the Edge: Memoirs of Everest and Beyond by Jim Whittaker. $16.95 paperbound. 0-89886-754-1.

Everest: Eighty Years of Triumph and Tragedy, 2nd Edition by Peter and Leni Gillman. $35.00 hardbound. 0-89886-780-0.

Everest: The Mountaineering History, 3rd Edition
by Walt Unsworth. $45.00 hardbound. 0-89886-670-7.

Fearless on Everest: The Quest for Sandy Irvine
by Julie Summers. $18.95 paperbound. 0-89886-796-7.

The Wildest Dream: The Biography of George Mallory by Peter
and Leni Gillman. $18.95 paperbound. 0-89886-751-7.

Everest: The West Ridge by Tom Hornbein. $19.95 paperbound.
0-89886-616-2.

Everest: Expedition to the Ultimate by Reinhold Messner. $24.95
paperbound. 0-89886-648-0.

The Crystal Horizon: Everest—The First Solo Ascent by
Reinhold Messner. $24.95 paperbound. 0-89886-574-3.

Fragile Edge: A Personal Portrait of Loss on Everest
by Maria Coffey. $16.95 paperbound. 0-89886-737-1.

Chomolungma Sings the Blues: Travels round Everest
by Ed Douglas. $14.95 paperbound. 0-89886-843-2.

*In the Zone: Epic Survival Stories from the Mountaineering
World* by Peter Potterfield. $22.95 hardbound,
0-89886-482-8. $16.95 paperbound, 0-89886-568-9.

Kiss or Kill: Confessions of a Serial Climber by Mark Twight.
$16.95 paperbound. 0-89886-887-4.

*Postcards From the Ledge: Collected Mountaineering Writings
of Greg Child* by Greg Child. $16.95 paperbound.
0-89886-753-3.

Sherman Exposed: Slightly Censored Climbing Stories by John
Sherman. $16.95 paperbound. 0-89886-852-1.

The Burgess Book of Lies by Adrian and Alan Burgess. $24.95
paperbound. 0-89886-641-3.

Rock & Ice Goldline: Stories of Climbing Adventure and Tradition
by Gregory Crouch. $16.95 paperbound. 0-89886-735-5.

The Best of Rock & Ice: An Anthology edited by Dougald
MacDonald. $17.95 paperbound. 0-89886-665-0.